Your Body Is Talking;
Are You Listening?
~ Volume One ~

How the Mind Works

For:

Miracles happen every day...
You could be...
Are yo...

D1315312

Handwritten annotations:

WHEN NEURO/CELLULAR Roprogramming Page 27

98 P139

Book #2

95

144

90

IMFO (T)

Cancer Cancer this is Not my Issue

Now Book Page 33

145 REjection SPINE

Book Page 168

97

SUPRING THE PAIN WITH LOVE & WATCH IT GO AWAY

What people are saying about this book and its author's work

"I have been a client of Art's for 25 years. His work has been phenomenal in helping me with my challenges in my life. A few years ago I had a heart problem and the doctor recommended drugs and possible surgery. Art cleared my heart problem and it has never recurred. This book documents his practice well."

– Ken Peterson, San Diego, CA

"Until I read his book, it was hard to believe anyone could do what Art does with releasing locked in anger. It makes one wonder why people are not beating a path to his door with the results he obtains with his process.... Many times I could not figure out what was causing the pain in my shoulders, yet he was able to find the cause and clear it in one session."

– Pat Drop, Milpitas, CA

"At his lecture, Art asked if anyone would like to volunteer. I did so, expecting him to do a little example of his work with me. I never realized that my mother rejected me before I was born and that I did not love myself.... In a session he released most of the pain in my left shoulder that the doctor had described as fibromyalgia.... I am pain-free for the first time in my life."

– Dottie, PA

"Being a therapist myself, I had doubts that he could do what he claimed in his lecture. I decided to try him at least once to test him out.... To my surprise, he dug into situations in my life I thought I had cleared. I had no idea they were causing problems in my life. His book is a whole new concept on healing. I thought I knew what Energy Medicine was, but he has shown me a totally new view of it."

– Sandra, Los Angeles, CA

"I had given up on taking the California teaching credential test, having failed it six times, with no idea why. When we discovered why I was failing the tests it did not make sense.

My father and my husband programmed me to fail! They told me I would never pass the test because I was no good at math. Wow that was revelation. He told me not study, I would ace the test. On the day before the exam, Art showed me how to take the test and helped me pump up my self esteem and confidence. I passed in the 94th percentile. I have never finished the test in the past. I finished with 45 minutes to spare. He is wonderful."

– Becky M., Sacramento, CA

"I went to the Omega Centre bookstore in Toronto looking for a book on Energy Medicine and/or Energy Psychology. They referred me to Art's book. When I read the book, I called him immediately to see if I could get him to come to Toronto. I got him a lecture spot at a local health show which started his practice in Toronto and the rest is history. He has been very successful here."

– Peter Myronyk, Toronto, Canada

"I could not do anything and stay committed to finish it. I sabotaged myself at almost everything I did. Art located the cause, but I still kept falling back. His books directed me to write down a long-hand affirmation, 21 times a day for 21 days. Each time, I would sabotage myself before I finished. It finally worked after five attempts. It worked very well. I do not understand why this book is not on the bestseller lists."   – Kitty Kartialia, Los Angeles, CA

"I have worked with Art since 1989 and helped him develop some of his concepts. We did research together until I moved to Ft. Lauderdale, FL. I developed prostate cancer in 2001 and the prognosis was surgery unless I could stop the growth of the cancer. Working with Art, we found all the causes and the activators that caused the cancer, and cured it. This is the best non invasive healing process I have ever experienced"

– James Landrell, D.C. H.M.S., Ft. Lauderdale, FL

"When I found Art's book in a bookstore in Sydney, I booked a flight to the USA with high hopes. The doctors had given me four months to live so I had nothing to lose. In a week of treatments, we had cleared my cancer. He did the impossible, but it seemed so simple when we found out what the cause was. Miracles do happen."

– Carla G., Sydney, Australia

"I had my doubts about what Dr. Art was talking about at his lecture. I decided to put skepticism aside try a session. To my amazement he was able reveal all the trauma I had experienced as child. My body told him all he needed to know to begin releasing and clearing the pain I had in my back most of my life. This is his special talent I had never heard about before. Doctors described it as Fibromyalgia but said you they cannot control your pain without drugs or surgery. Dr. Art has discovered a method that is easy, painless and works in hours instead of years or even a lifetime." – Mildred Kroger, St. Augustine, FL

"All I can say is when you are ready the teacher appears. He did in the person of Dr. Art Martin. I read his book in two days and called him. I flew into Sacramento to see him and stayed two days. All I can say is I got my life back in two days after suffering for 15 years. What a miracle!"

– Helen Markstein, Boston, MA

"I was a prisoner in my own body. I contracted polio when I was fourteen. I was in an iron lung for a year and was unable to walk. I spent five years in a wheelchair until I was able to learn how to walk. For the last 25 years I don't have the strength to lift my legs. I have dragged my feet unable to lift my legs. I had considered suicide because I don't really have a life. I told Dr. Art I did not want to pay for a session if I did not know it would work. My parents and I have spent $40,000 for treatments which did not work. He challenged me with an offer I could not resist. 'If I can't clear the polio symptoms that cause your disabilities there will be no cost to you. If I do release them so you can walk normally, then the fee is double.' I could not resist the double or nothing because I did not think he could do it. In two hours, we found the causes and I walked out his office normally. After spending all the money I did for nothing $500.00 was a real steal. I got my life back."

– Janet S., Elk Grove, CA

"I did not think there was anything wrong in my life as I had come to accept what happened to me in the past was the way it is. The concept of accepting yourself as you are was a way of life for me. I did not realize I had stuffed so much resentment and anger at my parents. When Art showed me how much of this anger and fear from the past was locked into my body it was amazing. I overlooked a lot of the problems I had because they were from the past. When we were able to get all the anger, fear and resentment removed from my body my Fibromyalgia disappeared, it was amazing how my life changed. People started treating me differently and I was happier. Opportunities that had passed me by in the past were becoming realities. My income increased and my relationships improved. What more can you ask for?"

– Jim Bentley, Austin, TX

"We have a hard time believing that we are the enemy. I did not want to accept this conclusion either, yet it was proved to me very clearly in two sessions with Dr. Art. I did not realize that my mind was controlling my life. I am successful in business, yet my personal life was not comfortable at all. When you are confronted with the truth and the pain that doctor described as Fibromyalgia totally disappeared I began to question all the things we have accepted in our life as the way it is and we have to accept it. Dr. Art proved to me that everything is changeable. Nothing is locked in, even genetic defects."

– George Sutter, New York, NY

"When you are confronted with a life threatening disease it changes the whole game of life. When I was in pain I could accept it and go on. I did not want to believe that it could be cleared so I lived in pain. But as Dr. Art told me, 'If you refuse to face the lesson, your mind will find another method to wake you up.' Since I refused to take notice of the first three notifications of a lesson being up, my mind decided to hit me with a life-threatening disease. When you are told you have three months to live, you wake up. Dr. Art helped me wake up and clear the colon cancer.

– Ray Mello, Redwood City, CA

"I have spent a lot of money and time trying to cure my allergies and environmental illness. I suffered and struggled with these afflictions for over 20 years. After reading Art Martin's book *Your Body Is Talking Are You Listening?* I realized he had the solution to my problems. I called him and ordered a StressBlocker and then set up an appointment to explore his theory and process further. I really did not expect a miracle, even though he said they do happen if I was to take responsibility for my healing. I just wanted relief. I did get a miracle. All my allergies and environmental illness cleared totally. I can eat any food I choose now. They have never returned since the sessions over two years ago. He is the master on how to release illness without drugs. It was a very simple process. He knows how to use affirmations that work."

– Ivar Ikstrums, Sammamish, WA

"When Dr. Art says he can find the root causes and the basic issues that cause a malfunction, he is right on. Not only that, he can pin it down to exact age and time it happened, and who helped you cause the incident that caused the malfunction. It is amazing how our mind will stuff and bury incidents so you do not even know they exist. Art is a master at finding a malfunction in your life. We never realize when an issue happens that it will cause a major breakdown in our life at a later date."

– John Neumann, St. Augustine, FL

"When your eyesight is beginning to disappear, you take notice of this lesson quick. I had diabetes which was causing my eyesight to deteriorate. Even though I knew what caused it, I could not stop it. It becomes even more of a conflict since I work at medical college and the doctors could not do anything for me. When Dr. Art began to check it out, we found the diabetes caused it, but the diabetes was not the root cause. We went back further and discovered that it was my need for love, attention, recognition and approval when I was a child that caused the diabetes. Since I did not want to address the issue of anger with my parents, it was telling me I had look at the issue. Not only that, but I married a man who was a duplicate of my father. When we cleared the issues with my family and my husband by forgiving them, and releasing my anger and resentment with love and forgiveness, my eyesight was restored and my diabetes was gone." – Myra Recovachecyk, Toronto, Canada

The co-author of my book gave me Art's book, *Your Body Is Talking, Are You Listening?* I asked him, "What is it about? Have you read it? What do you feel about? He had not even read it. "He makes some pretty controversial statements about his process" At this point I was ready for anything to alleviate my 24/7 pain. I read his book in two days. I could not put it down. I realized he had the answer. He healed himself of the same back problem I am dealing with and he did not submit to surgery. I called him with question "how can I get together with you as soon as possible? Where are you? His reply was "If you set up a lecture for me so I can make some money I can come to you." That won't work I wanted relief now, so I booked a flight to Sacramento. It was excruciating painful over five hour flight, I had to walk up and down the aisle every 45 minutes to ease the pain in my back. When I arrived Art asked why I was wearing a neck brace. I told him "doctors had tried to fuse my back by putting two rods next to my spine to hold it straight. It did not work and I was not willing to go that route again and subject myself to their butchery again when it did not work the first time." "I trust you can do what you have described in your book. So let's get to work" I just wanted my life back so I could get on with my career. I could not work or travel the way I am now. In two days of intense work he had cleared 85% of my pain and had me feeling good. I threw away the neck brace the first day. I was finally getting on track after 20 years of back pain. This situation was not about money or time. I had been trying for 10 years just as Art had done. As he has discovered no practitioners be they doctors, physical therapists, or any other healers, alternative, spiritual or otherwise did not know how to accomplish what he did for me in twelve hours in two days. I received what I came for and more. People saw my recovery from where I was before I went to see Art and were impressed. Their questions were "how do we get Art to come to Orlando?" "That is easy all we have to do ask him." I wanted him to come on spring break so he could work with my adopted children. I wanted to get out of the hornets nest I had created by adopting children from Russia. He did that too. He was able to free them from birth mother rejection, self rejection, fear of intimacy, lack of trust and respect, fear of commitment and many I am not all right, not acceptable and feeling rejected. Now we get along great and they are now exceptional students in school. His work has set me up in a place where I can now become a best selling author and present seminars all over the US. This was not a one session go around. It took two years. This is an ongoing story He came to Orlando every three months for the next three years and still coming now. He helped me create my success story. What I would like to know is, if he was able to help me not only with my back pain and all aspects of my life to create my success story why are people afraid to confront their issues? He has the process and the formula for success in your life. Why are people not beating a path to his door?

– Heather Forbes, Orlando, FL

"I ended up with type II diabetes at 56 years old. I had to carry an Insulin pump to keep my blood sugar in balance. Dr. Art cleared the Diabetes in two sessions. He found the cause was set in place when I was 16 years old. It did not sprout until I was 56 due to rejection by my wife. In three months my Diabetes was gone. Six Months later I called him to ask him what he might suggest what he could do for me. I had crushed my ankle from trying to move a 400 pound iron part from a Pug Mill. There are 26 bone fragments. "The doctors want to amputate my ankle. What can you do for me." I told the doctors I needed a few days to work with my friend. They were baffled but since it was a weekend they agreed. Dr Art did a Tibetan Surrogate Session with me. The pain went away in less than an hour. I did not know what had happened. On Monday the doctors did one X-ray. They took two more an hour later. They would not say anything about what the X-rays indicated.

Finally they took another one on different X-ray machine. They finally showed me the X-ray. No bone fragments or fracture showed on the X-ray. They did not even ask what I had done. They asked the nurses if somebody had visited me. They did not want to discuss with me what I done. I am sure many people ask this question: "If he can create Miracles like this, why are people not keeping him so busy he has no free time?"

– Frank Donley, Denver, CO

Disclaimer:

All the examples in this book are from people who were committed to heal themselves. They were expecting miracles and they received them. Many practitioners want to take credit for the results of the healing. I do not agree with this since I believe we can only provide the basic guidance, support, direction. We may be able to supply the information to activate the healing, we do not make it happen. Our mind either accepts or rejects the results of the healing. We have to realize that all healing is self healing. In a sense we could call it placebo effect. I am only a software developer and facilitator I can- not cause healing to happen. I provide the method and the support. I cannot guarantee you can achieve these results. You decide if you want cause them to happen. You create your own results. I can provide the software, you have to decide if you want to use it. Some people do not want to get healed. That is not the fault of the practitioner.

Your Body Is Talking; Are You Listening?

~ Volume One ~

How the Mind Works:
Behavioral Mind /Body Medicine Connection.

Here is the answer to healing and releasing frustrating emotions, feelings, discomfort, pain, stress, illness, disease and failure to accomplish goals with the power of your mind by reprogramming your mind in hours, not years.

Art Martin, Ph.D.

Personal Transformation Press
Energy Medicine Institute

Your Body Is Talking; Are You Listening? ~ Volume One
How the Mind Works: The Mind/Body Medicine Connection

by Art Martin, Ph.D.

Published by Personal Transformation Press
9936 Inwood Rd.
Folsom, CA 95630
phone: (916) 663-9178

ISBN-10: 1-891962-15-9
ISBN-13: 978-1-891962-15-8
Published January 2014
First published June, 1997 as Your Body Is Talking;
Are You Listening?

Revised edition Volume One published January 2009
Second edition published January 2014

This book explores the body/mind connection as the actual cause of all mental/emotional dysfunction and physical disease. However, the author in no way makes any diagnosis of medical condition or prescribes any medical treatment whatsoever.

Printed in the United States

Table Of Contents

Dedication

This book is dedicated to all the practitioners of Neuro/Cellular Repatterning who learned the process and provided the support to heal my body/mind, and to all my sponsors who have supported my work and helped me present lectures, workshops and seminars

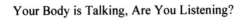

Your Body is Talking, Are You Listening?

Acknowledgments

My first introduction to healing came in 1978 at an acupressure workshop taught by Iona Teagarden. That same year, I met Paul Solomon, who would be my teacher for the next fifteen years. He was my mentor and, along with Ronald Beesley, he gave me a deep understanding of how healing works. I am indebted to them for starting me on the right path. In great physical pain at the beginning, I also worked with Frank Hughes, owner of Nance's Hot Springs in Calistoga, California, and am grateful for his intensive work with me.

I formed the Wellness Institute in Sacramento, California between 1984 and 1987 I began to incorporate hands-on therapy in my verbal counseling; I thank those who let me experiment with the process I was developing: Body/Mind/Integration, later to become Neuro/Cellular Reprogramming (N/CR). If it had not been for those who attended my classes and came to me as clients, none of this would have happened. I learned more from working with my clients than I ever did at a class or seminar.

When we closed the center, Chris Issel asked me if I would teach the process to a group. This landmark seminar proved to me that N/CR was not a special gift of healing I had; it was possible to train others to do the same thing. Suddenly, sponsors popped up everywhere as the original seven seminar attendees in turn set out to teach the technique. In a domino effect, Chris Issel introduced me to Jim Ingram, who turned out to be my major sponsor in Southern California, putting on workshops and introducing me to even more people. Many thanks to Jim and Chris for their invaluable support. (Jim has passed on to the spirit world now,

while Kitty Kartiala is providing support in the Los Angeles area.)

Mary Best introduced me to Pattie Marshall, who offered to bring me to San Diego, and she took care of me as if I were her son. I thank her so much for getting me established in San Diego. I am especially grateful to Amy Kinder, whose support went beyond what most people would offer. For many years, she set up clients and workshops and provided me a place to stay when I was in San Diego.

The list goes on: Helen Phelps, Joline Stone, Betts Richter, Lesley Gregory, Joy Johnston, Oshara Miller, Nancy Worthington, Araya Lawrence, Ilene Botting, Robert Perala, Joyce Techel, Barbara Stone, Nadeen Gotlieb, Ruth Johnston, Sally Machutta, Karen Arnold, Mindy Cantor, Nicole Cooledge, Sherri Decker, Jim Dorobiala, Marilyn Grow, John Hammer, Marilyn Henderson, Bill Irwin, Barbara Ikeda, Jeane Joregensen, David Kamitzer, Kismit, Angel Kay, Susan Moulton, Morningstar Black, Kate Moyers, Janette Nash, Joan Noel, Oshana, Joy Polte, Terry Pierson, Jean Rossman, Rita Raimondo, Karla Spitzer, Sara Sherman, Krita Sheyk, Bertha Taylor, Dave Thompson, Susie Taylor, Janet Tully, Ro Thompson, David Weisman, Wally Wallace, Rebecca West, and Ken Peterson (one of the best examples of someone who took what I had when I first started and ran with it, he has supported my work in many ways and continues to inspire me to this day).

When the workshops got larger than I could handle alone, Mike Hammer came along. He seemed to be a natural for N/CR and quickly learned the process. I appreciate all the help he provided during his tenure with me.

In 2001, we began to spread the word across North America. Your Body Is Talking; Are You Listening? opened up many new opportunities. People began asking me to come to their area and present lectures and workshops. My book was talking and people were listening. I appreciate the support provided by Peter Myronyk in Toronto, Canada; David and Donni Shultz in Phoenix, AZ; Joan Noel in Tucson, AZ; Betsy Lobes in Brookfield, CT; Dr. Jonathon Curzon in the

Philadelphia, PA area; Sandra Reis of Akron, OH; Karen Herberling in Santa Fe, NM; Dr. Larry Herbig in Kansas City, MO; and Heather Forbes, who really saw the value in my work who used it to become a very successful writer and speaker. Plus all the many who have invited us to their cities where we had not visited before.

With the help of my clients, Neuro/Cellular Reprogramming continued to evolve over the years into Energy Psychology and Energy Medicine, thanks to all the people who allowed me to work with them. Everyone taught me the process by working with me. Without any formal training program for N/CR, I depended on the people who participated with me. For example, Bernard Eckes came to a 1993 workshop with the attitude that he could not learn the technique. He is now one of my research associates. I thank him for his perseverance in sticking with N/CR so that he could work with me in developing the process. With his help, we have now refined N/CR to the point that we can clear and heal any dysfunction.

To spread our message to the public, I began presenting lectures and workshops at conferences and Whole Life Expos and many other venues. I appreciate the support my wife, Susie, gave me by spending countless hours running booths at the shows and traveling with me.

Finally, the help I needed to get this book out came from two people: (a) the editor of the original edition, the late Tony Stubbs, who smoothed out my language, tied the book together and laid it out; and (b) Mark Nardini who has re-edited and formatted this newest edition. I really appreciate their support and help.

Your Body is Talking, Are You Listening?

Foreword
by Mark Victor Hansen

Many times when somebody presents you with a new concept, it takes a while for it to become acceptable. After spending time with Art over two years in our Inner Circle group, I finally decided to try out his process because I had pain in my Achilles tendon area. Many people had tried to help me release the pain without any results.

In about an hour and a half, Art was able to release the pain, and it has never come back. I have heard many people talk about Energy Medicine but few get results like Art gets.

If something is blocking or limiting your success in your life, he has the ticket to remove the limitations too.

His theory that all of our problems begin in childhood makes good sense. Many of the incidents that Art helped me release were from my childhood. I overcame many obstacles in my life, coming from an immigrant family from Denmark. My father was a baker but he did not limit my options so I could go for the success I have now.

Art's process with Energy Medicine works well. If you need help in uncovering or finding your limitation, he has the process.

– Mark Victor Hansen

Preface

It was not my intention or goal to become a Practitioner, therapist or Psychologist. This just evolved as I was searching for the key to heal my 24/7 back, neck and leg pain. I also never had set out to be an author. I have no training in creative writing of kind. I did not have any training in English structure either, I only had one good English teacher in the ninth grade in school. When I first started writing I had to use a typewriter as Computers were not on the market yet. It became easier when IBM brought out the Selectric. We could make changes without having to retype the whole paper. I would run my newletters on a mimeograph. Or later we could copy them copy machines came out. It really became easier when I bought a computer in 1982. This amazing computer had a removable disc with 161 kilabites of storage. It had no memory so every thing had to be stored on these eight inch discs. I wrote my first book in 1992 and took it to Office Max and had them bind it with plastic comb bindings. I am still binding my session manual with comb binding. It makes it easy to update and revise the affirmations. I feel I finally have finished the work on it. We will publishing soon.

I wrote my first published book in 1997 after all my clients kept asking me to write a book about my work. The book has been revised four times. This is the fourth revision.

I do not follow the conventional method of writing. I just sit down at my computer and start writing. It just seems to come out in the way it should with very little revision, Sometimes I have to go back and rewrite it or change the chapters around. I have written seven books in this manner.

When we rewrote this book we realized it had too many pages. Most people are not willing to read large books, so we decided to split it into two. This volume is the introduction to the concepts; Book Two is about the protocol and the practice. We are also introducing four more books about Energy Medicine and Energy Psychology, to round out the series. The next release, *Behavioral Mind Body Medicine,* will provide the format and the therapy process.

I have been on this journey for over 30 years. My goal is to balance all four quadrants in my life, so that I will be successful at every challenge I embark on. These quadrants must all be balanced on a solid foundation for personal and financial success:

1. Physical Health: Nutrition, Diet and Physically Fitness
2. Mental Health: Psychological and Emotional Relationships
3. Financial Health: Abundance, Prosperity and Business Success
4. Spiritual Health: Spiritual Enlightenment, Transformation, Connection with Higher Power/GOD Source.

This volume, subtitled Behavioral *Mind/Body Medicine Connection: How the Mind Works,* examines the body/mind as a vehicle for spiritual transformation. It looks at the origins of illness, disease and behavioral dysfunction, in terms of how body cells communicate and how beliefs serve as agents of cause and effect. We will examine how the mind functions, and the origin and effects of sub-personalities. And finally, we will look at meta-communication and how we project our deepest self-image to anyone sensitive enough to pick it up.

Volume Two, subtitled *N/CR in Practice*, begins with a deeper understanding of the human condition, the history of Energy Psychology and Energy Medicine, and how I coupled these fields with the new therapeutic process of Psychological Acupuncture to develop the unique practice of Neuro/Cellular Reprogramming. Years with N/CR have produced countless remarkable—some claim miraculous—recoveries, many of which are documented in the Appendix titled *Case Histories.*

Your Body is Talking, Are You Listening?

Are you ready for a miracle? We create them every day.

With love,
Art Martin

January, 2014

Introduction

If we were to view our lives as a stage play entitled This Is Your Life, with ourselves as the scriptwriter, stage director and producer, we might see how they were created. We are each the lead actor/actress in the play, along with being the scriptwriter, so we can create any form of play we choose for our lives to follow.

This concept was presented to us in 1978, in a seminar by Paul Solomon. I consider it a really great way to show us that we do create our lives, and can change them any time we want, taking control of them to reclaim our personal power. Of the 200 people at that seminar, all but two were from basically dysfunctional families. Only two had had parents who'd been loving and supportive during their formative years. Most of the people there were in their thirties to fifties.
Many had young children and recognized they were passing on the same patterns they had inherited from their parents. (This type of invaluable training in the 1970s has helped turned the tide, so that children today have a better chance than their parents at becoming successful individuals, i.e., the generational chain has been broken.)

When we were children, we let our parents set up and write our scripts for us, and played out their scripts in our plays. In fact, many times we still play out their lives, not ours, as we are copies of them. When are we going to take control of our lives and rewrite the script? We cannot change the past, but we could accept, love and forgive our parents for doing what they did, and then rewrite a new, successful script for our lives today. Paul Solomon showed us how to set up that process and begin to change our lives immediately.

This seminar created such a ground swell in changing all of the attendees' lives that many became seminar junkies and attended every lecture or seminar that Paul's group presented.

Many people had the same reaction I'd had, and we 'regulars' continued to meet each other at future seminars.

I realized at that time that I'd never really told my wife, Susie, that I loved her. She'd had to draw it out of me, and even then, I would not say the actual word 'love.' Until I went to the Inner Light Conscious Seminar with Paul Solomon, that word was as foreign to me, and it actually scared me.

When I came home from this five-day experience, I told her, for the first time in my life, "I love you." Impressed with my new-found reality, two weeks later, she asked if there was an upcoming seminar that she could attend. There was, two months away, which we attended together, and it totally changed our life patterns. We had been married for 13 years and now recognized we had been 'coexisting.' The seminar changed us from roommates to loving, supportive partners.

This experience set a new career goal. I noticed I felt better and had a more positive outlook on life. I decided to go back to college to get a degree in psychology, along with attending many seminars on every form or type of healing I could find for my back and leg pain.

The problem was that every person I had contact with said they could heal me, yet not one could produce permanent results. This was very frustrating, because the pain was becoming more intense, and the doctors were telling me that if we could not stop the deterioration of my spine, I would end up in a wheelchair.

As with all my books, this one is about my journey to issue a challenge to conventional medicine, psychology, the human potential movement and to all the success marketing trainers, to find a way to heal people from illness, emotional dysfunction, and lack of success in relationships, to financial prosperity.

On that journey, I have discovered that fewer than 40 percent of those who recognize they're having conflicts and malfunctions will actually follow through to create better lives for themselves. This figure may seem high, yet only about 15 percent of those same people will follow through and admit to having conflicts in their life, so that 40 percent drops down to six percent really seeking help.

Many more will go to seminars and workshops, as a way to receive information without standing out in the crowd. The figures here are higher since 20 percent of those who attend seminars and workshops actually use the information from the programs. More than half never even open the material they received at the seminars, with some never even cutting the shrink-wrap.

In my research over the years, I have discovered that success at anything requires that we take control of our lives and reclaim our personal power, so we can empower ourselves to find out who we are.

Only one in 25,000 people have grown up in a functional family; the other 24,999 have walked out, abandoned their true selves, and taken on other identities, to escape from the real or perceived traumas they were experiencing. (This is my projection based on the percentage of the number of people I have worked with) Shedding all the mental and emotional trauma we have experienced in our in our childhoods is hard work. A major challenge is that most of us do not even remember what happened to create the trauma, because it is locked away within denial files.

Now that I have found the path to success, my desire is to show everyone how we can rewrite our scripts for success, at every level of our lives. In doing this, I have become a historian, helping people go back to recover the lost files and forgive the people who created their early life traumas, so they can get on with their own agendas of success at every level of their lives.

My interpretation of success is: (1) being able to do what you desire, when you desire, without any concern for how or when you are going to accomplish the goal; and (2) being able to accomplish the adventure with total trust and acceptance, so that you achieve your goals with peace, happiness, harmony and joy, in a total-wellness state of being.

When we find ourselves being blocked in our attempts to accomplish tasks or goals in life, we tend to look outside ourselves for why something happened. We tend to blame others and outside situations, rather than looking inside at ourselves for the cause. (How could we h a v e created a situation where we lost our life savings or did not get that job position we applied for?)

Are we going to take responsibility for the trauma t ha t has happened to us? Or are we going to blame and complain that *someone did this to me*? The only way out is acceptance, forgiveness and unconditional love. The more we hold on, the worse it gets, which o n l y causes more pain.

Every time most people suffer with pain, illness or depression, they run to the body mechanic (aka *doctor*), not realizing their bodies are talking to them. They have messages that can be understood if we can listen to the information being presented by our computer-based minds. Rather than block or relieve the symptoms with drugs, we need to look at what happened to cause malfunction in our life.

This is not about our bodies, but about beliefs, situations or tasks we are ignoring, or something we want to get attention, recognition and acceptance for. We want a payoff so we can get what we want out of the situation, usually tied into an attempt to control that situation. The base need is for acceptance and unconditional love, which most people do not have in their lives. Getting past this block is really about self-empowerment. You are the only one who can empower yourself; nobody can do it for you.

When I started this journey, I thought good nutrition and becoming a vegetarian would heal my body. Little did I know how much we were all controlled by computer programs that set up our behavior patterns. It's not about what we eat; it's about *what's eating us* that controls how we feel.

I also did not know that everything in our minds is coded into files, in a database known as the Subconscious Mind. Nor did I know there were such things as functional and dysfunctional families, though I had noticed that some of my friends were lucky to have parents who had given them affection and support, and had really enjoyed going to their houses because everybody was happy and treated me well.

My first teacher was actually the night manager in my restaurant. He had quit his $40,000-a-year job to come to work for me for $6.00 an hour. This was in 1976. He had done it so he could 'find his lost self.' At night, while we were cleaning up the restaurant, we talked about this concept at length. The more we discussed it, the more I wanted to sell out, so that I, too, could get on my journey to finding *my* lost self. I could not do it working 12-to-18 hours a day, six days a week. So, after a year of debate, I finally sold the business.

Over the last 30 years, I have discovered that you cannot work with only one discipline to get to clarity. All four quadrants of our lives must be balanced for total success. As Pogo said in the famous cartoon: **"We have found the enemy and it is us."** That is to say, we are our own worst enemies, until we wake up and empower ourselves to take control of our life. When we do, we can reclaim our personal power.

Paul Solomon did not describe it as balancing all four quadrants. His description was t ha t we must feed all fo ur bodies equally at all times. We feed the physical body all the time, but we neglect the mental, emotional and spiritual ones. (I have described these as forms of health that we must properly feed and care for.)

Over the years, I have demonstrated how I created perfect health for myself, through balancing out all four quadrants. If we take notice and follow a disciplined lifestyle, we can live illness-free lives, with abundant peace, happiness, harmony, joy, unconditional love and wealth.

In terms of achieving success, whether you come from a dysfunctional or a functional family makes no difference. It is up to you to take the bull by the horns and ride it. No matter how the first act in your play was written by your parents, you can change the script and write a new one for the balance of your life. You are onstage every day during your life. How successful you are at rewriting your play depends on your ability to empower yourself to take control and reclaim your personal power.

When you entered this life, you came in with a blank book, with only a few agenda items in it that were set up before you were born. In the first act, when you were born, your parents were the directors and writers of the script for your life. If you were a child who allowed your parents to control every action in your life, you had no choice in how you were treated. The way they wrote the script in your database still makes up much of the programming on which the balance of the play hangs.

We all want love, recognition, acceptance and approval. We have the ability to receive love as babies. Since our parents have been programmed, they've lost their own concept of what love was by the time they were four years old. How could they provide love for their children if they do not know what it is?

They are not able to do so. So, what do they do? Threaten you with the same basic behavior patterns they were brought up with. If they were strong controllers and manipulators, you will usually have given in to their control. Instead of showing you the way, they've ordered you to do what they want. You were not given any choices. Did it work? Probably not.

There will have been traumatic incidents that caused you to escape from fear and separate from self, going into magical child and inner child. When this happened, you lost control of your life. You went on autopilot, with no control over your life. You were upset that your mother could not provide these qualities of love, so you became angry, and the terrible twos began.

You kept pushing for love, because you were sure she was withholding it from you. This made her angry, so you were disciplined for acting out. You began to feel that maybe she did not know what love was, or she would not get angry and reject you. During that three-year period, you lost the concept of love and sank into self-rejection, feeling you were not acceptable. If you were all right, you would get love, acceptance and recognition from your mother. Something was wrong: you couldn't understand why she was angry, when you had done nothing wrong that you could see.

However, if you were from a functional family and your parents were able to provide love and acceptance, this creates a totally and completely different script. The difference in a functional family is that the parents model good behavior and gently guide their children in the proper manner, by suggesting and communicating about effective behavior.

In raising children this way, parents create respect, trust, self-esteem, confidence and self-worth. This helps a child develop good habits and behavior patterns in life. All the scripts that govern our lives were written before we were four or five years old. All the material we can draw from to write the play that controls the rest of our life is drawn from this period.

To write the next act in our lives, we must have a database from which to draw our information. To build this database, we will also draw from the people around us and how they respond or react to us. How we get validation and acceptance will also control how this database is created. In the dysfunctional family, there is seldom any validation given to the children, so they begin to reject themselves, thinking they are not all right. In the dysfunctional family, parents are always criticizing or making the children wrong.

In the functional family, however, children are supported and given love and validation, which builds self-esteem and self-worth. When parents disapprove of their children's behavior, they will make an effort to correct it, while maintaining the show of love, so that the children may understand that that they can trust and respect their parents. (This did not happen to me as a child, so I'd had to build a whole new set of behavior patterns to avoid falling back into my parents' own patterns.)

In a dysfunctional family, children learn to lie and cover up to protect themselves; if they tell the truth, they will be reprimanded or abused. Force does not work, yet most parents treat their children in this way, since it's the way they were treated. We will act and work within our frame of reference. (Most parents do not see anything wrong with physical discipline because that is their frame of reference.)

In the family I've gone on to co-create, Susie and I have made it a point never to yell at or hit our children, for any action or behavior, no matter how much we've disapproved of it. Long before, she and I had decided we would not get married until we had some time to understand how to make good decisions about our lives. We did not have children until we were able to overcome our own parents' behavior patterns. As a result, our children were born when I was age 34 and 39. They grew up self-empowered, with self-esteem and self-confidence.

I started on the path to personal development when I was 34, since I knew we had to correct our behavior before our son began growing up. Since considerable negative programming had been installed in the database during my childhood, removing this took many years.

Our lives are divided up into seven-year acts for each scene in our play. Our first two acts (0-to-7 and 7-to-14) are usually controlled by our parents. In the third act (14-to-21), some children begin to write their own scripts. It was not until the end of my third act that I finally realized how to take control of my life. As with many people, the first act in my play had been tragedy. (Apparently, I had known something was wrong and wanted to exit, as I'd had a near death experience when I was four years old.)

People often wonder what causes children to exit from life at an early age. I have worked with many parents who have lost their children during their childhood. Based on my own experiences and that of my clients, we have found that when children feel rejected by their parents, they can even lose the will to live.

In my case, my father had been having an affair with his secretary. When my mother had found out about it, she'd just picked up and left us, claiming she was going to take care of the children of a friend whose husband was in the Navy. (This was during WWII.)

She had then decided it was more important to take care of her friend's three children than her own. This was the illusion that had justified her actions, and I did not see her again for almost two years. (My second near-death experience pulled them back together, but my mother's anger and resentment created a continuing tragedy during the second act of my play.)

Beginning in the 1970s, we saw a major change in how children were deciding to handle their lives. With a new awareness, they did not let their parents control them as much. Many of these children caught on during the second acts of their lives (which was very disconcerting if they had controlling parents). With the advent of the computer age, children were being given tools to learn with at an early age, so they were becoming more adept at learning. The advances in communication were bringing everything to the forefront.

When I was young, the Industrial Age was in full swing, which made progress a slow evolution. It was the time later depicted in *Happy Days:* The war was over, and everything seemed to be 'hunky dory,' as portrayed by TV shows of the time (*Ozzie and Harriet, Leave It to Beaver,* etc.). Most high school graduates were not thinking about college or making it big; they just wanted to get married and make a living. Jobs were easy to get and paid a lot of money, or so we thought then.

I worked at a GM parts warehouse, making $2.07 an hour, which in 1957 would support a family: bread was 25 cents a loaf, hamburger was three pounds for a buck, and a new car cost between $1,000 and $1,500. When the Soviets launched Sputnik, 'science' became the hot word, and everything began to speed up. (I was then in the fourth act of my life (21-to-28), and so decided to go to college with everyone else.)

Back then, the business climate was much less aware than today; younger people now have more opportunities than they did 50 years ago. (I wish I had the knowledge that the young have now when I was their age. However, that has not stopped me, as I always intend to go back, learn it all, and begin my new life.)

How did I come to this knowing that we can change our paths and rewrite the scripts for the plays called our lives? It all started in 1978, and began to unfold as I became more aware of the opportunities before me. Through my studies with many teachers and mentors, I learned that I could succeed.

The most important and significant event was with Paul Solomon, learning his meditation techniques for making contact with Higher Source. This became a close link to support me in my search for a process to heal myself from my back pain. As I developed this connection with the GOD Source, as Paul called it, I found that I could tune into there anytime and ask questions.

Over the last 25 years, this link has become a high-speed data-line into what I call the White Brotherhood as well as to the GOD Source. I can obtain direct information any time I choose, and do not have to set up any special prayers or meditation. These resources are at my request, anytime I want to ask anything. (In fact, they monitor me, and will 'ring my ear' just like a telephone. As soon as I acknowledge the call, the ringing stops and I can hear them as thought-forms in my mind. I can then carry on a two-way conversation with them on any subject about which I want information.)

With the advent of the computer, I recognized that our minds are computers. The main difference is that our bio-computers are multitasking, and can store millions of times more data than the desktop computers we use today. In my books, I describe how to use these computers and how to rewrite the operating instructions. We are a set of four operating systems, with a common database that networks with all the cellular structures in our bodies. Each cell is a tiny network computer, controlled by how we think and feel.

We had been working on cracking the mind's codes for 20 years. In 2003 we finally discovered all the codes, which told us how the mind functions and interfaces with each operating system. We have since developed a manual with 27 basic affirmations to clear up the breakdowns in communication in the mind's ability to function at its highest level of competence. When we cleared up our ability to intercommunicate with each level of the mind, we were then able to clear all the programs that were blocking success at every level. (The Manual has now grown to 65 affirmations or Dialogues.)

Seldom is the outward manifestation the base cause. Being a therapist takes considerable clarity. Just having a degree and/or some acceptance in a field of therapy does not guarantee effectiveness. To be effective as therapists, we must ourselves be in recovery. Many therapists assume they "have the knowledge," and forget they must work regularly on their own recovery processes. (I have found very few therapists actually pursuing recovery in their own lives. We all get into healing work to find ourselves, but very few are dealing with their own issues.)

I attended a workshop at an Adult Children of Alcoholics conference designed specifically for therapists and counselors, the instructor asked the participants to fill out a

40-question profile about therapy. They did not know it was about them as therapists. Before his assistant went over them, he predicted this: "We will find that only about eight to ten percent of you participants will qualify as effective therapists." During the three-hour workshop he went over the questions, explaining why this would turn out this way. He said all questions are interlinked so there is a pattern you have to answer the questions. If you do not answer honestly it will show up when my assistant goes over them. He was right on. He shocked most people. "You know who you are," he said, "since we went over the questions he found only nine out the 101 people attending this seminar answered the questions correctly. You know what answers you provided. If you are one of the 90 percent who need help, you'd better find a therapist you can work with." I realized I had better find out whether I had more programming that had not been cleared. I began working with a friend of mine who was a therapist. We found that most of my programming was locked up in the denial files It was about my relationship with my mother. (We will expand on this in the later chapters).

I have become aware that healing is entirely up to the client. We can suppress or cause a dysfunction to go into remission as I did, but is that a cure? In my research, I have discovered that we cannot heal anything unless the client has made the decision to heal at the subconscious level. There are no conditions that cannot be healed, just clients who will not allow themselves to accept healing. So it is up to those clients to decide if they want to make that commitment. Once that commitment is there, anything can be healed with love and forgiveness.

Many of the miracles in the past 30 years have seemed to happen when the clients were "at the end of their rope" and made a desperate commitment to change. At this point, it seems that anything is possible: We have seen bones, vertebrae and discs re-form; we've seen metal rods, screws and wire disappear. We have yet to find any dysfunction of the body or mind for which we cannot locate a base cause.

We tend not to describe diseases by names, because they are due to the same thing: lack of love and acceptance. There is always a payoff. Our biggest problem is to get the Conscious Mind to see that its programs are not serving the body well. If we can get that across, and the client has made the commitment to be healed, a miracle can happen. It could be spontaneous or take hours, weeks or months. People have asked me, "Why does it seem that no matter what *I* do, nothing happens, although others have experienced miracles in their lives?"

Some would get angry at me, or at God, for withholding the miracles. But we have no control over the results or the effectiveness of the work, since it is all self-healing. Only the individual has total control over those outcomes. My intention in developing N/CR was to give the practitioner a set of tools that could, if used properly, heal any dysfunction—from mental programming that seems to have no viable cause, to emotional codependency and addictive relationships, to physical breakdowns in the body, to life-threatening diseases, to physical and genetic dysfunctions. (It is very easy to release physical pain, because it reveals itself; emotional or mental disorders are much harder, since they are non-tangible.)

So far, we have not been stumped by any dysfunction. We can always get to the base cause and the core issue, but healing will not happen until clients display commitment and intention to heal themselves. (In the early days of N/CR, we focused on ego as being the enemy with an agenda to control our lives, mercilessly beat it up as the villain and enemy: "We are not exactly sure who is the problem, but we know it is in the mind." Since then we have learned differently.)

When we start to participate in true healing, we find that clients unwilling to take responsibility for their own healing will find every excuse to avoid being healed. Most of the time, the practitioner is blamed, but whatever the excuse is, it makes no difference—anything will do, as long as we can find somebody to blame. I also have found that some people refuse to be healed no matter what we do. I call this secondary affect. They are getting some payoff no matter how they justify it. It could be attention and recognition. They can be punishing themselves for something they have done in the past and they do not want to or refuse to recognize it.

That is the mind's trap: justification, excuses and self-righteousness work every time when clients do not want to see their path clearly. Placing our self-worth on the line with a client who has no commitment to healing can be discouraging and frustrating, so I have found detachment to be very important, if not essential. We must become compassionately detached. Then we can understand our clients' dilemmas, but we cannot rescue them or save them from themselves.

Chapter 1

Listening to the Messages the Body/Mind Reveals

This book is based on a commitment to let the body/mind tell us the story of our life histories, as recorded in detail within the Subconscious Mind, and an exploration of how we can rewrite the scripts on which we base those lives. Your Subconscious Mind is a computer recording system that records every word, action, and reaction, from the time you were a fetus up to the present time. It is on, 24/7; it does not miss anything. It will tell us what we need to know to correct our course, so we may achieve peace, happiness, harmony, joy, unconditional love, and success.

Some may find the following concepts and theories unacceptable or controversial, and even at times unbelievable. They come from thirty years of work with clients, as documented in the case histories and examples. After four years of practice, I discovered book-based psychology techniques were not working. This process is a totally new protocol, based on the theories I have developed over the last thirty years. In addition to the example of how we worked with some of the people throughout the book, there are eighty case histories. Some of these cases are listed in the chapters as examples; eighty of them are presented in Appendix A. Some clients have opted not to have their particular cases revealed, so these listings are limited to those people who allowed me to write about their cases.

The basic paths of our lives are planned before we even enter the body. Life can be compared to a crossword puzzle. All the open

squares represent free-choice decisions, while the black squares are lessons that we as a soul elected to learn. As we work through the puzzles of our lives, we may decide to avoid a black square and duck the lesson. We may even get into the lesson and then call for a time-out. The catch here is that we have only a limited number of those time-outs in our lives; when we've used them all, there are no more to take.

Our minds will reveal all the lessons we have to learn if we allow them to do so. We have to be able to ask the right questions and then accept the answers. (In our process, we ask these questions using Behavioral Kinesiology, a specific form of Kinesiology that makes contact with the Subconscious Mind.)

Avoiding the minor lessons will usually cause discomfort, unhappiness, or lack of love and abundance in our lives. If we choose a detour or denial to block a major lesson, we may instead manifest a severe, even life-threatening, disease or illness. However, if we seek out the lessons and reclaim our personal power, we may experience discomfort at times but will ultimately achieve peace, happiness, harmony, joy, and unconditional love and acceptance into our lives.

Your mind will provide the lessons. The question is, are you listening? Can you understand the message? Or for that matter, are you willing and open to change if the lesson requires a change in your life? Many times, it will require a change. It is your choice.

How Do We Choose Our Paths in Life?

Your life path is a macrocosm, covering many thousands of years, during which you make great strides and many

2

mistakes. This, in turn, creates karma that you can balance in future lives. You choose the place and the time to work out the lessons, and you have as long as you need to do a thorough job. The progress you have already made in the past allows you to make more effective choices in future lifetimes. Belief in reincarnation or not is irrelevant, since the cycle of return is a universal law. You know this at the soul level, and you will continue to return until you finish the journey, even if you do not accept or believe this concept about life. (For more information on these subjects, see my other books, *Becoming a Spiritual Being in a Physical Body* and *Journey Into the Light.*)

Choosing Your Family of Origin

Before birth, you as a soul chose your parents for the lessons you wanted to learn from them; they did not choose you. However, parents *can* influence the child to be born, by reading material and meditating on the qualities that will attract an evolved soul.

For example, in one Idaho family, the father was a potato farmer with barely a high school education, and the mother was a Korean war bride from a very poor background, also with little education. They had three children, two of whom were genius-level students, and all of whom attended college on scholarships. (The parents did not have the income to send even one of them to college.) The oldest child graduated from high school at fourteen and left graduate school at nineteen with a PhD. The second finished school almost as quickly. The third graduated in the normal timeframe with honors and also went on to earn a PhD. All three found very good positions in industry.

Their mother had programmed these children by teaching herself English and then reading aloud from the Bible and many scholarly magazines and books. (She admitted that she hadn't understood much of what she was reading when she'd begun her program.) My wife and I undertook similar measures and turned out two intelligent, well-adjusted sons. Unfortunately, most parents just start a family with no thought as to whom they are attracting as a child.

At the time of your conception, your body had a defect-free set of programs and blueprints to produce a perfect body. The lessons you wanted to learn (and the lessons your parents had to learn from you) determined the result in the body you were born with.

It may seem that you had no control over the defects that might have been in your body at birth; at the soul level, however, you were in total control of the outcome, based on the choices you made prior to birth. (Many of my clients with genetic defects have been able to totally release, heal, and correct them, so I know that those clients had created the lessons during the pregnancy from the "flight plan" that they filed when they chose to enter this life.)

Consider the case of a couple who delays having children until they graduate from college. The husband receives a good position as an instructor in the Department of Journalism of a renowned university. After a few years, they have accumulated significant wealth and decide to have a child.

They are both instructors in meditation and dream interpretation, so as soon as the wife is pregnant, the husband begins a dialogue with the soul that has chosen to come to them. This soul already knows much about how the life will unfold and describes what will happen once he or she is born and the nature of the lessons that will have to be learned—but without revealing what those lessons are.

The soul tells them it will be a boy and what his name will be. They do not like the choice of name, but they go along with it, since the soul is so accurate in his description of the lifestyle. The events he describes for their future are upsetting, so they check during meditation with their Source to see if this is true. It is all validated, which upsets them more. They now know what will happen but not how to stop or deflect it.

The soul tells them he will become seriously ill when he is six months old. If they do not get the lesson, he will drop back below his birth weight and die. It adds that when he is eighteen months old, he will have another medical emergency and that the father will also lose his job. If he does not get the lesson, they may both die. The father begins to doubt all this, since he is healthy, follows a good dietary program, and exercises daily. He begins to lose confidence, but in other areas, the information is getting more definitive, so he continues the dialogue.

The dialogues stop when the child is born, but what the soul has predicted happens right on schedule. At six months, the infant begins to lose weight and drops below his birth weight, but doctors cannot find anything medically wrong with him. (Their physician refers them to a homeopathic doctor, who has come up with miracle cures in the past, although the physician must officially disapprove of him.)

The homeopath is unable to help but referred them to Paul Solomon, a medium who does readings in the style of Edgar Cayce. Solomon tells told them to feed the child raw goat's milk, mixed half-and-half with lime water. This makes no sense at all to the parents, but it's all part of the lesson they have to learn, so they follow the direction. The child begins to gain weight.

After two months, New Jersey (where they live) passes legislation banning the sale of any kind of raw milk. They switch to pasteurized goat's milk, and their son begins to lose weight again. They now unsuccessfully scour health-food stores for raw goat's milk. The homeopathic doctor knows of a farm in New York selling it but warns, "You are perfectionist clean-freaks, and although the dairy is sanitary, do not be shocked at what you see. This may be your lesson."

Upon entering the farm, they are appalled. As they drive up to the house, a goat ambles out the front door. Cats and dogs run loose all over the place. As they get out of their car, two goats come up to them like dogs, looking for attention. They consider leaving, but know it's the only source of raw goat's milk in the area; they go up to the house to contact the lady about buying milk she comes out of the house and, in conversation, tells them about her own situation. She had married right out of high school and had several children, but then her husband had had her declared incompetent as a mother, put her on disability, won custody of her children, and run off with them. She has not seen them since. Without skills or training, since the disability payments ran out she's had no way to earn a living.

She has wanted to stay in the countryside, since she hated the city, so she's made her mind up and focused on what she wanted. She has also let go of withholds and limitations on being willing to receive whatever came along. As a result, a friend has given her some goats and the farm to manage. She now considers the goats her children, and treats them as such.

Now that raw milk has been banned, the goats she raises for sale and for milk are providing her a good income; the county inspectors have overlooked what she's doing, since it keeps her off welfare. She and the parents become good friends, and they begin helping her on her journey.

For the next five years, the story unfolds exactly as the soul predicted. They have many hard lessons to overcome, because they both have come from rule-controlled, compulsive families that had to have everything clean and perfect. But they learn to be more laid back and take life in stride. When the son is old enough to talk, they are amazed that he is able remember everything since his birth.

Children, up to the age of seven (whom adults would not consider very aware), often say the oddest things. One client told me that her four-year-old daughter said, "Mom, when I was your mother, I took better care of you than you're doing for me." (The story checked out under regression.)

In another case, a young girl called her grandmother "Mom," and her mother "Diane." It turned out that the grandmother was supposed to have been the little girl's mother, but had had an abortion at age thirty-four. The child was unaware of the situation, yet she was committed to clear this lesson with her would-be mother, now grandmother.

When we cleared all the lessons around the abortion and she forgave herself for having the abortion, it all cleared up. The next time she visited her daughter she was addressed as "Grandma". The child had never entered into the process, yet she changed her relationship with her grandmother herself.

Some children are aware and can control the situation to some extent. Two twins raised in the same way will respond differently, depending on the lessons agreed upon at the soul level between them and their parents.

You get to choose how you respond or react to how your parents treated and raised you. You can be a survivor or a victim. No matter how a child is mistreated and abused, survivors will eventually take control of their lives and succeed. (On the other hand, victims may suffer much less or not at all, yet claim some minor abusive treatment they blame for failure in their lives. Victims always have excuses to justify their failures.)

You made the choice prior to entering this life, but you have probably lost the directions and the checklist you made for your flight. You may remember why you're here, or may not know until you cross over out of this life. (Unfortunately, after-death hindsight does not count toward evolution.)

Granted, if you were raised in a functional family, you will have fewer problems succeeding in life. But how did you choose this family of origin? It all has to do with the intentions you built into your prenatal flight plan, and the progress made during the lessons you presented to yourself in past lives. You start each life exactly where you left off when you left the previous one. The level to which you aspire in this life determines the type of parents you choose and their genetic background, so your choices also govern your body makeup and your physical attributes.

A sad fact I've discovered from the thousands of clients I've worked with in the last thirty years is that seven out of ten children were rejected before they were born, and one in five was rejected after birth. Thus only one person in ten gets a fair start in life The longer I have worked in my new practice of Behavioral Mind Body Medicine, the more I've discovered that these numbers were far worse than I had thought originally. Further, only one person in 25,000 comes from a family functioning well enough to give a good start in life. (This is projected based on percentages from the people I have worked with.)

Over half my female clients did not want children, yet most did not even know this was programmed into their own minds. They often had children anyway, mainly due to erroneous programming instilled by the church and their parents, plus the societal pressures and religious dogma that have overlaid our society for centuries. By far the greatest cause of our problems today is childhood rejection and abandonment (more on this in later chapters).

When a soul realizes its choice of family was a mistake, it has two choices:

- If it decides not to proceed, it can choose not to enter the body, resulting in stillbirth.
- If the soul perceives that stillbirth will be rough on the family, it may accept that it chose to learn the lessons and opt to continue.

Later, if the child's life becomes too unbearable, the soul may still leave, resulting in a crib death (SIDS) or some form of respiratory failure. Very seldom do medical doctors find a reason, even though they will always assign a cause of death. (In my own case, as noted before, I had two near-death experiences trying to back out of my family.) This is not a common situation, yet it does happen. Many times it is a lesson for the parents to deal with as well. I have run into those lessons with clients.

Choosing Your Race

Whether we like it or not, there is a pecking order in today's world, in which some races are subjected to more poverty and suffering than others. Of course, no one race is superior to another, and it has been proven repeatedly that people can succeed, no matter what their origin. We choose our race, as well as other external characteristics, based on what we want to learn, or have not yet learned from the lessons presented to us already. Every soul must undertake lives of subjugation and oppression, just as lives of mastery and dominion. Karma is also a part of the lesson.

A black woman, who had excelled in college and had many good positions, found that many times she had lost her job due to racial favoritism; often, the person who replaced her was also black. She could not figure out why this was happening, since she was sometimes far more qualified than the person who replaced her.

When looking at the past lives, we found she had been a white slave trader in her last past life. When we were able to clear this Karma, her life smoothed out and returned to normal. (Western cultures have been trying to level the racial playing field for the last fifty years, but it will not work in the long run if there are lessons to be learned, since we must have choices in learning certain lessons.)

So how do I feel about these concepts now? To me, life is a workshop. We come here for fun, and soul-evolution. Some people have life naturally handled; they say their lives work and I applaud them if that's true. For success,

9

you must be in contact with your true self, which most people are not, because of subtle and insidious denial. Breaking through the denial usually takes an outside person. Even then it is difficult, because the mind is so clever at stopping or blocking programs. To me, life is a series of lessons. (If the word "lesson" irritates you, substitute whatever word you want, such as "experiences.")

I know one thing for sure, however: When you file your pre-birth flight plan, you must then follow your defined lesson plan. If a storm blows you off course, or you decide you don't want to follow the plan you submitted, you may then choose to rewrite it, as long as you still follow the lessons you must learn. If you decide to add a few detours, you might not get to your desired destination in this lifetime, but that is free choice.

If your detours result in a crash or you hit a storm, simply pick up the pieces and head back out. When that particular storm is over, you might have to correct your course. (That can be done easily if you have contact with guidance. Higher Self and your Subconscious Mind impose no time schedule on you. In fact, they don't care how many lifetimes your overall plan takes you.)

A final note: When you recognize the illusion, you can leave denial behind, and create a life of peace, happiness, harmony, joy, unconditional love, acceptance and financial abundance. If you do not have it now, then I hope the rest of this book provides you with some guidelines on how to get it. But that, too, is free choice. Have a great flight!

Chapter 2

The Body/Mind as a Vehicle for Personal Transformation

Everybody would like to live in happiness, joy, harmony and unconditional love; that was my goal, too. So why do most of us continue to follow paths that do not provide peace, happiness, harmony and joy?

Most of the time, we feel that if we have a concept down and a goal clearly in our minds, we can accomplish the task. In my research, I have found that most people put honest effort into changing their attitudes and behavior, so as to reclaim their self-esteem and self-worth. But many do not seem able to accomplish their goals, so they become discouraged, frustrated and disappointed.

When we evaluate what's needed to empower ourselves, to change our paths and reclaim self-esteem, we overlook the fact that our belief systems, along with the Middle Self (coupled with Subconscious Mind), are very powerful. The challenge is that we may have the concept down in the Conscious Decision-making Mind, but we must have acceptance from *all three* minds (See Chapter 6 for details).

I have found that Conscious Mind must be aligned with Subconscious Mind, or we will be sabotaged. We are unable to get our minds to work for us until we remove Inner and internal Conscious Mind. However, we will be unable to "see" the Middle Self and how it fits into the situation until we can recognize it and believe it. If we suppress or stuff our feelings, an illusion or denial will block our recognition of a problem situation. If we deny the problem, it does not exist in our realities.

11

Of course, that doesn't mean that the situation doesn't exist; it just doesn't exist for *us*. It still exists separate from our willingness to recognize it. Young children have little or no control over how their primary caregivers' treatment impacts them, and they form their beliefs in reaction to that early treatment. The programs thus laid down continue throughout our adult lives, or until we change them. We lose our self-esteem and self-worth by giving away our personal power and allowing others to control how we feel.

However, few of our parents realize they are programming us through the negative emotions of rejection, disapproval, scolding, shame, guilt and fear. Some children are so sensitive to how they are treated or what is said, their lives can be programmed for failure or success. As a result, they may relinquish their personal power and begin to reject themselves, *even before the first birthday.*

This happens to adopted children in almost every situation. During the second year, children will begin to push their mothers for love, acceptance and recognition. They assume since they were born with the knowledge of what that recognition, acceptance and love are, their mothers should know this, too.

The terrible twos erupt because the mother is withholding these qualities from the child. At least that's their perception— the child does not understand this, so he/she keeps pushing for love and recognition. Mother does not recognize this, so she begins to get irritated as the child keeps pushing.

We end up with a standoff, with the mother thinking the child is acting out: yelling, crying and putting on tantrums. He or she feels Mother is denying love and recognition, because as children they are not all right. This causes them to feel rejected and abandoned, which leads to self-rejection. This sows the seeds for losing any recognition of what love is. By age four, ninety-eight percent of us have lost this concept of love with which we were born.

Most people assume love is indifference. This has been proven out with most of my clients over the last thirty years.

By the third year, many children have already set up their life paths to become self-destructive. If this happens often, we separate ourselves from Source, and when we experience separation from the presence of God within, we separate ourselves from our pipeline to unconditional love. Many people have an illusion that any focused and concentrated form of attention is love (even physical abuse); for healing to occur, their ideas of love must be re-established.

I have found that over 99 percent of my clients do not love themselves. Becoming "all right" with themselves requires unraveling the negatives created by isolation, rejection, frustration, discouragement, disappointment, fear, invalidation, guilt and humiliation. We can attempt to give others praise, strokes, support and recognition for empowerment, and try to help them to recover their self-esteem and self-worth, but many will discount and reject such validation if they feel they're unworthy of it.

Contrary to popular belief, self-esteem, self-worth and self-confidence are not learned or something you can teach someone. We all have positive self-supporting qualities at birth, as well as the ability to experience peace, happiness, joy and harmony. We are born in love and acceptance, not in sin as many religious people would have us believe.

As we grow up, our perceptions and interpretations of how we were treated by our primary caregivers begin to shape our beliefs and our view of reality and ourselves. We do not lose our self-esteem, self-worth and self-confidence; they are overwritten by negative contrary experiences as a child. Our perception of self either destroys or enhances our "self" qualities.

To compile a "Self-worth Inventory," we must look at the qualities that make us feel all right with ourselves. I use the term "all-rightness" to encompass all the positive cluster qualities that give us the ability to feel and claim our self-esteem. I have separated them to list them, but generally, if we have one, we will have them all, as they are cluster qualities. They cannot be separated:

13

1. Self-esteem: feeling good about yourself with no need for external validation or approval.

2. Self-love: ability to recognize, support, respect, trust yourself, and take responsibility, knowing you are all right without outside support. You empower yourself to be kind and caring of self, following a wellness program such as exercise and eating properly, and listening to and respecting your body.

3. Self-confidence: You know you are able to accomplish your goals, and you take responsibility for them.

4. Self-approval: You do not need anyone's approval or sanction to know that your actions are acceptable.

5. Self-acceptance: You can be happy without another person's love, support or acceptance.

6. Self-validation: You are all right. Nobody has to validate you or tell you that you are all right or loved.

Seldom do we know the base causes of any dysfunction in our lives. The body is a vehicle that will always tell you your history and the truth, for every sensory input has been stored in your cellular memory. Your Subconscious Mind's video/audio recorder has recorded every incident, reaction and response that has ever happened to you, along with actual voice and pictures in absolute accuracy; nothing is ever overlooked, discarded or deleted.

Figure 1 shows that we can deal with conflict in our lives in one of two ways:
   a) Defensive and closed, which leads to the intent to protect against anticipated pain and fear, or
   b) Non-defensively and open, with the intent to learn from the conflict.

With low self-esteem, and self-worth eroded by a negative environment, our primary motivation is the avoidance of future pain. We employ three main pain-avoidance strategies:

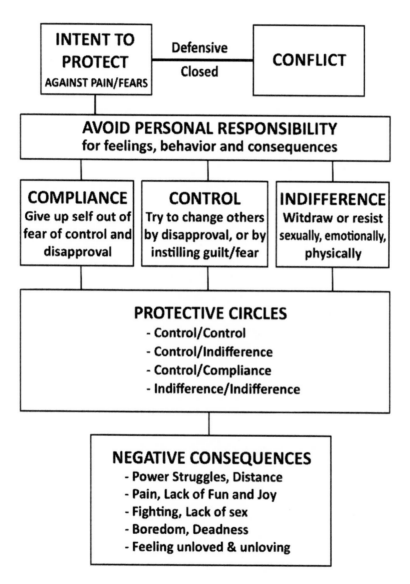

Figure 1a: Defensive, closed approached to conflict

- *Compliance:* we comply out of fear of retribution and disapproval, which can lead to a "see-saw" of control behavior and retraction. We give in and comply.

- *Control:* we try to manipulate others by instilling guilt in them, as in "You'll be sorry when I'm dead or when I run away from home."

- *Indifference:* we withdraw, which can lead to sullen, unresponsive behavior.

In all three strategies, we develop mechanisms to cope with outer rejection and the negative consequences of our coping mechanisms, such as fighting with siblings, meaningless activities such as "hanging out," and appearing as though nothing matters. On the other hand, with self-esteem and self-worth intact, we are eager to learn about the world and how we can best interact with it. We take responsibility for our actions and their consequences, seeing life as a learning experience. This leads to three main areas of exploration:

- Ourselves and other people, accepting any transitory pain that may result as part of the rich tapestry life.
- Why we and others act and feel as we do, and seeking the reasons behind what happens.
- Such areas as childhood, fears, expectations and personal responsibility.

This openness leads to being able to share love in intimate relationships, accepting them as arenas in which to resolve conflicts and explore personal freedom, with the overarching goals being growth of self, other and the relationship itself. The main conflict is that we must know what unconditional love and acceptance are before we can give love to our families, friends, partners and children.

The word "love" is used very flippantly by most people. They do not have the slightest concept of what love really means, because 99 percent of us have lost the meaning and understanding by the time we are four to five years old.

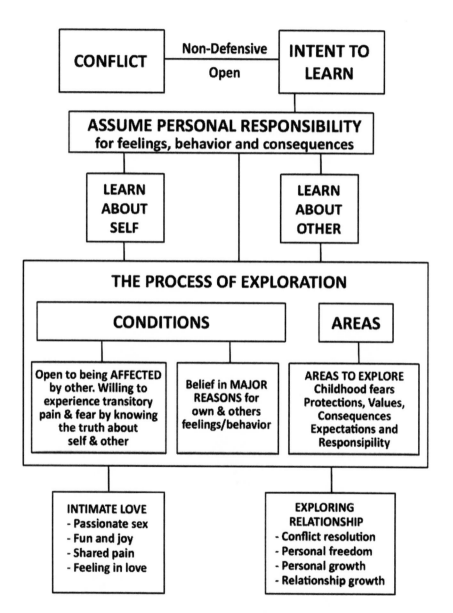

Figure 1b: Open, non-defensive approach to conflict

Your Body is Talking, Are You Listening?

Chapter 3

My Journey Into Healing

As a healing researcher since 1978, I use myself as my own laboratory to try new concepts. For the first seven years, being unable to find any alternative therapy that would totally relieve the pain in my body, I believed the doctors' prognosis that I would have to live with the pain for the rest of my life, and if it became unbearable, take painkillers. Their final prognosis was that my spine would deteriorate to the point that my muscles could no longer support my weight and I would be confined to a wheelchair. *I proved their prognosis totally false. The battle with your body can be won.*

I have achieved that end without surgery or drugs. Let's say that doctors are not wrong: they can only understand what their training and research gives them. Since few doctors do research, their education ends when they graduate from medical school. I was not willing to accept their diagnoses, and so I went beyond what the linear mind could comprehend. *"If my body can create this pain,"* I thought, *"something is making it do this, and I want to know what!"* I had no idea how I would accomplish this, but I did know this: "when the student is ready, the teacher will appear."

In a 1978 workshop, Ronald Beesley asked any participants with severe pain or a major dysfunction affecting their life to submit a written description and he would select six people to use as demonstrators. One of those was me, and after twenty minutes, for the first time in seventeen years, I was miraculously pain-free. However, it only lasted for a few days. One of Beesley's students, Reg Newbon, had an office three-and-a-half hours from my home, and I committed to a session every other week. I went to him for about two years for treatments.

Newbon's treatment revealed many of the causes for my pain. He used hands-on methods, touching the various points on my body that he said held the imprint of the experience that was causing the pain. By holding the point, he was able to release the charge held in that location, massaging along each side of the spine, and pushing into its center from both sides. He also cleared the etheric fields and the chakras. I was so impressed by the process that I attended three one-week workshops—an important stepping stone on my path.

The problem was, the pain would return if I did not keep to the schedule. Why, I wondered, did the pain keep coming back? I started going to the hot springs in nearby Calistoga in the Napa Valley, and had a deep-tissue massage from Frank Hughes, the owner of Nance's Hot Springs. Going far beyond just a relaxing experience, his technique was more manipulation of the muscles and bones, similar to osteopathy.

When I started out, I had a double "S" curve in my spine, and had shrunken a full inch in height between ages thirty and forty. The vertebrae were so tight that he could not move them by himself; he needed an assistant to hold me down as he tried to relax the muscles. It was painful, but my posture slowly returned. I explored many other alternative therapies to supplement Frank's work, but few people were willing to use the necessary force. I was frustrated because most physical therapists claimed they could heal me, but none did; the pain always returned.

In hindsight, my expectations may have been too high; the practitioners were doing the best they could, but their best wasn't good enough. I studied many alternative therapies with very little results. Most of the practitioners said they could help me but very few did. *I wanted the pain gone now.*

In 1978, I became involved in *A Course In Miracles*, but after the first five lessons, I found it too intense and threatening, and stopped reading. Later that year, I attended a seminar in San Diego—the Mandala Conference, at which Dr. Jampolsky presented a workshop—and was so enthused that I started going to his weekly groups. I was amazed at the energy in the group some nights; all we did was hold hands in a circle asking for help, and people would be healed on the spot.

I also first met Paul Solomon at that same seminar; three months later, I got a call out of the blue: "Paul is holding a workshop today in Palo Alto; you're supposed to be there, but we forgot to let you know. The introductory lecture was last night, but you can attend the first day of the workshop for ten dollars. Sorry about the short notice."

After that message, how could I not go? The workshop was far more than I expected, and changed my life forever. It was being repeated the next weekend, and I canceled my plans so that I could attend. I became deeply involved with Solomon's work, almost to the point of addiction. I attended every West Coast event for the next ten years, including one- and two-week residential workshops. In 1982, I even attended a two-week teacher-training course in Virginia Beach.

The most memorable aspect of his work was what he called the "X-Factor in Healing": the need to integrate all levels of body/mind and spirit to cause healing to take place, and the need for clear and focused intention to the purpose of healing. He talked about spontaneous healing miracles, in which clients were brought to an intention so complete that they let go of fear and anger, resulting in instantaneous healing. (This has since happened to me a few times with my clients.)

The next most important ingredient, he said, is unconditional love. When this is present, miracles also happen. My experience with clients since has shown me that healers must have their own "love issues" resolved, and be coming from 100- percent unconditional self-love. Then the clients will have amazing results. When clients can feel the practitioner's love coming to them, with no withholds or needs attached, healing miracles can take place. The practitioner must be able to project this caring, so that more than fifty percent is directed toward the client. (To me, this was the critical factor in healing: How can I do love-based work if I do not know what love is?)

RIGHT BRAIN

With Paul's guidance in mind, I set out to understand love. No one in my family had known what love was, let alone demonstrated unconditional love. My parents had given me material things and called it love, but there had always been strings attached. (There had been no love in their childhoods, either; they were doing the best they knew how.)

My first task, then, was to recognize the love deficiency in my life, so I started to attend workshops that involved vulnerability and support, beginning with a week-long workshop with Paul Solomon. When I saw men hugging, all manner of fears came up, and my first impulse was to leave. My family had been judgmental, with no intimacy, so all my childhood programs were challenged. However, I stuck it out, and when I went home, the first thing I did was to tell my wife Susie that I loved her. Up until then, she'd had to dig it out of me. For some reason, even saying the word "love" had scared me.

A surprised Susie responded, "Can I attend one of those workshops? I'd like to get some of what you got!" We attended the next workshop together, and it totally changed our relationship. We realized that for thirteen years, we had simply been living in the same house. The more I dug into what causes healing to happen, the more I learned about love.

I now wondered what it was that drove my body back into pain between my bi-weekly treatments. I realized that although they both had the same end-result in mind and both worked to release pain, Reg Newbon and Frank Hughes were coming from opposite ends of the spectrum: Reg from a purely spiritual orientation, and Frank from the position that if you press hard enough on the body's trigger points and adjust the muscles, the tension will release. Frank was having more success, so I stopped going to Reg. But I knew there had to be more to it than weekly treatments. Why were my muscles tightening up all the time?

Between 1977 and 1981, I studied more with Paul Solomon, along with my training for a Masters degree in Psychology. I came to realize how much the emotional component of dysfunction needed to be understood. However, there were still no teachers talking about how to apply psychological principles to pain in the body; only in the late 1990s would people become more aware of somatic (body/mind) oriented therapy. I decided to apply all the guidance my teachers had offered, and take some new directions as well.

I attended seminars at UC Berkeley on Chinese and Tibetan Medicine, as well as a workshop on Homeopathy with George Vithoulkas. He looked at a person as an integrated unit in which the body is a manifestation of personality, thoughts, emotions and sensations. This was the right direction, but the training was too long and arduous. (I tried Ayurveda with the same results; going through all the processes—just to find the cause, let alone treat it—would take many years.)

In April of 1979, I attended Solomon's two-week live-in seminar on Advanced Inner Light Conscious. It was a real eye-opener: on the third day, I started feeling very cold; as soon as the session started, I turned white as a sheet and passed out. When I came to at the break, I was unaware that I'd passed out, and even denied it. When the session resumed fifteen minutes later, however, I passed out again. When I finally came to at the end of the session, I felt as though I'd been hit by a truck, and went directly to bed.

The following morning, I could barely move. I skipped breakfast and finally got to the morning session late. All I wanted to do was go home. Something in me was extremely scared and did not want to be there. (In fact, over the next two weeks, ten other people left, but I'd paid my money and was determined to finish the course, no matter how much my body/mind resisted.)

One of the instructors agreed to work with me to find out what was going on. We found that every concept I held about who I was felt threatened. The concentrated energy of being with those people and the intensity of the work were forcing my whole being to change all of its beliefs, and my fragile reality was being threatened. (For just one example, I hadn't realized until

23

then that I was both a control addict and, by today's standards, a counter-dependent.)

The following days were a little easier, but I was still on edge. I was rebuked for talking too much and monopolizing conversations. More processing revealed that I only felt accepted if people let me control the conversation. That workshop taught me many painful lessons around acceptance and validation. Of course, I came out of it a very different person. However, I was now addicted to such high-intensity workshops, so I attended three more. I just couldn't seem to satisfy my thirst for a new life, and couldn't understand why others lacked the same drive.

In 1982, we settled a legal action that freed up some funds, and my family and I spent almost four months traveling around the U.S. We attended another two-week workshop with Solomon's group in Virginia Beach; it was another eye opener. This workshop was for people who wanted to teach his concepts.

It was a real emotional shocker, as we worked on communication and how to clearly present a concept without any need to be validated. It was like confrontational group therapy: if we justified a position, the trainers would work us over to show us our misconceptions, and why we w e r e defending ourselves. At times, it was really hard to respond and not react, as it would hit my feelings very hard. Their intent was to break down all our needs to hurt others or feel put down by what someone else would say. Their contention was that you cannot be a good teacher if you have any need to be accepted or validated for what you present. You must be above judgment, control, reaction or having any need to be "better than."

This was a "walk your own talk" seminar at the highest level. Being there gave me time to take stock. With five people confined in an RV, we were able to work out and practice what we had learned. By the end of the trip, I understood why my pain always returned: resurfacing beliefs and the programs that drove my life were continually refreshing it. Frank would release the pent-up energy by working my trigger points; my body and muscles would relax, and healing would seem to have happened, but the driving force was still there. Over the following days, the stress and tension of daily life would rebuild, and the muscles would tighten up again.

At a 1981 seminar on Hawaiian Huna work, a man asked me to help his daughter, who suffered from prism vision. I discovered it was a genetic condition caused by a past-life experience with her father. Through hypnosis after the fourth session, the condition cleared up in two days, and has never since returned, even after twenty years. This was my introduction to miracle healing.

Suddenly, in 1982, my whole reality shifted as I saw clearly how programs had been driving my life. We also purchased a computer, which opened my mind about how it was operating. Over the next two years, my understanding clarified. In 1984, I decided to change my whole practice over to somatic (body) based therapy.

As I began to shift to hands-on work, I lost those clients who'd simply wanted a therapist to hold their hands and commiserate about how bad their lives were. I now decided to work only with clients who demonstrated progress in each session.

My first experience with this new integrated process was with a male client having trouble dealing with women. He had lost two jobs from this fear, and was about to get fired for missing work at his present position. I focused on his situation and went directly to the problem at hand, but still could not help clear his fear of women. I asked him to lie down on my massage table, and found a large painful lump on his back near the left shoulder blade.

I put my hand on it and an affirmation came from my inner self: "*I know that my mother treated me badly, and I felt rejected and abandoned by her. I recognize she was doing the best she could, and I accept that now. I realize she did not know the effect she was having on me. I am loving and forgiving her now, unconditionally.*" Immediately, the lump and the pain disappeared completely. Not only that, he was able to return to work. Of course, clearing one program brought up many more, but after many sessions, we had cleared the whole situation.

This experience confirmed my decision to abandon talk therapy, since it was only marginally effective. I realized I had discovered why my own pain h a d returned after each release—it was the programming! As I explored this further, I discovered it was the reprogramming by affirmations that released the pain. I also realized that I could not do the reprogramming for my clients; I could develop the program for them, but they themselves had to delete the old program and install the new one. The big "ah-ha" for me was that in saying the affirmation for the client to repeat, I was reprogramming myself at the same time. During the next five years, I was able to cause my own healing by working with my clients.

Many of my colleagues were suspicious of what I was doing. Some resented my success, while others referred clients to me when they ran into immovable blocks. As word spread of my results, my client-list grew quickly, and my own back pain started releasing because I'd been able to include myself in the therapy process along with clients with similar programs and patterns to mine. Over the next four years, I cleared much of my pain. Stating the affirmations for the clients to repeat helped me almost as much as it helped them.

My next miracle came shortly after I began my body-based therapy. I was giving a weekly lecture, and an attendee asked, "Can you do something about back pain that was created by surgery? I understand your problem is similar to mine, but the difference is that the surgery was not successful."

She had four vertebrae tied together with stainless steel wire. Because her back would not fuse after the first surgery, the doctors h a d removed the discs and wired up the vertebrae, forcing them to fuse. The pain was now so intense that she was on the verge of suicide. She ended her question with, "I want you to heal me."

I told her I was not able to do that. "Only you can do the healing. It is your mind that does the healing." (I was saying this in 1986. Now we get Bruce Lipton validating this, both in 2006 and again in the DVD interview he did in 2013.)

Until then, I had called myself a healer, so my response surprised even me. "I can't heal you; only you can heal you. I just show you the way. I am a software developer for your mind."

I didn't know what to think when, after our session, she called to say that the pain had gone away that day for the first time in ten years. When we went into the process, we found that many of her problems were past-life, with others tied in with her parents in this life, both of whom totally rejected her. In fact, they had not wanted any children, so she'd been rejected before birth. Both were Colonels, hard-line lifers in the Air Force. She had been a mistake. After her birth, she got little time with her parents, as Air Force nannies took care of her.

I discovered that all her back problems were caused by this rejection and abandonment by her parents, plus her own self-rejection: *If my parents didn't want me, why would anyone else?* She had so many "I'm not all right" "I'm not accepted" and "I don't fit in programs" factors, all attached to the self-rejection, they had actually been eating away at her vertebrae and discs. (This was the same thing that had happened to me.)

She set another appointment, but later called to cancel. She had been in a car accident the following day and had been taken to the hospital for x-rays to see if she had any injuries. She later called me, bursting with excitement. "Do you believe in miracles?" she asked. "The latest x-rays show that the wire is gone, and all the discs are back, perfect, as well as the vertebrae. What do you make of that?" If she could have crawled through the phone she would have.

Removed discs grown back? Wire disappeared? Yes, it was a miracle, but at the time, I had no idea how it had happened. I now know that this happens all the time with N/CR. The infinite power of the mind can heal immediately if you are committed to healing, which is indeed amazing.

As I continued working with the process, I was making great progress with my clients, but there was nobody to work on me.

In September 1987, Chris Issel asked me to teach a workshop on the process, if she could get a group together. She then became so proficient in N/CR that we began trading sessions. My progress in becoming pain-free quickly became a reality I could know. At this point, the N/CR process also made a major leap; I was now on the road, speaking at bookstores and giving lectures and workshops all over California.

In 1989, I met Mike Hammer, and he learned N/CR as if he had already known it. I needed a workshop co-presenter and Mike was a perfect match for me. We learned much during our three years together, and by trading sessions with Mike, after 30 years of agony I finally became pain-free.

With all the new practitioners trained in NCR, my horizons rapidly opened up. My body was now really talking to me. Odd pains still surfaced, but in different places on my body. In each case, I had plenty of help in understanding the causes and releasing the pain.

From 1991 to 1996, the information floodgates opened. I had a steady stream of partners with whom I could do research. We found how to release pain, anytime it appeared, by looking for the lesson or the cellular memory that w as talking. Many times, we found, it was a Middle Self fear-based interpretation, which had no value. In an effort to protect us, Middle Self will set up what it thinks is a valid reaction. This requires us to take it to task over making decisions about our health and direction without our permission.

At one point, a friend asked me if I'd worked out all of my mother issues. I said yes, because I'd been working on them for over ten years. That really sparked a reaction that brought up issues I had no idea were still active, such as my unwillingness to tell the truth, especially to my mother. Once I saw my habit of telling people what they wanted to hear, so that I would not get rejected, my left shoulder locked up so badly that I needed painkillers for the first time in over twenty years. Over the next week, eight people worked on me for a total of fourteen hours to clear the old programs. This opened a whole new area in

N/CR: denial. We bury issues we don't want to deal with if they are too painful or fearful to handle. (We also found this connected to experiences with my mother. I knew I needed to talk with her and make peace with her.)

A good example of this was an incident that had caused me a lot of pain, so I had denied it, locked it up in the files. It began to come out when we started working on my mother issues again. I had no recollection of this, nor did I remember anything about it, until I talked with my mother about the incident. She showed me pictures of the tricycle, which did not bring up any recall either. Apparently, in 1943, my father had bought a used tricycle, fixed it up with new paint and given it to me for a Christmas present. My mother had been gone, taking care of her friend's children, so there had been no problems at the time.

When she had returned, two years later, it had really caused conflicts. My mother had objected to me letting other children ride it, so she'd locked it up in the basement and told me, "When you agree to take care of it, I'll give it back to you." I don't feel it was about the other children riding it at all, I think it had reminded her about her guilt of abandoning me. This happened three times. The fourth time I came home from school to ask for my tricycle, it had was gone; she had sold it, to teach me a lesson. Fifty years later, she still contended that she had done the right thing.

How does a six-year-old feel when his only big toy is sold out from under him? *"I am not all right! She does not love me! She has abandoned and rejected me!"* Many more feelings like this had caused me to block the whole thing out.

To this day, I don't remember anything about it, even though it was brought up during a session, and I then talked with my mother about the situation to clear it. She showed me a picture of me sitting on the tricycle. That did not bring up any memories either.

Shortly after she had sold my tricycle, however, the NDE had happened, the catalyst that caused my near death experience. A boy had been chasing me in the schoolyard and I had run into a square garbage can. It had looked like a bruise, so nobody thought much about it. I was having severe abdominal pain; my mother took me to the doctor, and he diagnosed it as stomach flu.

Two weeks later I finally told my mother that when I went to the bathroom the bowel movements were black. She called a friend whose husband was a doctor. "Get him to my office immediately," he said, "I will be there in half an hour."

He told his nurse to cancel all his appointments that day, took me to the hospital and put me in surgery immediately. What he found was a ruptured intestine that had been bleeding; my abdomen was full of the peritonitis from the break in the intestine. After ten hours on the operating table, the doctors were able to sew up the intestine and clean out all the peritonitis. During the final phase the monitors showed my vital signs disappeared, and they assumed I had died.

They attached a ventilator and tried to restart my heart. For twenty one minutes I was flatlined, with no vital signs. I was then revived and came back, but went into a coma for six days. They told my mother since I had had no respiration, I might have sustained brain damage, and would likely have learning disabilities.

When I came out of the coma, they began checking me for brain damage and communication, as well as eyesight and hearing disabilities. The only thing they found was that I was dyslexic, and could not read or write effectively. (Since then, during my practice as a healer, I have found that many clients have had similar things happen in their lives.)

New areas keep opening up all the time. For example, in July of 1996, I mysteriously started to lose my hearing; by December, I was stone-deaf. Refusing to accept that any dysfunction is final, I continued giving lectures and workshops, and by September of 1997, with the help of Bernard Eakes, I had recovered my hearing completely, only to lose it, again in December.

We located the internal programs and I recovered it again, but then in July of 1998, I again partially lost it. In the spring of 1999, I recovered the hearing in my left ear, but it continued to

30

come and go as more programs surfaced; I had some form of deafness seven times from 1995 to 2008, twice being stone deaf for six months at a time. I have since finally overcome the fear that caused the deafness.

Each occurrence has been due to fear: of presenting the N/CR concepts and my new devices from electronic medical research, and of publishing my books. It's a deep fear program, that people will not be interested in the books and they will not sell, and has been an obstacle for many years.

I would sit down at my computer to work on a book and pass out, as the survival-oriented programs and beliefs in Middle Self tried to prevent me from writing, in case I might make a fool out of myself. However, once I knew what was happening, I could deal with the multiple personalities responsible and remove them.

As of the reprinting of this book, I have not had any recurrence of deafness as I finally made it over the hill into my own alrightness. After over twenty years of trying to prove my concepts, I realized that I do not have do this anymore; I do not have to prove anything. The concepts can stand alone in the world of alternative healing, as proven by my books being sold in many countries around the world.

It's only a start, but acceptance is now building, and we receive calls, from within the U.S. and Canada plus many countries around the world, asking for information about our work and when we plan to be in the caller's country. (Ironically, while I now appreciate the validation, I no longer need it.)

To understand why we separate from self, we must reconstruct our childhoods. The reason psychotherapy does not get to the cause is that it cannot reveal how our childhood programming affected us as it did, since we seldom accurately remember our childhood experiences. Therapists can only work with what clients tell them, and, most of the time, clients describe the results of how they felt about an incident in their lives, which is the result of the programming. They don't understand the programming but they are reacting to it.

This has to do with how we react to a stimulus before us. Two twins can react totally differently to their parents even though the parents claim they treated the twins exactly the same. As a therapist, because I was clairvoyant, I was able to actually read the program files and describe them to my clients. However, I wasn't able to reprogram the mind's files at the time, but I now have the tools to do exactly that.

A good example of this is the following childhood experience. In the 1940s, schoolteachers favored right-handed children and looked down on left-handed children as aberrant. I was ambidextrous but favored my left hand. Thinking they were helping me, my teachers forced me to use my right one. The result was total dysfunction in my bicameral brain interpretation.

Added to this was the stress of my mother leaving the family home. The fragmentation caused by feeling that I had to please the teacher destroyed my self-worth, and I became totally dyslexic, unable to read or write. Whatever I wrote came out backwards, and the teacher had to hold the paper up to a mirror. When I read aloud, the words were reversed and sounded like some code language. This appeared after the near-death experience.

Instead of understanding the problem the teachers had caused, they classified me as "learning disabled." They had no program to deal with, so my mother was told to keep me out of school until they could teach me to read and write. I had a tutor come to my home two or three days a week. By adulthood, I did not even know this had happened to me, because I was suppressing it to the point of denial-of-denial. After clearing this incident, my residual dyslexia with numbers disappeared and I can now even speed-read without any problems.

It is difficult for men to show emotion or express their feelings if it shows them as vulnerable. I broke this barrier when I realized that sub-personalities were causing me to act with a macho male attitude: having to be strong, never showing emotions, and always having to be right. These are what one would call Ego.

Once I understood Ego and realized what was creating these personality self-traits, it was not Ego at all; Ego was just the file manager. It had no agenda, nor was it the enemy that many people make it out to be. I was able to overcome this false concept and allow myself to become open and vulnerable. When this happened, I also realized that I had become more accepted and trusted.

One of the major breakthroughs came with the movie *Field Of Dreams*, which brought up so much emotion that my wife, Susie, took almost a half hour to process it out. I realized that I had not cleared with my father before he died. He had been my champion, yet I had not known it, since my mother had verbally beaten him up so badly that one day he had just walked out and died.

I had known at the time (1976) that I had something to do, the day before he passed on, but I had not known what it was. We had cleared him of three life-threatening diseases, yet we had not won the battle. My mother had won the battle, though, and she had not even known what she had done. I talked to her about it, but she did not understand what I was talking about. She had no frame of reference to understand it.

I was very disturbed because I had helped heal him from three life-threatening illnesses. The doctors had given him three months to live after they found pancreatic cancer, but he had lived for many years after the cancer was healed. Until I saw this movie, I had stuffed all my feelings, but now they all came pouring out at once. One of the most troubling feelings was that my son had been deprived of his grandfather, who had adored him. They had had a bond that was building a supportive relationship, which my son had missed for a long time.

When I worked with a client who had the same experience, or described my experience in a lecture, emotions would start and tears would flow. It did not seem to bother me anymore, and it actually drew people in more when they saw that I could be vulnerable in front of them and allow my feelings to surface.

A client recently brought Wayne Dyer's new tape set, *There is a Spiritual Solution To Every Problem*, to a session and insisted I listen to it. "It sounds like you're talking to me in a different voice," he said. "This is what you've been saying for fifteen years. Why is it that Wayne Dyer gets an audience and you don't seem to get the exposure?"

I asked him, "How many of Wayne's books have you read?"

"All of them," he replied.

My response was, "Well, what does that tell you? He's been writing books and speaking to audiences for over twenty-five years. My books have only been in stores for three years. (This was in 2009.) You don't get recognition until you get books published."

"I guess your time is coming then."

As I was revising this book and listening to the tapes, some of the stories and anecdotes brought up many tears and emotions. When these emotions have come up, I have realized that denial-of-denial programs are surfacing. I had not dealt with these issues. The tapes are catalysts, and they will always bring up suppressed files. We must be willing to deal with these files when they come up, as they are limiting our enlightenment and evolvement.

Sometimes in sessions, I've had an emotional reaction when the same issues I had not yet worked out surfaced for clients. It seems now I have worked out most of my issues, as I have not had a reaction while working with a client in over ten years; we both have the chance to get our feelings out and clear them. Some therapists find this embarrassing, because they do not feel they are the strong leaders they should be. However, the result of their avoidance attitude puts clients in a hard place from which to deal. There is much more to my journey on this path, which appears in my book *Becoming A Spiritual Being In A Physical Body*.

Chapter 4

There Is a Way Out: Healing Miracles

To some people, a miracle is something with no reasonable explanation. Something happens that, under normal circumstances, would not take place in an ordinary way. Some people would say, "God caused healing to happen." Does that make sense as an explanation for miracles?

In my practice, none of these make sense, because we are assuming that some outside force is at work. In my experience, miracles are ordinary happenings that take place all the time to people with the desire, commitment, and discipline to clear all the programs, beliefs, doubts and skepticism that block the effects of total transformation.

The best explanation is that miracles are mechanical effects that happen when there is nothing to block the effect of healing. Recovery is possible. We do not have to live in pain, emotionally or physically. Dysfunctional behavior, illness and disease are states of mind that we accept and allow to exist in our bodies and minds.

We must recognize that healing is possible if we will allow the body/mind to heal itself. As we saw earlier in this book, healing does not happen if we have resistance, resentments and unresolved emotional attachments that we have not let go of. Detachment and forgiveness are the keys to healing, happiness, harmony, peace and joy in life.

To reiterate, this process is not spiritual healing. We are following rules that produce the same results every time, in double-blind experiments, as long as people commit themselves to following the protocol and guidelines, and to disciplining themselves to obeying the directions provided in the process. Most people view healing as a spiritual process, but it is not at all. We carry baggage we brought in from past lives and/or emotional issues encountered as a child. We clear these by changing the programming and writing new life scripts.

Whatever you believe forms your reality, and generates the programs and patterns that drive your life. You may not even believe that you created your life as it is, but are you willing to unload all your false beliefs and transform your life now? There is no time other than now. Again, as Walt Kelly's cartoon-character Pogo said, *"We have met the enemy and it is us."*

If you think you are not ready and will wait to do it when you are ready, you may wait until your next life. You must decide, and there is no better time than now. Do it now and see what happens; you have nothing to lose except your pain and discomfort. Once you find your path, you can get on with your mission in life.

Of course, change causes fear because most people would rather suffer than change. If you are in denial, you may not even be aware that you're not on the path. Sometimes, playing victim can get you many rewards—you can control other people and manipulate them to give you attention even though you deny what you're doing. *You can be in denial of denial, which gives you the illusion that you're living your truth—"There's nothing wrong with me; I'm all right just the way I am"—and nobody can break that illusion except you.* Of course, you must first recognize the illusion.

How do you confront your illusions? There is a way out if you want to reclaim your personal power and take responsibility. No one can heal you; it's all on your shoulders. When you decide that life is not working the way you are now, all you need do is decide to confront the delusion, the umbrella you're living under. But people can seldom see their own illusions because denial obscures them. When you are inside your illusion, you can not see you are in an illusion. Some people have been able to break through the denial themselves, but it takes tremendous personal power to reclaim responsibility and be willing to fly into new territory.

It is like jumping off a cliff and knowing you can fly, or what I call the "Jonathan Livingston Seagull lesson," because you're jumping into the unknown. Very few people are willing to do this, so they continue in their dysfunctional lifestyles. Transformation requires you to jump out of the nest and fly. Looked at from the outside, it may seem simple, but trying to fly while holding onto the fear of letting go will bring up fear of the unknown. You can find many reasons not to fly, including blaming other people for causing your reluctance.

In an effort to stop you from threatening your safety and security, your mind will set up myriad reasons why this is happening. *Remember, your mind considers the status quo as security* and works to prevent anything that threatens that security (such as change), so we must confront that fear and work through it.

An excellent example of this happened during a session with a new client. When we began the basic clearing of programs, she would leave her body (a common occurrence when a person does not want to confront or deal with the issue we are working with).

As we began clearing the shadow self, she again left, and I could not get her to come back into her body. She started shaking and began to experience intense abdominal pain. When I checked to see if her file and program managers were functioning, we found all the sub-personalities and programs we had just cleared were all back in place, and Instinctual Mind had taken over again.

After a long talk with her Conscious Mind, to persuade it to let go of fear and allow us to rewrite the operating system, we found that she had zero control over her life and was afraid to reclaim control because it was foreign to her. We reinstalled the file and program manager, and everything went all right until we asked Inner Child to release Magical Child. Reading the affirmation triggered an intense emotional reaction, and everything we had just cleared crashed again. We had to start over again, beginning with getting her back into her body since she'd left it again and crashed all the new programs.

Eventually, we discovered that she had been living her life through Inner Child and Magical Child. Our attempts to release them had crashed her whole means of coping with life (her "operating system"). We started over again and worked through the fear, reinstalling a new operating system and programs as we went. She stuck with the process, even though her feelings of fear were trying to get her to leave.

In fact, many people *do* leave in fear and I lose them as clients but, in this case, we were able to get all the way through the fear and start her on a new life path. (If I had known then what I know now, from all the new information and protocol I have developed over the last fifteen years, we could have walked right through it with no problems. I had to work with what I knew at the time.)

I have worked with many clients in this situation with great results, if they just stick with it until we have cleared the fear of change. This client felt that a miracle had occurred because she had never before felt in control of her life, and didn't know what it felt like. She had tried other therapies but none had been able to help her break through the fear and take control of her life.

If you have been on autopilot for most of your life, reclaiming your personal power is a threat to the power structure in your mind. However, when you deprogram all the denial sub-personalities, the results may seem miraculous, because there is then no resistance to change.

Most people need help in confronting the programs that are controlling their lives. Some will seek help in the form of psychotherapy or some other counseling, but few practitioners can get to the base cause and core issues, because they're not trained to go beyond the surface issues presented by the client.

How can clients explain to the practitioner what is causing their problems, unless they have an obvious symptom? If the symptom is obvious, most people will consult a medical doctor first, as they are unaware that all symptoms are caused by an emotional reaction, usually some form of anger or fear. Feelings do not always indicate the cause either, so how does a therapist understand the client's problem?

As we saw earlier, everything is caused by a program, and we must get to the base cause to locate it. This is where Energy Psychology and N/CR shine, since we can use our detective ability with Neuro-kinesiology to locate the cause, and then release and clear it.

An excellent example of someone facing this challenge was a client we'll call Fran. She'd had a laser face peel a year earlier because she was concerned about skin cancer. Her doctor had advised her that if he removed the surface skin, all the moles and skin disfiguration would be removed, which would thus clear up her complexion. (This might be true in some cases, unless we have a program that is causing cancer. If that is the case, no surface removal will stop it. It will reappear until the program is cleared.)

Fran did not have a cancer program, but a past-life program that had not been cleared, which caused her face to burn, inducing considerable pain. Her mind had equated this procedure with a past life, where she had been burned at the stake for opposing the Roman Catholic Church's ruling that it was also the government. She also now felt that she had made a mistake by having the face peel; she blamed the doctor, who defended himself by telling her she had an incurable skin disease so she should let the matter drop there. (He did not have the courage or self-confidence to tell her he did not know what was causing her reaction.)

She had consulted another doctor, who had no answers either, and then with alternative practitioners who had also been unable to help in releasing the burning or the pain. Finally, in desperation, she had turned to the Internet to find some answers, and found my book, which she had ordered. After reading the book, she had called me to make an appointment.

"I'll go anywhere to meet with you," she told me.

"I'll be in your state in two weeks," I told her, but she said she couldn't wait that long, and made an appointment for the next day, despite the nine-hour drive to where I was at the time.

We found and released the past-life programs, along with some conflicting beliefs and programs. She had gotten some short-term relief but the burning had returned. When I was in her state two weeks later, Fran saw me again so that we could get to the cause of the resistance behind the burning and the pain.

It turned out that her mind would agree to let go of the pain and heal her face in thirty-six hours, but we could not clear her disbelief that clearing all the programs would actually work. Her Conscious mind was not about to believe this new concept; she was also still getting payoff from holding resentment and blame toward the doctor.

I gave her some homework intended to break her disbelief and skepticism about my work. (My standard process is to write an affirmation in longhand, twenty-one times a day for twenty-one days. This works well ninety-five percent of the time if clients can discipline themselves to actually do it.) But Fran would only have her miracle when she also forgave the doctor and let go of the blame. Her next step would be to accept that she created everything that happens to her. When she accepted that her body could heal itself, then she would become healed.

Over the years, we have found that the statistics on loving ourselves have changed. In the past, about seventy percent of our clients had told us that they understood what love is and that they loved themselves. Once we began using the affirmation, to release "I need to suffer/be punished" programs, the number dropped to thirty percent. (Apparently, this affirmation gets around the conscious beliefs and accesses all the denial files, so we get a more accurate percentage.) When we ask Subconscious Mind if the client loves him/herself, the number of people who love themselves and can receive love drops to less than ten per cent.

How do we overcome these tragic odds? By rewriting the program and releasing the Split and Multiple and sub-personalities, and then locating the base cause, the core issue and the other people with whom you have participated in the situation to put you on your current path. To release the program/belief, we must locate how you reacted in the base cause/core issue situation. How you are currently handling the situation in your life will show us how we must proceed to release the program.

We then form an affirmation to describe the situation, and move into loving and forgiving those involved—and loving and forgiving yourself for allowing the situation to happen. Bingo, the condition is healed and released. If this seems simple, in fact, it is. All we do is guide you to reprogram your mind so it can create a different response. To many people in their condition, however, this seems impossible.

I work with many female clients who are in physically abusive relationships yet refuse to break up and leave, despite their intense complaints about how their partner treats them. Why do they stay in abusive relationships? They ask for miracles, but they refuse to leave. Why? Fear of change: *"I know what I have now, and how to deal with it. Where would I be if I left? Alone, rejected, abandoned and unloved."*

Few of them know what love is, so they misinterpret abusive attention as love. When you have never experienced unconditional love, you interpret any form of concentrated attention as love. If these women were in control of their lives, they would be able to recognize the abusive situation. If sub-personalities are in control, *they* dictate the path to take, and not her Conscious Rational Mind. Some of these clients will stay with the therapy until they break the bond with their abusive partners and step into new life. The basis of these relationships is usually an over-controlling parent and/or a karmic contract by which the couple is drawn together to clear the karma. However, if you do not know that this contract exists, how do you break the attachment?

Releasing and clearing past-life karmic contracts frees the client to empower herself and start a new path. This may seem like a miracle as she breaks free of the abuse and is now able to evaluate the relationship as it is. If nothing can be done to resolve the issues that remain, then she has the personal power and new understanding to avoid choosing the same type of partner again.

Many of these women come from large families. As girls, they often fell into a mother role to younger siblings; in their adult relationships, they pick men who need mothering. If the men had controlling mothers, they will choose these mothering women for partners. (There will always be exceptions to the rule, but we usually find clients operating from one of several broad patterns.)

Relationship patterns (mother-son, father-daughter, etc.) are common because, as adults, we have not cleared the lessons with our parents so we partner up with a surrogate parent in the hopes of working out our unresolved childhood issues. Over ninety-five percent of adult relationships start out as dysfunctional, and the parties can resolve the issues only if both commit to working through them in therapy. A one-sided approach to the process cannot lead to a miracle relationship.

There are exceptions to the "both partner" rule, but this presents a major challenge to the one partner who does want to work with us while the other refuses. One such case involved my son, who began seeing a girl who kept threatening to kill herself if he broke up with her. Wanting to help her with her problem, he asked her to have a session with me, but she resisted. He finally did set up a session for her, at which she put up such resistance and had so many shields to prevent her from getting hurt that we did not accomplish much.

Coming from a functional family, my son was unable to figure this one out, so he asked me to help him break free of this relationship. We found that he had spent four past lives with her, and she had been pursuing him for three of them. Now that she had finally caught her prize, she was not about to let go. Once we cleared the effect of the past lives, he was free to go, but then he felt guilty and couldn't understand why. Once we cleared the karma, the guilt disappeared and he was able to move on to a new relationship.

Some of his friends called the transformation a miracle; to him, it wasn't one, since he knew that I could unwind his predicament. He was able to get out of the conflict because he had grown up with my work. (Unless we are aware of the intensity of karmic addiction, we cannot understand what pulls us into a dysfunctional relationship.)

In other cases, karma works in the opposite way. The rejected partner threatens to kill the other for wanting to leave the abusive relationship. Resolving this issue requires delicate negotiation. I explain to both partners that the only thing holding them in the relationship is their own fear, and that, if they work with me to release all the attachments that hold them in the relationship, we can unwind the fear and they will be free from the karmic binding. When we clear all the present and/or past life connections, the abusive partner fades into the sunset, never to be heard from again. This outcome seems unreal, but it works by clearing all the attachments that drew the two into the addictive relationship in the first place.

Miracles do happen every day. Transformation is instantaneous, and recovery from anything is possible. I experience about twelve to fifteen miracles a year. Why not make your life one? All it takes is desire, commitment and a willingness to consistently discipline yourself to follow through with a plan for taking responsibility. Pain will disappear instantly when you recognize your "all rightness." You have your life back! Self-esteem, self- confidence, and self-worth return. You never lost them; you just wrote over them with dysfunctional programming.

Self-esteem is one of the cluster qualities that is always accompanied by self-worth and self-confidence. It is a quality that allows you to know who are, so nobody can break you down. Other people's opinions, rejections or attacks do not affect you. You do not have to be right, self-righteous, the authority figure, or in control of any situation.

Jeri, a colleague, attended a conference on self-esteem and relayed to me the following amazing example of lack of self-esteem. Jeri had been invited to present a seminar and workshop at the conference regarding the self-esteem program she had developed for a school district. Her seminar drew a standing ovation. Afterward, one of the conference directors accosted her with the question, "Did you read the protocol and guidelines for this conference?

Jeri replied, "Yes, I did. Why do you ask?"

"Because you didn't follow them."

Jeri was baffled, because her presentation had received such a great reception, and she asked for more detail. The woman's reaction was this: "Your central theme is that you cannot teach self-esteem, because it's an inner quality that is suppressed by negative training. That is wrong!"

"Are you telling me," Jeri responded, "that you know more about my subject than I do? What are your credentials. I can't hold my workshop because you disagree with my premise?

"Are you saying you can reactivate self-esteem, self confidence and self-worth, merely by changing beliefs? Do you recognize what you're trying to do to me right now?"

The woman's reply was, "I'm only telling you that you must follow the conference rules."

"Please answer my questions" was Jeri's response. "It's obvious you want to be in control, and that you're trying to destroy *my* self-esteem right now. But I'm not going to let you do it. Apparently, you're putting your need to be in control and be recognized ahead of the theme of the conference.

"My workshop tomorrow will go ahead as planned, Jeri continued. "I am *not* changing the content to suit you. I know what I'm presenting works because I've been the director of a successful self-esteem program for over fifteen years. If you choose to ask me to leave and have the authority to do so, I will, but I am not changing my workshop. And I'll make sure that the conference chair and committee is aware of your controlling behavior."

Seeing that her attempt to control Jeri had failed, the woman walked off in a huff. When Jeri checked with the conference committee, she learned that the woman held an administrative position with the conference, but apparently did not understand its theme. They said they were going to replace her.

Jeri was well-anchored in her own self-esteem, so the confrontation did not get to her in any way, but she was disappointed that a person representing a self-esteem conference could act the way she had. (In my experience, when I check clients for self-esteem on a scale of 1–100, I find that most of those from a functional family test in the twenty to fifty range. If they have been rejected before birth or been adopted, they usually test much lower, in the zero to ten range.)

When we erase and rewrite the programs, the real you emerges. You came here to be a spiritual being, taking on a physical body to learn some lessons and resolve karma. So why not get on with it? There is no better time than *now!* If you wait until you feel ready, though, your denial may cause it to be delayed, and it may not happen in this lifetime.

You can make the commitment now. No one is stopping you except you. This is the right time. In fact, there will never be a better time than right now. The only limitations are your own beliefs and denials that create the limitations. Yes, it will take some hard work and a strong commitment, but it can be done. You can be a miracle; you have the ability. All you need do is let go of anger, control, manipulation, authority issues, judgment, justification, righteousness, rebellion, the need to please people to win acceptance ... and the addiction to these types of behavioral patterns.

The most complex thing for people to understand is that we never lose anything, positive or negative. The sub-personalities and the programs just go into denial or get written over. Unlike computer files, a program or habit pattern is not deleted by writing over it. When you erase and overwrite indigenous operational programs, they can immediately reconfigure and remain operational unless you clear the belief and sub-personality, too.

We discovered this, once we became aware that beliefs, programs and patterns reactivate and become operational again. You must move negative programs and sub-personalities into the trash bin, and then delete and destroy them by incinerating them, burning them up. By doing this, we have deleted the program forever. It cannot reconfigure or reactivate unless you recreate the same habit pattern over again.

Summary

In this book, I am not only providing the miracle success stories. I am balancing those with examples of average people who had conflicts in their life, some of whom I was not able to help, and giving the reasons why. Most people list only their few success cases and avoid writing about the failures. With over one hundred examples, however, you can get a good cross section of what N/CR is capable of providing.

In Energy Medicine, we do not heal anybody. All healing is self-healing (see Chapter 8 on the Placebo effect). We can provide the tools and the directions, but our clients must take responsibility themselves, and reclaim their personal power. Energy Psychology is about self-empowerment and recovering your lost self that you lost when you were a child. (The more I work with this protocol, the more I feel that all healing is placebo effect.)

Chapter 5

Understanding the Theory of Healing

Before we begin, let's dispense with the term "spiritual healing." There are many ways in which people describe this process; the main conflict is in the basic viewpoint and interpretation. Twenty years ago, I worked with what I thought was spiritual healing; over the years, I have redefined my interpretation, because the more I delved into and came to understand what healing was, I realized what Paul Solomon had said about healing made sense. He said, "It is the separation of self that creates the breakdown." What we are really healing is this separation.

Back then, we did not have sufficient knowledge or the basic terminology of healing to explain how it takes place, so the term "spiritual healing" was a catch-all phrase that covered the field. But then I discovered that we were misusing the term, since "spiritual healing" was a very advanced process, one with which that few people would ever have contact, because only a tiny minority of people ever get out of the morass of the physical world.

I found that we were misinterpreting the concept, since our spirit and soul do not need help or healing in any way. They have all the the answers for us if we will listen. They talk through our body and use it as a communication device if we listen.

As Paul Solomon, one of my first teachers in the healing field, described the process, "Until we clear the hurdle of our childhood emotional trauma and start building a foundation for our spiritual life, we can't even address the spiritual aspect of healing." Too many people want to skip over the foundation-building and evolve to the spiritual aspect of their life-paths. For most of them, their denial of their own shortcomings will stop them from making this transition. Even though they may convince themselves they are on the path of spiritual enlightenment, most people are deluding themselves, because they have not dealt with the basics of building a solid path on which to anchor their spiritual journeys.

Many of my clients claim to be highly enlightened spiritual beings, yet live in suffering, survival and illusion. They tolerate their lives, rather than enjoy them. Very few have real peace, happiness, harmony, joy, unconditional love, acceptance and financial abundance in their lives. Health and wellness do not just mean being clear of illness; it is an integrated totality of being. The question we must ask ourselves is, *"What am I really here for?"*

Many people I meet believe that we are here to suffer and be deprived of happiness and joy. Yes, I have found many people w h o believe this. Yet consciously they don't even know it. We must be really objective in evaluating our life-path, since so many of our experiences are locked up in denial or even denial-of-denial files that we do not or cannot even recognize the programs or their content. With Energy Psychology, however, we can open these files and reveal the information we need to rewrite the programs, beliefs, habits and scripts from which we operate our life. This book deals with the basics of healing in the physical world.

The personality self lives in an illusory world of suffering, pain and denial. Our intent is to eliminate and delete the programs and sub-personalities that personality self functions through, and reinstall the client's true self. We are healing the separation from self; when we can accomplish this, miracles happen.

When we walked out during the traumatic experiences in our childhood, we separated from self, which caused our minds to shift to a "safe mode" system, just as our desktop computers do when a file is corrupted. We have to take back the control, deleting the autopilot and Inner Conscious mind, which took over during the trauma.

Many people would like to believe that miracles come from the spiritual realm, yet this has proven to be false. Over the years, I have worked with thousands of clients, many of whom did not understand about enlightenment; some were not religious or spiritual in any way. Once they committed to following my directions, though, miracle healing occurred.

We must turn on our "God-switch" (how ever we envision that concept) before miracles can take place. The presence of God is in all of us, but most people have it shut down. Disease, illness or any form of lack is not a reality for a person who is truly on the spiritual path.

In my client base, I am working with less than 0.5 percent of the general population. When I narrow it down further, I find that the aware people who come to see me, just once, is only one in four out of that tiny sample. Even among people who are aware that they can change their paths, only twenty-five percent will stay with it, work through their issues and really get their lives on track. So now that 0.5 percent drops down to 0.125, or one in eight hundred.

Few people realize they could take a different direction in their lives, so most slog along through their life lessons not recognizing that peace, happiness, harmony, joy, unconditional love and acceptance are available to them. (For example, most people do not know it but the files in their mind have set up a program that states: "I am not entitled to prosperity.")

Only one in 25,000 people even knows what unconditional love is, and fewer still have it anchored in their life. Self-love is the key. Love and forgiveness are the basic door to happiness and healing, yet these concepts are foreign to most people, which explains why we have so much conflict, anger, resentment and hatred in society today. The ruling church governments have fostered fear in us for centuries, to the point that most people are overrun with "I have to suffer" programs.

I have a hard time believing religious people can believe that they were born in sin. It is next to impossible to build a positive mental attitude if you are laboring under a heavy build-up of programs that say, "I need to suffer" or "I must suffer in order to learn the lessons of life." Healing is a process brought about by releasing the programs and core beliefs that drive our life. There is no disease, illness or dysfunctional behavior that just comes in and affects us by happenstance.

Your mind controls every action you take and every situation that happens to you. Pathogens, bacteria, viruses and fungi do not cause disease; their proliferation is the result of a breakdown in the body's immune system, again caused by the mind. We would like to blame our problems on someone else or "a disease going around," but it doesn't work that way.

Growing up, my children were exposed to many contagious diseases but I would not allow them to be vaccinated for childhood diseases, yet they were never affected by any of them. We had to sign an agreement to accept that if a contagious disease got into the children at school, we would keep our children home so they would not be infected and become carriers of the disease. Illness and disease are all caused by how you feel about yourself, and we set *ourselves* up for disease, illness and other dysfunctions.

We set everything up to get a certain payoff, usually without knowing how or why, or how to get out of the resulting situation. There are qualities that will provide us the immunity for diseases, illness and malfunctions in our personal behavior. They are also the ingredients that build self-esteem, self-worth and self-confidence. If you did not get them provided to you as a child, then you will get sick to draw attention to yourself, in an effort to get someone to give them to you. These are approval, acceptance, validation, acknowledgment and recognition. If you did not get these from your parents, you go through life looking for outcome-based validation.

The only problem is you can't get it from someone else. You are the only person who can validate you. If you can't get it, you will get sick to get it. Your mind does not care who gives it to you, either. Anyone will do. So we get pain from various symptoms; we assume they are diseases or whatever you want

50

to believe, when in reality, it us doing it to us. (Again. as Pogo said it, "We have met the enemy, and he is us!")

In fact, most of the time, we are so deep in illusion that we cannot even understand why or how we ended up with our afflictions in the first place. Our first thought is, *It is physical, I can feel the pain (or whatever is surfacing to cause the discomfort). I must have gotten it from something or somebody.* Malfunction or pain is just a signal that something needs to be heard. It is also resistance to locating the cause.

Your body is talking to you but, rather than listen to the message to locate the cause at the mental/emotional level, you run to the doctor for a drug to mask the symptom. Anything that removes pain or discomfort without addressing the underlying cause is simply removing the charge, and side-stepping the symptom.

We will stop ourselves with strokes, heart attacks, cancer, organ malfunctions, MS, ALS, MSD and many other forms of illness and disease, to get someone to take care of us, or s i m p l y to gain attention and love. Very few people recognize the base cause of the dysfunction; they are running away from themselves and the illusion driving their behaviors.

The base cause is what happened in the beginning to cause you to react. The base cause of fear of fire could have happened in a lifetime several thousands of years ago, or during childhood. How you respond or react to the catalyst governs how it affects you, and your interpretation sets up either a belief or a program. It may be many years before there is enough charge to cause an illness or a mental breakdown but, each time you run into the same catalyst, you will react based on the program or belief. Over time, programs and beliefs become patterns that cause you to react in the same way each time.

The payoff for all illness and disease is the attention and approval you receive. Most of us will do anything to get attention, and are searching for someone who will provide the attention we crave. The attention may not be love, but that's how our mind interprets it. Children get sick to get attention

51

because they know it works. If they are getting enough love, recognition, affection and acceptance, they do not get hurt or sick.

One of the most devastating situations for children is to hurt themselves to get attention, then get ignored, scolded or disciplined for doing something wrong. The parents or caregivers are quite often reacting to their own guilt and taking it out on the child, which causes major rejection and a feeling of "I'm not wanted," or "I'm not loved." The proper behavior would be to hug the child, ask what happened and give him or her the attention and affection he or she is asking for.

Many female clients come to see me, complaining that they are in an abusive relationship. Sometimes they have had a string of abusive relationships, in which they change partners but not the underlying lessons. We repeat the lesson until we learn that we do not need to suffer. There could be a major misinterpretation operating in these relationships—one where the mind interprets attention as a substitute for love. If we have known only abuse since childhood, then we mistakenly identify any form of attention as love.

These women can't break out of their abusive relationships because some attention is better than the unknown. When we empower them to stand up for themselves and take control, reclaim their personal power and take responsibility for their lives, they have a new perspective on the relationship and find more functional partners. (One client told me that her husband was beating her up, but that it was better than her childhood because her father had used to beat her even worse. What we will accept as a love-substitute amazes me.)

True love is acceptance without judgment. It is kindness and caring without any put-downs or attempts to control and manipulate. *Conditional love* takes on many forms, such as controlling a child's behavior with authority. It could be abuse at any level, even physical.

Our viewpoints about love are based on how we interpreted our treatment in childhood. If, as children, we were never picked up and hugged, or received no pats on the back, we grew up not knowing what approval is. As an adult, we may be lacking a basic unconditional love program. Without this program, people frequently get sick. Their lives do not work, yet they cannot find the cause. It is their body/minds trying to get someone, anyone, to give them attention, which they interpret as love.

Underlying any healing process is the ability to accept unconditional love, but most people are unable to accept love at a deep level of their beings. Healing can only take place once we have released all the rejection and abandonment we perceived throughout our lives. We cannot receive approval and acceptance from others until we are able to give it to ourselves. As long as we believe others should give love to us, they will not do so unconditionally.

Many people seek out someone they can cling to and manipulate in an effort to get attention, but almost everyone who offers them support or help has a hook or a cord connected to it; they want something in return. There is a basic human desire to have our existences recognized, and people will do anything to get that recognition. Sickness is an obvious way of getting someone else to recognize we are alive. Total rejection will cause death; if you think you are not accepted and wanted, why be here? (HIV and AIDS are forms of total self-rejection. Society does not accept you, so you reject yourself.)

Most diseases are caused by selective immunity. AIDS is caused by total breakdown of the immune system, so there is no protection from disease. When the T-cell count drops to a level where the immune system cannot attack disease organisms, those organisms will flourish and overwhelm the body.

What then is the answer to the dilemma? Quite simply, the answer is unconditional love and forgiveness. It's that simple, and it is the only way to heal the body permanently. To achieve this, we must remove all the programs, patterns and records from the Subconscious and Conscious Minds and the other 25 files where programs are stored, any one of which can house the causes and precursors to disease and illness. The encrypted and encoded programs are the most damaging, because they were laid down before you were born. *In utero* programming recorded how your parents felt about this new child they created, and whether they were going to accept this new addition to the family.

Seven out of ten children are rejected before they are born, so they will interpret this input as: "I am not all right. I am not acceptable. I am not wanted." This follows with, "If they wanted me, they wouldn't treat me this way." This in turn is followed by self-rejection, which degenerates into, "I have no value."

If your parents considered abortion or even just talked about it, this destroyed your self-esteem, self-worth and self-confidence, as well as your validation of yourself, before you were born. If you feel you have no value, you will continually bring people in your life to confirm your worthlessness, and invalidate your credibility as a person. We always choose people who will validate who we perceive we are. As a result we will see ourselves as not having any value.

Bonding with your mother at birth is very important. Your earliest relationships with, and your treatment by, your primary caregivers now control your life. How you interpreted the way people treated you set up childhood programming that, in adulthood, causes most people to reject themselves. By the time you are four to five years old, you have set up your life pattern. For most people t h i s includes "I need to suffer" programs, that play out in their lives over and over again. We can remove these programs, but you must be willing to open the files.

The conflict is more evident in adopted children who were rejected by their birth mothers. They do not trust anybody, which causes them to reject any type of affection. You have to gain their trust and respect before you can get close to them. If you do not know where these files are located and what must be done to clear them, you have a challenge. It takes a skilled therapist to ask the right questions and know how to help you delete, erase and destroy the beliefs and programs that cause the malfunctions in your mind's database.

An interesting case began when a young woman (whom we'll call Sheryl) came to work for us at our center. She became interested in my work after attending a few lectures, and set up a few appointments to clear her rejection by her birth parents, since she and her twin sister had both been adopted. I met her adoptive parents and found them to be delightful people who obviously had created a functional family for their children.

In fact, I would describe them as ideal parents. They had provided a loving supportive environment with plenty of affection and validation for the children, yet they commented on how the twins had both pushed them away. In the beginning, the adoptees had been uncomfortable with the level of acceptance they were being given.

Thinking they had failed, the parents were critical of themselves. When I explained about the rejection felt by adopted children, they understood it had not been their fault. This marked the beginning of my work with adopted children in the middle 1980s and, over the next 17 years, I worked with many more, which has validated my contention about adopted children.

Adopted children often feel that they were rejected by their birth parents: *I have no value, or they would not have gotten rid of me!* The question in their minds is, *If my birth parents gave me away, why would my adopted parents want me?* Or, *If I let them into my life, get close to them and depend on them, they might reject me, too. If I depend on them to give me acceptance and support, they might abandon me and hurt me again.*

Since most adoptive parents do not know about this inner dialogue going on in the child's mind, they get frustrated, thinking that *they* are being rejected. If the parents are not strong enough in their own convictions, this fear of intimacy and commitment can backfire and make the situation deteriorate, causing further rejection because many parents are really only adult children who want to extract love and acceptance from the children. In these situations, there is no love from or for the parent or the child.

There are exceptions to the case, but most adopted children have a hard road to navigate, because their fear of commitment and intimacy blocks them from functional relationships, causing them to enter into relationships with people who validate their feelings of unworthiness and lack of self-esteem. Almost all of the adopted children or adults with whom I have worked have these challenges. We can overcome them, but it takes time.

An excellent example of this case is Sheryl, mentioned earlier. As we saw, she came from a functional family and, when we had released all the birth rejection and cleared up the fear of commitment and intimacy, her life really smoothed out; I thought she was in for clear sailing.

However, ten years later she called me up, because she and her twin sister were baffled by the abusive relationships they were both in. According to my contention, they should have chosen functional partners, since they were from a functional family. It had not worked out that way at all. Sheryl knew that I could unwind their "soap opera" dramas and find the cause, so she made an appointment for herself and her sister.

Their session proved to be very enlightening: they had both chosen marriage partners who duplicated the birth father, whom they had never met. They had past-life lessons to learn from and had chosen the biological father with whom to work them out, but that lesson plan had been aborted when they'd been put out for adoption. Therefore, they had had to find someone else with whom to work it out.

Not only did they have the father lesson, there were also past-life issues with the men they had chosen for husbands. Sheryl's sister said, "I cannot accept that I set it all up, and I still blame my husband and his family for the abuse." She disputed the information I presented to her and continued in the abusive relationship, complete with her "I need to suffer" program.

These are good examples of how Energy Psychology works, and how we can unwind and back out all the programs and beliefs set up by the past-life lessons. We cleared the birth trauma and the rejection and abandonment in both of them, but I have no feedback or knowledge as to what happened with Sheryl's sister.

During the time I was working with Sheryl, the sister was often sick, due to the anger and resentment she held. I assume she is still suffering in her abusive relationship and holding onto her resentment, anger and blame. Some people just cannot let go or accept anything new. Change brings up fear of the unknown, and people often prefer to stay in something unpleasant they know than strike out into the unknown, for fear that it may prove to be worse. This is not always the case, as we see from what happened next.

Meanwhile, as we worked through Sheryl's programs, we found that her relationship with her husband was a mother/son connection. This type of relationship can be explosive and dangerous if the adult child is not given his way. When she started taking control of her life, reclaiming her personal power, unwinding this addictive relationship and standing up to her husband, he crumbled because his personal power was bluff. Being a counter-dependent, he became physically abusive to try to maintain control, which scared her at first.

When she empowered herself to tell him she was leaving the marriage, he threatened to kill her. He reacted violently because he was losing his power, his surrogate mother and his "medicine." He could not replace it, and was shocked because he had to face the truth. She tried to explain to him why she was no longer willing to put up with his abusive behavior, which inflamed him even more, because he could not see anything wrong with himself.

He did not even recognize that he was being abusive. It was obvious that he was on autopilot, operating from Magical Child Syndrome. (This is the cause of many so-called "crimes of passion," in which someone says, "If I can't have this person, then nobody will!" It is the final mother-rejection, and often results in murder/suicide.)

Sheryl called me in a panic, asking, "What can I do now? I told her to move back with her parents. She did move back her parents' home and her father obtained a court-ordered restraining order, but that did not stop her husband. He was stalking her and harassing her, so she was afraid to come to work.

I explained to her, "If we can release all the addictive connections you have to him, he will just fade into the sunset." She was willing to try this, though it was hard for her to believe that if we could clear all the lessons that created this obsessive/compulsive addictive relationship, then her torment would cease.

In the session, I told her, "You have three options. You can stay in the abusive relationship, as your sister decided to do. You can try to get out of the relationship and avoid the lesson, which could result in your death and the lesson would recycle in another lifetime. Or, you can face the truth and release the lesson, so that you can go on with your life in peace, happiness, harmony and joy."

She chose to face the lesson and release it. We found that all the time-outs had been used, and the lesson was up to be dealt with. Over three sessions, we cleared all the past lives, and the beliefs and programs that had been programmed into her mind. These had caused her to attract this type of a person into her life. When all of that charge was released, the programs disappeared, so it no longer made any difference how charged up her husband was. All the connections had been severed, so his mind had to let go.

She divorced him, and he faded out of her life. She went on to a new one, attracting supportive people commensurate with her newly found self-esteem. She was willing to confront the issues that caused her continual physical ailments, so they stopped, and her life became filled with peace, happiness and joy. (This case-study proves that past life relationships do exist, and that we must clear their issues to move on with our life.)

I thought we had her on the path to success, yet as it turned out, we had not cleared everything. I recently had an opportunity to work with Sheryl again. (This was fifteen years since our last encounter.) What we found was her life had deteriorated and she had not accomplished her goal of finding a compatible relationship.

She had a job that got her by, but she was not any better off than she had been nearly twenty years earlier when I had worked with her. She also did not have the funds for the sessions she needed to clear the conflicts blocking her path, so I bartered with her for two sessions.

Even then we still had not cleared all the problems. Even though I thought we had cleared up the conflict with unconditional love, the rejection was back again. Due to my lack of basic understanding of the complexities of how much programming can be covered up in adopted children, I had not cleared everything twenty years earlier.

Even after moving to another city 1500 miles away, she had found the same garbage following her. After many failed relationships, she was now about to give up ever finding a suitable relationship. (We will find out more as this case unfolds. Adopted children have a tough journey to reach success with peace, happiness, harmony, joy and unconditional love.)

I tell my clients contemplating marriage that they must clear the skeletons out of their closets before the parties make the commitment. We then evaluate and clear any current and/or past-life lessons that have addictive and/or compulsive attractions that might create dysfunctional patterns. If Sheryl had done an evaluation of her connections with her fiancé before the marriage, she would have cleared them all and would never have married him; she therefore would not have had to confront the abusive relationship. (This is a good example of the "I have to suffer" programs from past lives.)

When I tell people we need to clear all the skeletons out of their closets, they do not understand this until we find what they are. If not cleared, they will start rattling later on in a relationship, breaking it up or at least causing a lot of problems.

Almost all marriages result from four basic situations caused by behavioral dysfunction:

- Looking for love in the wrong places (i.e., wanting to be taken care of or codependency)
- Past-life addictions based on karma (the last example)

59

- Physical attraction
- Looking for a mother or father replacement. (Mother-Son or Father Daughter relationships make up about seventy per cent of these partnerships.)

We will always seek out the person who best suits our needs in resolving issues and lessons in our life. Very few choices result in satisfactory relationships, as the relationship deteriorates when the needs of the partners are not met. In fact, ninety per cent of all relationships do not work, even though the partners stay in them. I have many clients who decided to evaluate their relationship before they committed to marriage. After we cleared the past-life addiction, the other partner was no longer as attractive. Quite often, they broke up because the draw was not there anymore.

If the dysfunctional relationship results in marriage, statistically it will have failed within ten years. We are now seeing a large increase in the divorce rate after twenty five or more years of marriage, as people decide to take control of their lives. They are no longer willing to "stick it out" if they do not feel accepted, respected or recognized.

If both parties are willing to work on the issues during the relationship, it can be turned around and progress to a loving supportive partnership. It takes work and both parties must participate. In our case, Susie and I had lived in a codependent, co-existing relationship for thirteen years. Fortunately for our children, we began to wake up and work on our issues, ten years after we were married.

When we review the information in this book objectively and without prejudice, we see clearly that illness and disease are states of mind caused by dysfunctional programs and relationships. They exist in the body only because the beliefs, concepts, patterns and programs driving them get locked into the cellular structure of the body. In actuality, illness and disease do not exist. There are no contagious diseases, only contagious people with programs, patterns, beliefs, interpretations and concepts about illness and disease that cause them to succumb to dysfunctional beliefs leading to physical breakdown.

I have proven beyond all doubt that allergies are beliefs with a causal factor (catalyst, trigger, activator) that, when activated, will flare up the allergy. Asthma works in the same way. We can blame some environmental agent, but that agent is tied to the core issue and base cause that created the allergy symptom in the first place. When we remove the causal agent (trigger, catalyst and activator), the allergy and/or asthma will totally disappear.

I personally have seen a doctor only once in over thirty-five years. That was to repair a hernia. I have been sick only once in the last forty years, and that was because I had worked twenty-six straight days without time off (while at the same time, being under intense emotional tension and extreme stress). Recovery that time took only a few days, once I realized what I'd done to myself. Full healing took about two weeks, since I had stressed my body out to the point that my overworked adrenals had to recover.

The challenge is being able to recognize the symptom and what your body is telling you. Few people can read their own "book" well, so the records are not accessible. Doctors will tell you, as they did me, that you have no recourse, and that the condition will continue to degenerate unless you have surgery on your back. I am happy I did not submit to surgery, as it does not work. (A new challenge is that because your body/mind wants you to get the message, it builds up immunity to drugs, which nullifies their effects.)

All we need to do is rewrite scripts by reprogramming the mind—simple when you have access to the records. If the script is coming out of a past life, you will have to release the karmic contracts and agreements you made with others in that lifetime. They follow you everywhere you go, from lifetime to lifetime. (You cannot talk them out either; they must be removed from cellular memory.)

The script could stem from a belief you accepted that is not a reality. You constructed a situation out of an interpretation, one not even programmed into your Subconscious Mind, nor is it in cellular memory as a body-based program. It exists only in your Middle Self's files, and such beliefs can simply be released with an affirmation.

To understand the theory of healing, we must first understand that nobody can heal us; we must do it ourselves. The "Catch-22" here is that first we must be willing to release ourselves from our past programming, without blame, guilt, justification or judgment. Fear will drive us to control everything we contact. For example, if security is a major need in life, this need will prevent healing. Another important factor for healing to occur is self-validation.

Many people believe that nutritional therapy promotes healing... and sometimes it does. However, this still discounts the awesome power of the mind. If someone takes responsibility and commits to recovery, what they eat is *four times* more effective in healing, compared to the person who follows a program simply because they were told it would work.

It is the discipline and commitment that make the difference, not the food, herbs or supplements. The power of your mind is awesome. If the programs and beliefs are set up with an end-result of rejecting the body, your mind will actually stop your body from assimilating drugs, herbs, minerals, vitamins or any useful products. The mind may allow selective acceptance if you commit to taking care of your health, which is why many nutritional therapies work so well. They give the body adjuncts to help it clear the toxic materials that have been deposited, so it will begin to heal.

You can also use electronic instruments or acupuncture that remove pain by allowing the body's electrical functions to return to normal. Many alternative therapies will help adjust the body through manipulation or energy transfer, but if you do not get to the base cause and remove the program, it will eventually cause the same condition to recur.

Many do, however, acknowledge the body component as the most important facet. This happened to me for over twenty-four years. The therapist would release the charge and the energy causing the pain and it would go away for a few days or a week or so, but it would be back again, sometimes worse.

You can rearrange the body fascia tissue such as with Rolfing and you can overwhelm and release a dysfunctional pattern, disease or illness with energy by the laying on of hands. That is true in part, but again, what is controlling the situation in the first place? The mind's computer may allow a situation to clear, but will it return when the same crisis becomes an issue again?

If we view how the body heals itself, we find that it communicates using neuropeptides, chemicals that transmit electrical impulses that are picked up by the body's cells. Positive messages heal; negative messages cause breakdown. We know that a scalar wave of between 50,000 and 100,000 Hz is a standing energy wave that promotes healing. However, we do not know what the mind might do to block the energy. We must go back to the programs and how they will affect the outcome of any process.

Visualizations and guided imagery may work well to recreate new programs, but the challenge remains to get the Program Manager and the File Manager (Ego) to agree to work with you, so that the new programs can be filed in Subconscious Mind. My books frequently make such statements as these: "You must take your power back. Reclaim your personal power. Take responsibility." To make a commitment and stick to it with discipline is hard for most people. They will confront the issues, then turn and run.

The most common problem in our society is the illusion: "My life is okay the way it is." Many clients have said to me, "I would like to change so long as it doesn't upset my life." This is a fear-based reaction to change. Money and power also seem to be important. "I can do it if it doesn't cost too much or cause financial difficulty."

So I ask, "What value do you place on your health and mobility in your life?" People want to control their environment, so power and control in relation to what they must do to clear the issues become a major challenge. Many would rather stay in pain and illusion rather than confront the unknown.

A client once called me after a session to say, "You really fouled my life up. It was a lot more comfortable before I had the session with you." We had opened a Pandora's box, and now she had to deal with some lessons and issues in her life she did not want to confront. Her mother was also seeing me and had overcome some big obstacles in her life, so she assumed her daughter was also ready to deal with her issues and had paid for an appointment. Obviously, she was not.

Other clients tell me they feel better and their life is working better, yet they do not want to go any farther. Quite often, it's due to feeling better than ever before, and they can't see how it could be any better than it is now. When you reach a plateau where you have never felt this good before, you may think that this is all there is, because you've never experienced this level of wellness before, but we all have higher plateaus to strive for.

With many clients, total change causes intense fear. Going into uncharted waters can cause someone to retreat to what is known and safe. You do not have to be sick to step into wellness. Wellness is not lack of sickness, but the absence of dysfunctional programs that run your life. Over the years, a few clients have stuck with me to clear most of their issues that were buried. As we peeled away the onion layers, more issues came up. This was not done in a few sessions, however, but took years of processing.

We can have anything we want out of life if we are willing to commit ourselves to positive mental attitude (PMA). This may look simple on the surface, but it takes considerable discipline. We may have good intentions, but are we willing to hang in there when the going get tough.

The following is a good example of sticking with it when the chips are down. A client we will call Joan called to tell me, "I'm in a bind and need to clear any blocks that could set up a fear program, because I'm getting depressed about my position at my company. The rumor going around the company is they are going to downsize, due to the coming bubble with the dotcom crash coming up very soon." (It did happen six months later.)

Following the crash, her company was indeed downsizing. "My department originally had fifty-four people and they've laid off over twenty people. Other departments are hit harder. My goal was to get a new position, but that's been frozen."

Joan was unhappy with her position and had hopes of transferring. It had hit her very hard because her lease was ending on her house and they were raising the rent $300 a month, which added to the distress. She was having trouble with her domestic partner, and was feeling rejected by him. Her car was acting up and she had been told that it would cost far more than she could afford to fix it.

In her precarious position, she couldn't buy a new car, so she had had to fix her current one so she could drive it. It seemed as if everything that could happen was now coming down on her. All the stress was having a major depressing effect on her immune system, which was causing many malfunctions in her body. Like clockwork, the neuropeptides were setting up a breakdown in her body, so she ended up sick and unable to go to work for a few days. To solve the challenge with her car, she moved in with a friend at work, which cut a big expense out so she could fix it. What she did next was proactive: we set up at a session on how to overcome her financial conflicts.

This is a good example of how psychoneuroimmunolgy works. We were able to release all the programs that had been causing the stress, installing new programming that supported her, so she could empower herself to stand up to the pressure being put on her at work. Overnight, she popped out of the depression and recovered immediately. I described what all the negative feelings were doing to her and showed her how to block them and support herself when the pressure was on.

We worked on creating a positive mental attitude, and how her employer's situation was a positive change that would result in fulfilling her goals if she was able to hang on. Her department was finally reduced to seven people, and she survived the cuts. Her supervisor was so depressed with her workload that she asked to be transferred to a lesser position, and was instead laid off.

Joan was now carrying her supervisor's workload, but could not do it anymore, since she had so much more work now herself. She then survived this cut when her department was disbanded altogether. At a reorganization meeting, the company announced there would be no more layoffs, as they were down to the core group of staff. Joan had survived all the changes.

Keeping Joan buoyed up during this period took about ten sessions. She stopped drinking and smoking and moved in with the friend to cut costs so she could see me weekly. A year later, she finally received her transfer from Silicon Valley to a Phoenix location, which had a lower cost of living. Not only did she get the transfer, she received a promotion and realized all of her goals as they came through.

She was now able to work at home and go into the office once a week, so she moved out of the city to the country. At their cost, the company set up all the necessary communication lines for the computer, fax machine and phones. Living in a less expensive place with no commuting costs, she was able to buy a new car and take a vacation, too.

Joan's case shows what we can do if we accept that we can have it all. She is now an administrative assistant to one the top people in the company. She starts work at 6 AM and is off by 1 PM, and she does not even have to leave her home. Her income is now four times what it was eight years ago. She just recently purchased a home, something she never thought would happen in her life.

When you know that you are entitled to receive the goals you set, they will manifest. Joan is one of many people with whom I have worked who would not give up and accept failure. I had worked with her for over two years before all this pressure came up, and we thought we had cleared most of the programming, since she had moved from a codependent to a strong, self-actualized, empowered, independent person.

It is obvious that the feelings and programs locked up in denial, along with many of the other files, will be inaccessible as long as there is no catalyst or activator to bring them up. When one comes up, the floodgates open, because there are no programs blocking their release into the Conscious Mind.

We can see the basic difference between Joan's situation and Sheryl's. Sheryl had given up and accepted where she was and did not take proactive action because her frame of reference did not show her it was possible. When she finally recognized she was stuck and could not find her way out of her dilemma, she called me . . . twenty years later. Fortunately I was going to be in her city in two months, so we were able to start clearing those twenty years of accumulated garbage that had since built up in her Subconscious Mind.

Conversely, Joan had taken immediate proactive action, so she could set up a survival plan based on what she knew was going to happen. I try to tell people you have to set up goals and follow through to reach those goals as she did. The main conflict as you will see throughout this book is this: "We don't know what we don't know" If it is not in our frame of reference, we do not see or perceive the conflict or problem.

Summary

There are no diseases, illnesses, allergies, physical dysfunctions or mental/emotional dysfunctions that are caused by an "intruder" from the outside. All viruses, bacterial infections and pathogens, although real, are enabled by the mind, which allows them to proliferate by compromising our immune and endocrine systems.

All malfunctions are controlled by the mind through the internal communication, which transmits signals to the body based on how we feel at all times. Negative mental attitude depresses body functions, which results in illness and mental depression. By the time we are four years old, our life patterns are set up, and we will live them out unless we change the programming.

Positive mental attitude is eighty per cent of the challenge; knowing what to do about anything is only twenty per cent.

Knowledge can help, but it is our intention, discipline and commitment that cause change to happen.

Nobody does anything to us; we set it all up. We have the free choice to live in survival, suffering and lack of abundance. It is our choice, as you can see from the example we illustrated with Sheryl. No one makes these choices for us.

Disease is a choice that our mind makes for us. When we take control, and become a self-activated person who takes proactive action and who is in control of life, we do not get sick or create malfunctions in our lives. We have the free choice to set up the pattern if we can get to the point where we understand that we do have a choice.

Most people go through life like a log floating down a river, hitting all the obstructions in the way. Many people do not have the frame of reference to see that is what is happening to them because they cannot see a way out. Once we realize that we must be the captain of the ship, we can begin steering our life through the troubled waters.

We eventually get to calm waters, where there are no waves to control. As you can see in Joan's case, she could have given up and would have probably been laid off. What the company was looking for was committed honest people who were ethical and in integrity with their desire to perform at their best.

As she told me, "It was the people who were just there to collect a paycheck who were laid off." Joan found out later they had had a team of specialists come in and evaluate everybody's performance, to decide who would make up this new team of professionals to run the company. " Thanks to the work you did with me," she said, "I have survived the cuts and downsizing." That was 2003. She has continued up the ladder and is now an executive assistant for two top-level people. Her salary has risen to the high five figures.

As you will understand, we have to expand our frames of reference to be able to understand all the new concepts I have discovered. I have had people tell me, "Each time you present a workshop on N/CR, it is like starting over again." There are so many new concepts and practices that have been folded in to the practice.

My feeling is that many people create a program and a protocol, but they never change it when our world is evolving. Their practice becomes out of date, yet they keep teaching the same program. Behavior Mind Body Medicine is evolving, with new information that makes it more effective and faster to work with. I can accomplish three times as much in one session as I did in three of them, twenty years ago. We have a wider scope of dysfunctions with which we can work. We are more effective in how we approach situations.

I am becoming more convinced each year that what we are doing is providing the software our body/mind can use to change its programming. We need more instructors and mentors than healers. We provide the same information and support to everyone, yet we get different results. I find that those who make a definite commitment and set a definite intention to accomplish healing are the ones who get healed.

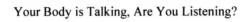

Your Body is Talking, Are You Listening?

Chapter 6

What Causes Illness, Disease and Behavior Dysfunction?

Medical researchers are right on track when they say that illness and disease are caused by a breakdown in the immune system. However, only a few understand why it happens and what the causes are. Research in the field of psychoneuroimmunolgy is limited to a few who have discovered that negative feelings, attitudes and sensory input cause the immune and endocrine systems to breakdown and malfunction.

In a weakened immune system, the T-cells, white blood cells and leukocytes that are our protectors do not have the numbers to attack viruses, bacteria, pathogens and other invaders. At this point, the researchers get lost, because they do not know how to boost the immune system. They have used all forms of drugs, and tried hypnosis and visual and guided imagery, all with marginal success.

Sometimes antibiotics or other drugs can suppress viruses. This may happen, but many times the body's resources will refuse to work with t h e drugs, because the awesome power of the mind is able to neutralize their effect. As a result, the outcomes are not consistent because the person must be committed to the process working in order to clear the activators. If the body is talking to us with emotional distress, pain and/or illness, do we listen? Rather than try to understand what our body is trying to tell us, most of the time we run to the nearest druggist, practitioner or "body mechanic" who gives us an adjustment, or prescribes herbs, supplements or drugs that provide suppression.

If a lesson is up for us to understand, we have used anything to suppress the symptom, until we have no more time-outs left in the game of life; the next step is a serious traumatic experience. If this does come up and we are faced with a life-threatening illness or disease, most people pass on, without ever knowing why they died until they get on the other side. (Once there, they conduct their life-reviews, during which they see the lessons that were blocked from view while they were in a body.)

We must detach from our need to be right and let go of the belief that the direction we're traveling in is the right path on our journey to enlightenment. We must allow ourselves to accept other concepts and opinions, without judgment.

The big conflict is that ninety per cent of the population don't even know they are in a school. They see or perceive the impediments or blocks in their path as something created by someone else, or as having an environmental cause. Even though we attract everything to us, we are our own worst enemy. They don't see that.

Some of my clients claim to eat a good diet, but when I question their habits, all I hear is justification for why they eat right only on occasion, or how they fell into bad habits. I describe that as illusion and denial. Denial is not just an emotional problem. Nobody likes to have their bad habits pointed out, so most people will justify their behavior with excuses, It all comes down to commitment, discipline, and responsibility for yourself. Justification does not work. The only person you are fooling is yourself. In any justification all you are trying to do is shift the blame off yourself.

Eating properly takes commitment, discipline, consistency, and the ability to follow through. The human body has not changed or adjusted its dietary needs in millions of years. Within a thirty-two-foot intestinal digestive track, heavy protein such as red meat will putrefy before it passe[.] intestines, and even then it requires a pH of two (stronger [...] battery acid) to digest it.

Then we wonder why we have an overly acidic condition, which in turn causes ulcers and rheumatism. Normally, the intestines operate best at a pH of five. Fish, nuts, beans and grains digest well in this medium. Fruits, melons and vegetables need no acid. If you mix fruit and protein in the same meal, you will create a winery in your stomach and it ferments, because it takes different enzymes and acids to digest each one. (Any form of sugar combined with protein will cause that protein to putrefy before it is properly digested.)

Sugar and white flour are poisons to the body. In fact, white flour products will turn to simple sugar in your mouth in 30-to-60 seconds, yet most people will justify consuming sugar and meat, making them the mainstays of the western world's diet.

Most people are sedentary individuals who eat the "Great American Diet." Yes, it is important to eat right, since proper nutrition supports the body, but very few people know what proper diet is. It is also important when you eat various foods in your diet that you know where your vegetables come from.

Most foods are devoid of minerals, so we need to supplement with minerals, but even with proper foods and supplements, you cannot heal your body. I have seen strict vegetarians with cancer, strokes and myriad other diseases. It is not what you eat; it is what is eating you *emotionally* that counts. (For a full picture of proper diet and nutrition see my forthcoming book, *Energy Psychology Energy Medicine: Volume Two—The Mind/ Body Medicine Connection*, to be published spring, 2014.)

The next ingredient is emotional well-being. Negative thoughts and feelings will break down your body faster than anything else. The emotions of fear and anger will generate more toxins in the body than a poor diet. Once received by the mind, negative sensory input will trigger depressive breakdown in the body in microseconds.

My mother lived to be ninety-four, and was in the hospital only once: for elective surgery. Her saving grace was that she had a positive mental attitude and forgave everybody. She ate a relatively good diet and did not drink or smoke, and her Christian Science background did not allow her to accept or believe in illness.

Life-threatening diseases are ways to escape from situations or conflicts. Most stem from suppressed anger, or from fear of having to face some insurmountable situation or trauma. However, the mind can make a mountain out of a molehill if it perceives something ahead with which it does not want to deal, even though the situation may be an illusion. (We are talking about the mind's interpretation, not about someone's rational mind making a decision.)

When people cannot claim their power and take responsibility for their life, they will back out. In fact, rather than confront a controlling person, many people will set themselves up to contract a life-threatening disease. Usually these are codependents, unwilling to break the codependent bond and stand up for their own views and desires. Rather than fight, they take flight—out of life.

Sometimes I can clear the situation and the client will take control and responsibility, as in the case of a woman whom we'll call Sherry. She had worked with me on many other issues that we had previously cleared, and a new issue came up where she was feeling down, with no energy. She was having a hard time accomplishing her work. I thought it might be Chronic Fatigue Syndrome, but it did not check out. It turned out to be "I want to die" programs.

Sherry had employed a caretaker for her elderly, invalid mother, and was having a difficult time working with the person. She did not want to fire the woman, as she could not find another person as well qualified to take care of her mother. So, rather than confront the dilemma, her mind set up an "I want to die" program that, if carried to finality, would have killed her.

We intercepted and cleared the program before it created a life-threatening disease. The problem stemmed from two past lives where Sherry had caused that caretaker's death, and from a number of other lifetimes where the two women had had conflicts. This is a good example of where an unwillingness to confront an issue can kill you, as it did in the following cases.

Four of my clients chose death rather than standing up for themselves. In my hospice work, I can deal with the trauma and be compassionate, but also remain detached. For me, working with hospice patients is not a challenge, since most of them have given up hope, so all I can offer is help in passing on comfortably.

I participate in their dying days and give them comfort, and offer them the opportunity to forgive themselves for choosing death rather than facing the issue. (In all four cases, little did their families know that the family's controlling behavior was responsible for the death. I did not tell the families this, however, as this would have only added to their grief.)

Quite often, those who cannot stand up for themselves and look out for their interests will take the ultimate escape. However, they will still need to address the issue in another lifetime. In my mind, this is legal suicide. The next two cases make the same point, with both clients not wanting to claim their personal power and confront the issue.

Case #1. The family owned a very successful printing business, which over the years and through hard work, the husband and wife had built up to a multimillion-dollar business. The husband was ill, and I felt that he should take a vacation to get away from his wife's control, which I saw was the cause of his illness. However, the wife could not accept that his condition stemmed from her controlling nature. His state worsened until he ended up with colon cancer.

Chemotherapy did not work, because the lesson was up and he had to deal with his anger at his wife's control. We cleared the cancer and I was finally able to persuade him to take some recreational time off. This infuriated his wife, so he made an appointment for her to see me and discuss the issue.

In the session, all she could do was complain about his not taking responsibility for the business, so I realized that we were not getting anywhere. I suggested that we try to find out why she was so angry at him and what was driving her workaholism. She agreed to try, but we failed to make any progress, because she refused to accept her role in her husband's illness.

This standoff lasted for over a year, during which the husband began doing very well. He delegated much of his work to his secretary and his assistant, who both did excellent jobs, which made the wife even more mad at him and me. He joined a health club and began to play racquetball in the mornings. However, his wife was getting increasingly angry at me for convincing him that he needed to exercise and take some time off. She was irate that he was sick, but unwilling to accept that her manipulation and control had caused his cancer. Nor was she willing to allow him the time off to recuperate.

Finally, he husband started losing the battle and began to get progressively weaker. I suggested that he go to Mexico to the Gerson and/or Contreras clinics, which he did. However, both clinics told him there was nothing they could do for him, because he had given up. Dr. Contreras told him, "You need to spend some time contemplating your future. You do not have cancer, but are just withering away."

Contreras asked him to evaluate what he was escaping from. The couple had just finished building a million-dollar home that they'd paid cash for, and the husband had everything to live for. However, because he could not confront his wife's control, he just gave up and passed on.

Case #2. I had been working with two women for about a year on the issues of taking responsibility and standing up for themselves. In any conflict, they always capitulated, telling people what they wanted to hear, rather than standing up for themselves due to fear of rejection. Both clients wanted a cleaning person to come to their homes once a week, but both of their husbands refused to pay for one.

One husband just flatly refused to pay for the help. He was very controlling, manipulating and abusive and, due to this, the wife had twice had breast cancer. She'd had a double mastectomy, and now had a tumor on her rib cage.

"You're killing y o u r self," I told her, "because you're unwilling to confront your husband. You're rejecting your femininity because, as a woman, you cannot stand up to him. If you were a man, he would respect you, as he does with his friends.

"When you tell the truth, back it up with commitment, and take responsibility, he will back down. Also, we have released all the programs that caused the cancer, yet it's returned because you're not willing to reclaim your personal power."

The next time I saw her, I decided to try another approach. We cleared all the programs about rejection by her husband that had caused her to back down. Then I asked her, "Give me the cancer and visualize love replacing it. Then let go of the anger that's holding it in place."

She replied, "I don't want you to get the cancer."

"It's not in my karmic or emotional pattern to contract cancer, don't worry." I told her, "I'll transmute into the earth."

I asked her to hold my right hand and visualize the cancer leaving her left hand. "I am going to replace the cancer with love coming from my left hand." Within a few minutes, she let go of the cancer energy, which was so intense that it knocked me to the floor. In a week, the tumor was healed. Then she hired a house-cleaner, paying for it herself out of her social security.

The opposite had happened with the second woman, who'd also asked her husband to pay for weekly cleaning help. He had refused, saying that he would help out around the house, but then he had never actually d o n e anything. She told me he was going elk hunting for a week in Montana. The last time I had seen her. I had asked her, "what is he going to do for you?"

"He has not offered to do anything," she had admitted.

I didn't hear from her for six months, until her husband called me to say, "My wife is close to death and keeps repeating your name. I will pay you to make a house call to come and see her."

When I arrived, I barely recognized her. She had degenerated to just skin and bones, and was barely able to talk. The doctor had told her husband, "Your wife is dying a slow death, albeit with no discernible illness or disease. I just can't figure out why."

I explained why she was dying, but I doubt she really understood me. I helped her forgive herself and forgive her husband, and release the fear of dying.

I tactfully tried explaining to the husband why she was dying, but I doubt that he understood, either. All he felt was resentment at her leaving him. I told him, "She will most likely pass on in the next twenty-four hours, once she makes peace with herself." He called me, exactly twenty-three hours later, to tell me she had passed on.

As I noted before, we set up our life paths by the time we are four years old, and few people are willing to break out of that mold and change. There are only two types of people: survivors and victims. Survivors will work against the programs, beating up their bodies because they will not give up. No situation will deter them. They will work through pain because they feel they don't have a choice. It must be done. Conversely, victims back out very easily, looking for someone to support them rather than push themselves. These are the people who die from life-threatening diseases.

Survivors will tend to put themselves in double-binds by working against the programs. They will use willpower to overcome dysfunctional patterns, until the body finally breaks down. The Middle Self and Subconscious Mind will do anything to divert them from the path they have chosen. These minds assume that if you keep on the path you're on, you will be rejected, abandoned or killed. This is unlikely, but your mind is unable to look beyond the current day. It cannot see into the future, so it projects the past into the future, assuming the past will be repeated.

In the case of past lives, your mind interprets the program created by the karmic contract or agreement, and acts as it deems appropriate for your safety and survival. Its fears may be unreal and ridiculous but they exist in your mind, so it sets up defenses against possible threats even though it may never happen. The mind evaluates situations as they come to you, and responds based on how it handled them in the past.

I find that many parents beat their children because they perceive a program that tells them the child killed the parent in a past life, and they are afraid that it will happen again. The parents and children reincarnated together again to create the opportunity to clear the karma. However, by mistreating the child who came to them to release the karma, they are actually creating more karma.

Past lives are one of most misunderstood causes of problems in our lives. In relationships, they can create relationship addiction, as we saw in Chapter 3. Karma can involve "an eye for eye," or being killed for killing someone in a past life, but it does not have to end up that way if we can access the lesson behind it. When we accept, forgive, and understand the lesson, we clear it from our files. We then claim grace, which ends the conflict and discharges the karma.

Killing another human is never justified, no matter what the consequences are or who orders it. Every person who flips the switch on an electric chair, drops the pellets in a gas chamber, or administers a lethal injection is responsible for that death until forgiveness is cleared.

A good example of this is the client who came to see me with neck pain so bad that she was beside herself. Drugs would not relieve it, nor did chiropractic adjustments do any good. Her doctors just could not figure it out. In our session, we found that she had been a hangman in *four* past lives, two of them for the Roman Catholic Church during the Spanish Inquisition, d ur ing which the church had executed twenty million innocent people. We cleared the past lives and the pain went away totally.

Another client could not move or turn her neck. We discovered she had operated a guillotine during the French Revolution. We cleared the past lives and she could move her neck without resistance.

One man came to me, suffering intense pains in his body that inexplicably moved around. We discovered a past life in which he'd been a rifleman in a firing squad and had killed many people. Once we cleared that lifetime, all the pain left permanently.

When your mind receives sensory input, if there are no programs to access, the mind will create one. The big IF here is: If *you* are directing your life, your mind does not have to make a decision for you. *You* act on the sensory input and make the appropriate decision. But, if you have sold your power out to autopilot, then Artificial Intelligence and sub-personalities will make your decisions for you, w h i c h may not be the decisions you would ordinarily make, given the same input.

The major causes of most physical breakdowns are feeling rejected, not accepted, invalidated and abandoned. We all want to be accepted by everyone we meet, and will go out of our way to set up situations so that people will accept and validate us, many times doing so subconsciously. Yet the harder we try, the more we are rejected.

Likewise, we do not intentionally mean to reject other people, but when we detect their need it can feel as though an unwritten sign comes up saying, "Reject them, they are not getting the message or the lesson."

It may seem cruel, but that is how our File and Program Manager and the Subconscious Mind's programs work. They have no morals, nor do they make any decision as to what is improper behavior. They play out their roles based on the stored programs.

The awesome power of your mind will either heal you or cause you to get sick, and even to die. Many times your mind causes illness without your conscious consent. If this happens, it is an autopilot response. If you do not clear the situation and find the base cause, it will continue until you give in and lose your will to live. At this point, it's too late to change the outcome.

My father finally died of lung congestion in the hospital after overcoming three life-threatening diseases, including pancreatic cancer. Once he had made up his mind to give up, there was nothing we could do. He wanted to be near us and his grandson, but my mother would not move. She controlled him just as she had tried to do with me. Rather than take his power back and just move where he wanted to be, he chose death in order to escape the situation.

Many years before that event, I had made up my mind that I would not follow my parents' path. Breaking out of that pattern was a major battle, because we generally follow our childhood model. Quite often, however, I would find my parents' behavior sneaking into my own.

My wife and I made an agreement that if we perceived our parents' behavior appearing in ours, we would point it out. As children, we accept the model we grow up with, which insidiously becomes such a part of us that most do not recognize it as such, so we continue in the same mold throughout life, passing the patterns on to the next generation.

When dealing with physical/emotional breakdown, disciplining ourselves to face the issues that affect us is a major challenge. The more fear exists in our mind, the more we will resist acknowledging the very programs that are blocking recovery.

Denial is the worst enemy of transformation, since it prevents us getting to the base cause of the breakdown, while creating a false sense of well-being. Denial-of-denial suppresses the cause totally, so we do not even know the program exists at all. When we do not know that a habit pattern exists in our mind, we will operate from it, not knowing that we are simply on autopilot, acting out a program that we choose not to recognize.

~ ~ ~

I often hear people comment, "My life is working, there's nothing wrong, and I don't have any (or many) problems" ("any" or "many" depending on how far the person is into denial). Denial has blocked their awareness of the programs that are running in the background.

When I ask, "Do you have peace, happiness, harmony, joy, unconditional love and financial abundance in your life?" they respond in many ways. Most people can recognize lack of money or job satisfaction more readily than peace, happiness, harmony and joy, even though they are all in one package. The answer I usually get is, "Well, I would like to have more money, or a better job that provides more income."

When pushed further, however, we find that most people are not happy with their positions in life and, as we dig even deeper, the more we find that unsatisfactory conditions do exist. (Remember, the originally the statement was, "There's nothing wrong with my life.")

The reason for the discrepancy is that most people live on the periphery of life, or in survival mode. Most are on autopilot, so they deny the very conditions that block emotions and programs from arising so they can be cleared. We suppress and stuff our feelings and emotions so that we do not have to deal with them.

Most people will deny that there is anything wrong with their lives, because acknowledging that would bring up fear. If something does not work, we prefer to shelve it or run away from it, rather than face the issue causing the challenge. I find that only five percent of the population is happy with their station in life, which leaves ninety-five per cent of people unhappy. Twenty per cent of those are trying to achieve change in their lives, but the rest do not seem to be aware that life could be free of struggle. (My findings align with the statistical sample Studs Terkel presented in his 1980 book *Working*.)

With today's unrest in society, I feel that most people's sense of futility and frustration may increase the level of unhappiness. Many people live in an illusion of happiness because they never delve into what happiness really is. They may laugh at many situations and instances and appear superficially happy, but does that denote genuine happiness and joy in their life?

In a workshop or during a session, when I ask the question and probe, suppressed emotions bubble up to the surface. Because this happens with a tremendous emotional release, few can deny what's happening. When we finally admit that we are not on our path, we find that there is a long road ahead to recovery.

Many therapy processes can provide a little help, but seldom do they erase the past so we can rewrite the script for our lives. We must remember that we are the lead actors/actresses in our plays of life, but most of us forget that we are also the producers, directors and casting crew. *We create it all; nobody does it to us.* We invite and choose the cast of characters and players into our plays. Everybody is in our life by *our* invitation; no "intruders" can sneak in. We choose them all.

The only way that we can change our paths is to thank and forgive all the major and bit players in our life's dramas, and let them go, because we invited them to be our teachers. But that does not mean we need to let them cause us pain, illness, disease and emotional turmoil.

The cause of dysfunction is our inability to detach and let go of emotional trauma during the play. We must rewrite the future scripts so we do not continue down the same path, saying the same lines before the same audience. The hardest concept to accept is that we created it all and can "uncreate" it with some guidance and help. It is all simply programming software, and we can easily rewrite the programs. We just need to know how. The body/mind will heal itself if given the proper support, but the support is not drugs. The support is *LOVE*.

During the winter of 1997, in a major breakthrough in the search for the cause for dysfunction, we located the most of sub-personality programs. My psychology training had taught Transactional Therapy, which focuses on the inner child, critical parent, inner adult and other sub-personalities that were assumed to be in the Subconscious Mind. Some researchers even advocated looking for disowned selves, or denied sub-personalities.

In 1983, I was introduced to Voice Dialogue, a therapy process developed by Hal Stone. His son Joshua was working with us at our center, which gave me a chance to understand the process. Stone had developed Voice Dialogue to get in touch with our disowned selves in the subconscious mind.

In the process, we talked with these disowned selves. (At least, we thought we were at that time. Now that I have delved more deeply into the function of the mind, and worked with people with Magical Child Syndrome and split and multiple personalities, I am not so sure with whom we were talking then. I doubt now that we were in contact with disowned selves all the time.)

Sub-personalities can run your life and appear very real. Chapter 6 describes how sub-personalities function and how we can rewrite their scripts. Suffice to say that we must review the nature of disease. The medical field defines "disease" as: *A malfunction in the body that causes an infection, a virus, bacterial growth, or abnormal growth of a cellular structure*—in other words, anything they cannot control or understand.

Researchers give names to the syndromes they study, then they try to find drugs that control them. Or, if surgery is possible, they will remove the offending body part without regard to the body's need for that organ or gland, on the assumption that removing the offending tumor or infected body part makes the person clear of the disease. While measures such as antibiotics and chemotherapy kill offending body parts, they also kill all the body's good anti-viral agents. This is all based on trying to stop the condition before it kills the patient.

I am beginning to think that a considerable number of cancer cases seem to become healed without medical intervention, because the person decides to overcome the fear or anger that created the cancer. Do clients go "into remission" as the medical field calls it, or are they healed or cured (see Chapter 8, "The Placebo Effect")? My feeling is that when you release the program causing the cancer, the mind/body deactivates the abnormal cell growth, and the cancer disappears.

In my father's case, he had one chemo treatment and decided not to continue. His doctor had given him a "death sentence" of three months to live, so he decided to go with my process, but also to see a doctor whom I recommended. (I knew he wouldn't accept my program only, so I recommended a physician to work with me.)

In less than six months, we had cleared the cancer totally. We worked with nutrition and positive mental attitude so he could get a handle on a new way of life. He changed his diet and, with a new attitude on life, was healed.

(The medical doctor I suggested he consult was overloaded with patients, because his track record had about an eighty per cent cure rate. Most of his patients, including my father, were healed with lasting results, so the inevitable happened: The AMA and the California medical licensing board ran him out of state; cancer is a big money spinner, and the medical establishment did not want him on their turf, someone with a methodology that was effective eighty per cent of the time.) He moved to Mexico.)

When my father finally did cross over, many years later, the doctors tried to pin his cause of death on cancer. But I forced their hand and demanded a full autopsy, which they did not want to do, presumably because they knew the truth. When both my mother and I formally requested an autopsy, they found the cause of death to be lung congestion and not cancer. There was not a trace of cancer in his body (which proves without doubt that the present cancer research will not find either cure or cause because researchers are barking up the wrong tree).

The medical profession cannot surgically remove programs from the mind; all they can remove is the physical results of the mind's programming. This, however, seldom stops the cancer from returning, but if we remove the program, as we did in my father's case, the cancer disappears for good.

Research with psychoneuroimmunolgy has produced amazing results that are staggering when one looks at what has been written on it. Yet very little money for research is directed to the researchers who are finding that it is the *mind* that causes almost all illness. Unfortunately, the researchers have not found a viable process that will cure illness yet, so the medical establishment does not currently give much credence to the research.

Energy Psychology and Energy Medicine are processes that will heal any illness, disease or emotional dysfunction yet we get little acceptance until a person sees the results of the therapy process. Miracles are created every day but we get no press coverage because we are considered on the fringe.

When I met Dr. Bruce Lipton at an Energy Psychology Conference in 2006, it was a breath of fresh air, Finally I was meeting a person who knew what I had been talking about for the past 20 years. He had started his research about the same time I had, and we had both come up with the same conclusions, from opposite directions: me from the psychological side and he from the medical arena, We both had discovered the same concept.

I was a little disappointed he did not have a solution, even though he had the right theories. I have talked to many people who have attended his lectures and workshops who are also very interested in his theory and concepts, yet they leave the lecture feeling lost because he does not have a workable solution. When they meet me, they ask "Why are you not working with him?" At this point, I have not made a strong enough connection with him or his people.

People will often object to or disagree with my findings, but we have proven the process repeatedly with people who are committed to becoming well. Those who are getting mileage from their condition or are intent on controlling others may not want to get well. This may seem irrational, yet it's true, so why would someone want to suffer?

We have discovered many "suffer" programs, all caused from pre-birth, in utero rejection, childhood programming and/or past-life karma programs I need to suffer:

- I really need to suffer
- I want to suffer (to get my needs met)
- I deserve to suffer (from being told repeatedly that I am somehow "wrong" or not all right)
- I *think* I need to suffer (a perception that I did something wrong and am guilty)
- I *believe* I need to suffer (a belief of my unworthiness or shame)
- I *feel* I need to suffer (usually from some feeling that I am not all right)
- I *know* I need to suffer (for some karmic contract or program).

Finding the "I need to suffer" programs opened another door to a new concept of healing. We have found that *everybody* has some or all of them. When we opened the door to "I need to suffer" programs, we found a veritable Pandora's box, as it gave access to the suppressed denial files.

Even with clients with whom we had worked in the past, we discovered new files that had not been accessed before, because they were locked up in denial-of-denial files. Again, why would someone want to suffer? Yet that is exactly the case, because the mind is irrational when we are not in control. If Inner Conscious Mind is running on autopilot, we will be run by sub-personalities and multiple personalities that see all their actions as payoffs. If we do not want to confront an issue, we will act in ways that are not in our best interests. And our mind will justify its behavior to avoid dealing with what it fears.

It does not consider that it is killing its host vehicle, and we will go along with it because we are not in control of our life. Quite often, I find clients with irrational control issues or "I'll do it myself" attitudes that are behind the refusal to deal with the issue. Since our mind is irrational in its thinking if we are not in control, it perceives anything that confronts its control as something it has to block or stop.

I have had clients refuse to continue with further sessions because they complain that I "needle" them, or that I'm arrogant and controlling. It is not them talking; it is the controlling personality selves. All I can do is retrieve the programs that are causing or running their dysfunctions, with no vested interest in making someone well. If we create a miracle, great, but it does not validate me personally because I know that I do not create it.

All healing is self-healing. I function from a compassionate-but-detached point of view, as a facilitator showing the way to wellness. The whole purpose of my work is to learn to tell the truth and empower clients to be able to stand up and take their power back. Our mind will gladly relinquish control to us if we reclaim our personal power and stand up for what is right. Healing only happens when our commitment and intention is to discipline ourselves take control. Nobody can do it for us; nor can anyone hurt us or reject us. It is our *interpretation* of their actions that causes the breakdown.

When we choose to see the truth, healing will happen. There are no blocks to healing when we are open to the information that caused the breakdown. What blocks healing is our perception of our needs and payoffs, and our resistance to them. In the case of depression or emotional dysfunction, doctors use mind-altering drugs, which suppress one function and activates another. This treatment gives a false reading that can cause a reaction in the body/mind, and may or may not work in the long term.

A good example of this was a person who asked in one of my lectures, "If your process does work, can people stop using Prozac and Paxil? They saved my life eight years ago, but I would like to stop taking them."

My response was this: "Yes, but we must clear the cause of your depression first. You may need a bridge to help you while we are clearing the emotional trauma and imbalances."

I provided her with a StressBlocker to help her stabilize her endocrine system while we released all her childhood trauma and the rejection. Her divorce had reactivated the childhood traumas that were the cause of her depression. (See Appendix for information on the StressBlocker.)The body is an integrated unit. If we remove or suppress any part, it will strive to regain balance, but that does not create wellness and heal the cause. My interpretation is: *There is no such thing as illness or disease.* (I also believe that there are no contagious diseases, only contagious people who set themselves up to contract illness and disease.)

Physical breakdown is caused by emotional trauma, a dysfunctional program or a lesson coming up that needs to be addressed. It is just a messenger. When we understand the message it brings, we can clear and heal the illness or disease immediately. The offending body part is only telling you that you are rejecting it for some reason. Do we take it out because it is malfunctioning? The medical field would say, "Yes." I say, "No." We need to find out what is causing the malfunction and then, when we clear it, the body will correct the malfunction and resume normal function.

A good example of such clearing is a client whom we'll call Sam, who was referred to me by his brother, with whom I'd had some amazing results. In Sam's session, I learned that he had kidney failure and was on twice-weekly dialysis, with no signs of recovery. One of his younger brothers had donated a kidney for him, yet he was destroying the transplanted kidney, too. We reactivated his original kidney so he could stop

Dialysis. Even though we successfully stabilized his condition so that he would not reject the transplanted kidney, Sam did not continue with treatment.

All the brothers had been raised by the same parents, yet Sam was the only one who had picked up the dysfunctional programs that were causing his physical breakdown. His older brother's path was one of great success. Of course, we had found the usual triggers from a dysfunctional family but he was not letting them hinder him.

When we removed those blocks to success, he made his dream-come-true of being an actor, and received parts in Hollywood movies and a leading part in a play. So what was the difference between Sam and his older brother? Sam was a *victim* of his childhood programming, and his brother was a *survivor,* able to rise above the same programming.

The body/mind will reveal the cause so we can correct the programming. Once we find the cause and release the program and/or sub- or multiple-personality driving the malfunction, the body will recover its balance and heal itself. All we need to do is rewrite the script from which we are operating—a false belief or interpretation—to delete or create and write a new program. Then we harness the body's own healing power and, as we operate from the new program, the body will heal itself perfectly.

Two clients I was working with fifteen years ago indicate how a dysfunctional pattern is created:

Case #1: This client first saw me about three years before regarding chronic pain in his back and one foot, which was always cold even in warm weather. Seven years earlier, his doctors had put an electrical stimulator in the nerve area that would activate the nerve to lessen the pain. When this was not very effective, they suggested surgery to open up the channel in the spine to relieve the pressure on the nerve. He decided against this because of the risk of paralysis if the surgeon made an error.

When he came to me, I did what I could for him, with limited success. He recently decided to work with me again because my process was the only one that had provided any relief at all in the last three years. Progress was slow until we found the denial-of-denial file.

In clearing sub-personalities during each session, we found that six in particular—judgment, resentment, blame, avoidance, disorientation and indecision—kept coming up each time, along with feelings of futility and frustration programs. This indicated that he was unwilling to deal with a lesson that was suppressed.

When we located the cause, we discovered he did not want to deal with it because he didn't want to get into conflict over the issue. I told him, "Your back problem will continue until you decide to work out the lesson. When a lesson is up, nothing can stop pain. When the lesson is released, the pain will go away."

In the next session, we were able to release all his resistance to speaking his mind, and we set up the lesson so he could take care of it. I wondered if he would have the courage to talk with the other person involved in the conflict and start the process of clearing the lesson.

We achieved some minor pain relief, and I have tracked his recovery to see how long it would take him to remove the denial so he could resolve the conflict in a forgiving manner. To this point he has not made another appointment so I do not know where he is in that process. With all the programs cleared he is able to confront his conflicts and recover with no pain.

Case #2: A very simple issue created intense back pain for a client whom we'll call Jane. I had seen her two years earlier and, in the meantime, she had gone to a chiropractor but the back pain kept returning. We discovered that the issue was her not taking her power back and voicing her needs to her husband. For example, two days before she came to me, Jane and her husband had taken her car to get it smog-checked, and it had failed. She assumed her husband would call the shop and, if it failed the test, bring it home and fix it, as he had done in the past. However, this time he had not called the shop. Jane assumed that it was a small item and that he'd left it for the mechanic to fix. When the car was ready, though, he said, "I can't take you to pick it up until tomorrow."

Jane needed the car right away, so she walked two miles to the bus to get to the shop. She was shocked when they presented her with a $300 bill. She needed the car, so she paid the bill and got her car back. That evening, her husband would not validate her efforts to pick up the car, nor would he respond to her question, "Why didn't you call the shop to see what needed to be repaired?" He could have fixed the car himself for about $35.00. Her mind took that as rejection, and her refusal to demand an answer to her question caused her back to lock up. That night, she could hardly move or sleep.

In just one session, Jane's issue came up about giving her power away and not standing up for herself. Her back pain was gone after that session. Her case is a good example of the power of Energy Psychology and Energy Medicine when coupled with Neuro/Cellular Repatterning. Her challenge began when her husband did not respond in the way she wanted him to, so she felt rejected. (Note: He had done nothing to cause her downward spiral, but just had not responded in any way. Her *interpretation* of his lack of response had started the reaction in her.)

As the strength built up in her, she started pushing him for a justification; their dialogue had continued, until he had just walked away, clamming up and refusing to take responsibility for not calling the auto shop. This had further frustrated Jane, causing her to feel depressed; her body went into anger reaction. Reacting to this negative feeling, the neuropeptides and cytokinins began to shut her body down and tighten up her muscles. As her anger and depression increased, she could not effectively voice her disapproval.

Due to the pain, she was unable to sleep, so her energy level had fallen to the point of lethargy and listlessness when she called. In one session, we were able to clear all the causes and reactions, allowing her body to return to the state of normality. Subsequent sessions allowed Jane to reclaim her personal power totally, because she ran into other tests of her ability to withstand rejection and respond effectively. She now no longer reacts to her husband's lack of respect for her needs and questions, nor does she push him for validation or acceptance.

In cases such as Jane's, the client can go to a serious illness if we do not clear the anger and rejection early in the buildup cycle. Jane recognized the cause of her locked back in two days, and acted to clear it as soon as possible, knowing what has happened to her in the past. Most people do not recognize the cause, however; if they cannot recover their personal power, they end up either in long-term depression, taking drugs to buoy themselves up, or they deteriorate further into a life-threatening illness and possible death.

Summary

We have found, as more information is revealed when we work with people, one may either rise above the programs that cause illness and disease, or be submerged by them. We cannot afford negative thoughts or feelings entering our minds, as they will set up a depressive reaction there. The body's neuropeptides and cytokinins will begin to send out negative messages that depress our immune and endocrine systems.

When negative programming begins to activate, it is deposited in cellular memory, which begins to break down the body. The process starts slowly at first but, if we don't recognize the inroads caused by negativity, fear, anger, rage and resentment, the process will eventually end up in a life-threatening disease. Many malfunctions are control-based, as the ailment brings the person the attention craved. We must rise above our needs and payoffs, to the point where we do not need others to validate our existence. As long as we depend on others for acceptance, recognition, respect and a feeling of being all right, we will be subject to situations that cause malfunctions in our lives.

When we rise above the need to get validation from others and can accept and love ourselves unconditionally, we will approach the state of total wellness. You do not have be sick to know you are not well.

In the last five years we have discovered many more situations that are critical issues in clearing programs and beliefs. The seeds that cause most of our problems are set in place by the time we are four to eight years old. Then they play out throughout our life unless we remove and delete the negative programs.

In almost all cases the cause of all breakdowns, malfunctions, illness and disease are caused by lack of acceptance, validation, approval, respect, acknowledgment, recognition, trust or unconditional love.

Two of the big issues for children are trust and respect. If they do not get this from the model their parents show them, they will not trust or have respect for their parents. The major problem and conflict is that parents do not know what unconditional love is, because they never received it themselves. How can you provide something you do not have yourself?

This is the first breakdown in family relationships that begins causing conflicts by the time a child is two years old. A child is focused on its mother totally for the first five years of life. Children are born with all the programs needed to grow up in a functional family: all the qualities of unconditional love, self-esteem, self-worth and self-confidence. They know who they are and expect their mothers to treat them with love, respect and recognition. Unfortunately, not all children are born into functional families.

Chapter 7

Energy Medicine: How the Body Communicates with the Cellular Structure

Each cell in our bodies is similar to a "network computer" controlled by the mind's mainframe computers. Sensory Input comes to us from our eyes, ears, skin and our intuitive ability. Our minds decide what this input is and the meaning it has to us. If we can comprehend and understand what the meaning is, we can control our responses.

If we do not recognize the meaning or understand what it is, our minds will search for an appropriate response in our Subconscious Mind's database. If there is not a program which applies, our Middle Self program manager will create one. At this point we've gone into an emotional state.

If we are in control of our behavior, we can provide the appropriate *response* with our Conscious Mind. We have thirty seconds to make a decision as to how to respond to the sensory input. When we are not in control, the sensory input drops to the next level and turns into a *reaction* as Middle Self assigns a meaning to the input.

At this point, we react according to the programs that are in the file and the input becomes an emotion. File Manager pulls up the program out of the Subconscious Mind's database and we react according to the programs from the past. This all happens automatically if we do not *consciously* decide how to handle the situation. Negative input, such as fear, anger, rejection or outward displays of resentment and blame, causes the body to suppress its immune system and shut down its endocrine function. The challenge before researchers is to find a way to prevent or clear, and then release the effects. So far, they have not found an effective process that will work in every case. What they have worked with has a marginal effect. With Energy Psychology and Energy Medicine, coupled with Neuro/Cellular Reprogramming (N/CR), we have the answer. We have proven over the past 20 years that N/CR has a 95 percent success factor on any issue if clients will cooperate and discipline themselves to follow through with the process.

Research has shown that, as adrenal activity increases to handle fear, stress or anger reactions, it will slow down or shut down the secretion of hormones and chemicals that our body uses to heal itself. Secretion of "happy" brain chemicals, such as seratonin, interferon, interlukins and even L-dopa are shut down by excessive adrenal output. The cell receptors begin receiving stress messages that tighten the muscles, ready for flight or fight, on receipt of messages that alert them.

If these messages continue for an extended time, adrenaline output increases to a level that can cause adrenal exhaustion and resulting depression. When adrenaline is exhausted we begin producing cortisol (as a replacement for adrenaline). If the output continues for an even longer period, illness and disease will result.

Medical researchers working in the new field of psychoneuroimmunology have proven without a doubt that positive input, such as expressions of love, kindness, positive support and acceptance, will activate healing energy within the cellular structure of the body. The implication is clear. We can't afford to hold negative, feelings, thoughts and attitudes. We pay a high price in destruction in our mental, physical and emotional heath when we allow ourselves to hold negative feelings and reactions to control us. We are giving our power away to people around us. Many major speakers including doctors and therapists proclaim the effect love has on the Body/Mind, yet they do not show us how to install it. Ten years ago, the medical community would have laughed at them; today, even people from the medical field (Bernie Siegel, Larry

Dosey and many others) are making these claims. We have found that love is the basis for all healing. When you rewrite the programs so that people can love themselves, miracles can happen. Medical researchers are now discovering that the body communicates positive or negative impulses to itself through chemicals such as neuropeptides (NP) and cytokinins. The cell receptors react to the messages sent to them by the body/mind's reaction or response to feelings and to how sensory input is interpreted. NEUROPEPTIDES NPs

For a long time, it was thought that only the brain released NPs, but now we know that all cells communicate with them. NPs are like the acid in a car battery—turning the ignition switch triggers a chemical reaction in the battery that is converted into electrical energy, which cranks the starter. In our bodies, the NPs release minute electrical impulses that tell the various parts of the body what to do. These messages travel around the body in microseconds.

Our nervous systems operate on electrical impulses, and messages of fear or anger create a destructive reaction in the body. The body cannot interpret this logically as, "Oops, this is a dysfunctional interpretation of incoming sensory data, so do not record." Instead, it records *all* sensory input without censoring the negative parts. This can cause us to go into a downward spiral of behavior in seconds as all bodily systems do exactly what our mind instructs them to do. But if we are able to intercept and block the sensory input before our mind activates the reaction, there will be no effect.

A basic human need is to receive love, so when we are in an accepting, supportive loving state, the NPs transmit a positive, love-based message, which heals the body. On the other hand, illness, disease and depression stem from lack of love. The next time you hurt yourself and feel pain, try this experiment. Focus your mind on the location of the pain and surround it with love. Send love to the point of pain and feel the love releasing the pain. The pain will subside very quickly.

For example, suppose you accidentally hit a fingernail with a hammer. Normally, bleeding occurs underneath the nail, but sending love to the finger will stop the bleeding more quickly. It will not swell up or get black, and you will not lose the fingernail. I have done this myself many times over the years and I have suggested this process to many people who have used the process. It works every time.

The main reason why researchers cannot find a cure for disease is that all disease is created by the mind's interaction with the body's cellular structure. You cannot remove a pattern from the mind with drugs or by removing the dysfunctional part of the body.

Conversely, a cathartic release can remove emotional pain by releasing the pent-up anger or fear energy, but it will not remove the program. The dysfunctional program is still operating, and the illness will be created over and over, until the program is released. If you do not release the program that caused the emotional pain, no amount of affirmation on forgiving and releasing a person will prevent recurrence. Identifying the cause of the program in the first place is just the first part of challenge. The program must then be released from the physical body/mind to affect permanent healing. (You will see this statement repeatedly in this book.)

Pain is an indicator of resistance; your mind is talking to you. All you need do is decipher the message and you can release the dysfunction. This is why Neuro/Cellular Reprogramming works so well. We tell the Subconscious Mind to release, and the NPs do the work for us, provided that some program or multiple personality does not intervene to stop the process.

The Body/Mind is an amazingly sensitive bio-electromagnetic machine. Medical research has yet to understand that the body will heal itself if you release the dysfunctional programming and allow the original programs to perform as they were intended to do. Each cell has an original blueprint (RNA) from which it can regenerate itself, and it retains this blueprint, even when we write over it by placing limitations on the cellular structure.

The cell then begins to recreate the limitations in itself from the existing programs held in its files. All we need to do is remove the limitations and healing begins. The mind holds the program and sends it to the cellular memory, which creates the dysfunction that causes breakdown in the cellular structure. The malfunctioning program continues until we rewrite the program. When the limitations are removed, our cells can regenerate themselves from their original blueprints.

Medical research has discovered that cells communicate with each other using NPs, that the mind communicates through the endocrine system, and that it mobilizes the immune system. But doctors do not seem to understand the research findings. They are baffled by most diseases, against which drugs and surgery have only selective success.

Admittedly, doctors do a fine job of putting broken bones back together and patching up bodies that have been damaged in accidents; when faced with a symptom that does not need repair, however, they are at a loss as to how to handle the situation. Granted, they do achieve some success with disease, but their work does little to isolate the condition causing the breakdown. Meanwhile, people who want to be healed can do it themselves if they are able to break through the negative programming and create a positive mental attitude.

Medical research is stumped on another matter: why the same treatment for same disease yields different results with different people—one dies and the other recovers. It always comes back to the question, "Why? Why this selective immunity or selective remission?" (This will be revealed in the next chapter.)

When we understand the mind and how it functions, however, why the results differ becomes obvious. As a result, we must be accurate in the program we are releasing and reprogramming, including their application in our lives.

Chapter 8

The Placebo Effect

Medical researchers and doctors do not yet completely understand the placebo effect, even though they are often faced with the results. The placebo effect is the mind accepting the intention behind the methodology of the practitioner. The product or the process may have little or no real therapeutic value, the controlling factor being whether the client accepts and believes that the process or drug *will* work.

On the other hand, some people do not consult a doctor or practitioner after the diagnosis, yet they end up clear of the disease that was diagnosed. How? A miracle? The power of their minds?

I used to subscribe to my mother's contention that God helps some of us but not all of us. Today, I do not believe it has anything to do with God, mainly because there is no selective God that favors one person over another in any way.

Twenty years ago, I believed that selective remission was somehow causing the healing but now I know from my research that the controlling factor is the programs that control the mind's communication with itself, and unless you remove the programs healing will not happen. In fact, I have found that people who have experienced frequent miraculous healings have erased the programs, even though no one had worked with them to rewrite those programs.

How do we explain that phenomenon? The power of the mind? If the belief becomes a knowing, we can heal anything. With the power of the mind, a strong belief system, and a committed intention, you can heal anything.

People with a strong intention and commitment make practitioners think they themselves have caused the healing, so the latter describe themselves as "healers" when it's really the placebo effect in action. Positive Mental Attitude (PMA) is the basis of all healing. The stronger the intention and the commitment, the easier it is to create a healing environment.

Positive thought and action can have amazing effects on the body because the response causes the body to support itself with positive feedback that activates all the receptor sites to produce healing energy. (Book two) in the "The Mind/ Body Medicine Connection" series, *Behavioral Mind/Body Medicine: Exploring The New Frontier of Energy Medicine/Energy Psychology and Psycho-neuroimmunology in Practice*, will provide further explanation.)

Pharmaceutical drugs appear to have little positive effect on the body unless patients taking them believe and accept that they will work. Doctors are finding that patients are developing resistance to many drugs that used to work in the past.

Simply reading about a drug's side-effects in the Physicians Desk Reference (a listing of all the drugs, their ingredients, uses, contraindications and side-effects) or having a doctor or practitioner explain the cautions may be enough to catalyze a particular side-effect. Then the patient would need to take another drug to counteract that side-effect even though the prescribed drug may not have its primary effect at all. So the placebo effect can work in reverse, too.

An example of this is a man who attended one of my lectures. He was taking a drug for high blood pressure and his doctor told him that a possible side-effect was diarrhea, which began as soon as he started taking the drug. He realized his high blood pressure was caused by arterial sclerosis and decided to use chelation therapy to clear his blood vessels. This worked well and his blood pressure went down and he avoided heart bypass surgery. However, he continued to have diarrhea and, every three hours, had to take pills to control it. In hopes that we could stop the diarrhea, he volunteered to do a demonstration with me. With a simple affirmation, we cleared and reversed the doctor's statement about the drug and forgave the doctor for the miscommunication. The result was end of the diarrhea. It stopped on the spot. Any statement your mind accepts will become programming; this is the basis for the placebo effect.

Some of my clients have had electrical stimulators surgically implanted in their bodies to stop pain, but they no longer work after a time. Hospital inpatients are often hooked up to an antibiotic IV drip for days, weeks and even months in order to kill a viral or bacterial infection, and they finally get well. Why? The placebo effect finally kicks in and they get well because they believe it will work.

In the following case history, however, it did not work. When Jim was told he must go to the hospital for chronic back pain, his girl friend gave him a copy of this book. After reading it, he called me to ask when I would be in Toronto.

When I asked about his problem, he told me, "The doctors say that it's a bacterial infection, but the daily antibiotic IV injections are having no effect." It had advanced to the point he could not turn over in the bed. The doctors claimed his spine so fragile that turning over could cause damage.

When I arrived in Toronto three weeks later, he had been in the hospital for four weeks, receiving a daily one-hour antibiotic IV drip, with no visible signs of recovery. In the fifth week, I was able to get to the hospital and work with Jim. (Since my tools are my mind and body, and I do not carry any equipment or briefcases, I looked just like any other visitor and did not draw any attention.)

We went through the manual so he could remove the saboteurs and reclaim his personal power. When I located the cause of his pain, we cleared the issues that were causing it; he began his recovery, and was released two days later. Before releasing him, the doctors took x-rays and ran an MRI. They would not discuss the results with him, because they could not understand what had happened: No results for four weeks, and then totally healed in two days with no change in treatment?

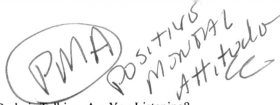

They released him the following day. They did not understand what had happened, nor would they discuss it with him.

They called it a "spontaneous remission." What is that? Doctors cannot explain it, and say it will return again. In actuality our minds have removed the programs, either by accepting release of the condition/ailment, or by acknowledging that we have released the programs that were driving and causing the condition.

I have since done follow-up sessions with Jim, and he attended one of our Level One Energy Psychology workshops, at which he commented, "You probably do not know how wonderful it is to be able to walk up steps without pain, and to know that I'm getting better each week."

We were able to help heal his chronic, debilitating back pain by clearing the anger and resentment he held towards his parents. It was the same old story of being rejected at birth, which continued into childhood. His family was controlling, dogmatic and did not know how to express love or even affection.

When the lesson is up, nothing will clear it unless we recognize the cause and release everyone involved, with love and forgiveness, accepting them as they are. When you clear the fear, anger and resentment that are the cause, the condition will not return because it has been cleared completely. The antibiotics would not work because he had to learn the lesson. (This was not the placebo effect even though it may appear to be.)

In many double-blind studies, researchers get skewed results because of the placebo effect; many times, the placebo is more effective than the drug. The most effective drug is positive mental attitude (PMA), regarding the process and/or the practitioner. If you accept the process, it will work for you. On the other hand, negative thoughts, feelings or actions will suppress cellular activity and the production of the neuro-chemicals that support immune system response. This in turn causes a build-up of cytotoxins that trigger cellular breakdown.

Since all systems are depressed by negative sensory input to our "databases," this will produce actual physical/emotional depression, as the endocrine system tries to cope with keeping up the body's energy. The result is increased adrenal output that eats up the body's reserves, producing the same effect on the adrenal glands that diabetes does on the pancreas. Doctors try to intervene with Prozac, Paxil, Zoloft or other mind-altering drugs as a stopgap measure to help a patient cope with the depression, but that does not get to the cause.

At a recent book show, I talked with a doctor who was writing a book on placebo medicine. He told me, "I have become more effective than most of my colleagues since I began using saline solution injections and placebos. I no longer prescribe any kind of drug, yet I have more success now than I did in the past."

He said a belief in the practitioner or doctor has an amazing effect. He related many instances when patients had come to him after the conventional doctor had given up on them. In response, I related the following astonishing story to him, to which he replied in a matter-of-fact way, "Oh, that happens all the time."

About fifteen years ago, the FDA began testing a new anti- cancer drug called *Kerbotsin*. In the first six months of the eighteen-month double-blind study on the efficacy of the drug, the results were spotty, ranging from total remission to no effect at all. Having exhausted all other possible treatments, a patient with metastasized cancer asked his doctor, "Is there any experimental drug that I could take?"

The doctor then joined the Kerbotzin test group, and obtained a free sample of the drug. He injected his patient with it, and a miracle happened: the cancer disappeared almost overnight! About three months later, the FDA released its preliminary report, saying that the drug was not very effective in its tests. Within days of the patient reading that report, his cancer had reappeared.

At that point, the doctor felt the patient had nothing to lose, so he conducted an experiment of his own. He called the

patient and said, "I've obtained a newer version of the drug that's stronger. It is a three-week treatment where I give an injection each week." All he did was to inject the patient with saline water, the cancer disappeared again.

At the end of the eighteen-month test period, the FDA did not approve the drug, claiming inconclusive results. Within two days of reading that report, the man died, after having been cancer free for a full year. The power of the mind is awesome; the placebo effect works in amazing ways.

~ ~ ~

Many books bear titles such as *The Cure for All Cancers*, while others describe the cure for this condition or that one. However, among those who have tried these processes, the success rate is not encouraging. Of course, some people do successfully clear up a disease using the products and processes that are advocated, but it's mainly because a belief is set up in their mind which becomes an inner "knowing." It is not actually the product or the process that heals them, but their commitment and belief.

We are finally understanding the placebo effect in healing. Once clients release the fear, their minds heal them. There are only two basic processes: healing, that eliminates the syndrome permanently; and remission, which puts the condition into limbo for a time. I often work with clients on whom the medical profession has given up. Each one has been given a death sentence and told to get their affairs in order, because they have only so many months to live—something that is then communicated to every cell in the body. (Having some authority-figure telling you, "You're going to die in three months" just about wraps it up for most people and they self-hypnotize themselves into compliance.)

Fortunately, some people have determination, and many of them come to me. We reverse the disease syndrome and release the doctor's death sentence, all without drugs or surgery. Because all dysfunction is caused by fear, anger, self-rejection, invalidation, feeling unacceptable (not all right) and the lack of love, the only treatment needed is unconditional love. When this is transmitted to you, your body feels a sense of security, and uses NPs to relay this love to your cells. The cells in turn release the disease or dysfunction and heal. Drugs and surgery simply cannot perform this miracle.

From the 1940s to the 1970s, Kathryn Kuhlman presented shows where she gave a lecture on how the Lord and Jesus Christ would be there and heal the people who came forward, come up on the stage profess their belief in Jesus Christ. I watched people get out of wheel chairs and walk for the first in years. She would say, "stand up and be healed now--you can do it; come forward. Jesus is here for you now." People with every type and form of disease would come up on the stage. It was quite a presentation.

This really was hard to believe. A little boy was sleeping in his mother's arms next to us. He slipped down from her arms and began walking—very shaky, but he was walking. His mother burst into tears and could not get up. An usher helped the boy stand up and walk back to his mother. She said he had been paralyzed since birth. She walked out after the event, holding her son's hand. How do we explain these healings? When you believe, anything can happen. What was it in the little boy that activated his mind and enabled him to walk?

People with a burning desire to accomplish healing can sometimes heal themselves with no outside help. I have seen this happen. How do you explain a theater full of people who stand up and walk, when they have been in wheelchairs and unable to walk for years?

An example of determination with a burning desire to recover: A woman called me and asked if my book was really true. (I receive a lot of calls like this.) She had read it in two days. Her statement was "I just want my life back. I do not care how much it costs, or how long it takes." She was from the East Coast, yet was willing to fly in to see me the following week, which she did. Over the next two years, she overcame all her blocks and limitations.

Her friends saw the miracle transformation in her life and wanted to see me, too. She invited me to her city so she could continue working with me and share my work with her friends. The rest is history. She came from an almost total disability when I first saw her in 2007 to an extremely successful career in her business, plus presenting seminars and trainings and publishing a book (This case is a testimonial in the front of this book and on my website.).

That is what I call determination and commitment. If she can do this, anybody can. It just takes intention, discipline and follow through. We do not give up, no matter what the roadblocks in our path are. My motto is I never give up until I win. I helped her win.

Chapter 9

Cracking The Mind's Codes

Since we are multifaceted, binary digital computers, every file is coded and locked in the mind's database. We do not hear or see with visual impressions or words; all our sensory input is transmitted through chemical reactions or electrical impulses through neuro-pathways in our bodies. The brain is a switching network that directs all the information to the various cellular points of contact.

The information is transmitted in microseconds from thought to action. We have control over how the information is interpreted and used to get the end result we desire, yet very few people use their ability to maintain control of their body and mind. About ninety per cent of the population is on autopilot and, as a result, have very little control over their daily activities. Almost all of their reactions are automatically decided by the internal Conscious Mind, with help from the sub-personalities.

Our databases in the Subconscious Mind contain all the files and programs that are used to direct our daily life. They can be accessed in microseconds. In 2003, we encountered a part of the mind we had not worked with before. One of our practitioners in Toronto asked me if I had ever worked with split or multiple personalities. I had avoided them because I did not feel they were in our field of work.

Little did I know this would make a major shift in our work. What we discovered was that almost everyone has them. We found we were not working with true self until we released the split personalities. We went back to past clients and released their personality selves; we were now back to true selves, but much of the work we had done in the past was now gone, too.

We had been working on the split personality, not the true self. In many cases, we had to start over again with childhood and the causes of the traumatic incidents that had caused the separations from self.

One of the limitations we must deal with is that the Conscious Mind can only record sensory input at 134 bits per second, which is very slow in comparison to the Subconscious Mind's 210 million bits per second. We can teach ourselves to bypass the Conscious Mind's limitations by learning how to scan.

Using a technique termed Photo Reading, we can read a 100-page book in twenty to thirty minutes. We must understand that since our Subconscious Mind never turns off, it records every bit of sensory input that makes contact with it, whether we want it to or not. We can maintain some control by setting up programs to block certain input. The N/CR technique contains a step to install a quarantine, a firewall and a spam blocker, which will help block information that is not in our best interests for our health and well being.

We can choose how we desire to respond to every thought and sensory input, yet very few people understand how this happens. In a sense, we are at the mercy of our mind's programs and most people do not even know it, so they justify or blame everything around them. Every minute of the day, we can either have total control of our life or give our personal power away.

Often we see a person with unlimited energy and enthusiasm, who seems to flow effortlessly through life with no limitations. Everything seems to fall into place for them with no restrictions. How does that happen? *PAMELA!*

I have direct experience with the situation myself. Twenty years ago, it seemed that I would never get to this point in my path where life was ease and peace, rather than struggle and battle. I knew that you must build a solid foundation. I tried to discover how to do this by studying as many alternative therapy processes as I could, and became a "workshop junkie," but I didn't find the answer until 1982. when I bought a computer. When I had started my journey, I did not know there are four sets of codes that must be mastered to get to the state of enlightenment I was seeking. To build the foundation for success, I decided I had to find the way to total wellness. Everybody told me they had the answer. Looking for this elusive key to success, I wandered through all the various disciplines from eastern to western gurus and teachers, but never found the key.

My physical pain was driving my life but I did not find that key until 1984. In my attempt to find the answer, I cracked the first code to physical wellness and success in 1978, yet I did not know it at the time. I started maintaining my current age and becoming younger. I accomplished feats that people said I could not do.

Even though I was feeling better, cracking the emotional/psychological code (code #2) took six more years of research until, in 1984, a client revealed to me how to do it. Working with her, I was able to heal my back pain. She was the catalyst to bringing this awareness to me. I was sailing along with this new awareness (that physical health is controlled by our minds) until I met the next lesson. My business went bankrupt in 1987, since I was not watching the hen house, and the foxes (my partners) killed the business.

It took twelve more years (1998) to crack the third code: mental control and success. Once I recognized that there was no one but me out there to show me how to succeed, I recognized the code. Many people had the formula, but I had to activate it in myself. I had released all the negating rejection and resentment programs from the past, so I assumed I should succeed. *How do you step up to the plate and hit a home run?* That was the elusive one for me.

In 1997 I published my first book, and I went stone deaf until I discovered the code. I realized there was a major file on: *"People will not accept what I have to say, so why stick myself out there, where I will fail?"* I would not give up because I knew I could make the grade.

I presented a seminar, even while being deaf, which really showed me I was accepted. Everybody was supporting me for not backing out and canceling my presentation. This opened the door, yet I was still not finding the key to financial success (code #4). My mind was fighting with me, because it felt it was protecting me from rejection. I finally broke this barrier in 2001 after going deaf twice more.

In 2003, we discovered something else that exists in 99 percent of us: *we are not who we think we are.* This major breakthrough came when one of my client-practitioners in Toronto, Canada, told me we have to clear split- and multiple-personality selves. We could describe this as a code, since the selves are set up in such a way that if you do not ask the proper question, they will not be revealed. (See description in Step 4 of Chapter 10 in *Energy Psychology/Energy Medicine*.)

Most of us have been programmed, as I was, for failure. We carry *"I'm not all right," "I'm not entitled to...," "I'm not accepted or approved of,"* plus fears of vulnerability, of being inadequate, of being rejected and/or abandoned, and myriad defective programs that cause us to react to get approval. We become saviors, rescuers and empathizers so we can draw approval from others.

When I was able to break the third code, everything opened up and I could see why I was limiting myself. The second and third codes are intertwined, and so they must be cracked before real success can take place.

The fourth code is spiritual awareness. Most people start here and forget they have to build a foundation for success. I started at this point, too. In 1977, I decided to sell my restaurant to go on the journey to find myself.

I was lost in this spiritual/metaphysical jungle until I recognized that enlightenment involved activating all the codes in order. When I started showing people that the spiritual aspect was the last one, many people rejected my contention. Twenty years later they are still stuck in the mire of their disbelief—and envious of me and my success. I showed them the way up the ladder when I was at their level but they did not want to take responsibility for their life.

Spiritual transformation only happens when you are capable of listening. This brings on the level of enlightenment where you realize that you get what you give. (My books *GOD Is Talking; Are You Listening?* and *Journey Into The Light* detail my work and research on the last code.)

When you get to this step, you open the door to another series of lessons and codes that must be worked through. True success and abundance at all levels of your life can be accomplished when you release all the malfunctioning programs that block you from success and abundance.

Once you get the doors of success and abundance open, everything falls into place. It seems effortless, as everybody and the universe seem to be at your service. Some people seem to ascend this ladder easily, while others fight and struggle throughout their lives. For a few people, the codes were opened when they were born, so they inherited a functional family. They seem to live a charmed life, yet others from the same family never seem to succeed. Why? We carry forward our file cabinet from past lives, with all the unresolved lessons until we confront the issues. We must clear the lessons generated by our past lives or they will block our success.

Many people may not have to go through all the lessons, as some of the codes may have been opened by their parents because they were shown what was to be loved and accepted. They appear to go forward without much hindrance. Other people desire to create the intention and commitment to discipline themselves to follow through, yet they never seem to make the grade.

If they keep their commitment and have to fight themselves until they reach their goal, they will reprogram their mind to build a habit that will result in a belief that, in time, will overwrite the defective program. Many successful people have taken this route, which takes a considerable amount of drive and will power to accomplish the goal in this manner. I know I accomplished my goals by never giving up or letting myself fall back as a victim.

Over the years, I wondered and was puzzled by people who seemed to have it made financially. Their success and abundance were obvious, yet they had meltdowns, failing in the physical, emotional or relationship areas of their life. Most these people would not talk with me or allow me to work with them. I discovered that they could not understand why they could be so successful financially yet their health was failing. I found that their focus was off base, because they had a special relationship with themselves.

They had used their willpower and the knowledge they had gained to make the proper decisions to get to their goal, and mastered one facet of their life, but they overlooked building a strong foundation upon which to anchor their success. We very seldom can perceive our special relationship, as it is in denial and is the basic operational pattern we live by.

When we make a claim about what we can do, quite often our mind put us up to a test to see if we can perform as we claim. If we cannot perform, it will throw us into survival. We are a multifaceted being and must work with, and take care of, every level of our life.

Why is it that only five percent of the population understands this process of success? We can go to endless seminars, workshops and boot camps on personal success and many streams of income, but will we follow through?

Statistics show that less than twenty-five per cent of attendees actually reach the goal of financial success. Less than two per cent reach the level of total wellness at all levels of enlightenment. Why?

When the book (and then the movie) *The Secret* came out, most people thought, *Now here is the answer to success*. It was the key, yet most people were not able to follow the instructions. Why?

The conflict was that if we have not built a good foundation to start with, even though the presenters laid down the concepts in the proper manner, most people do not feel they are entitled to money and success. It is why this whole book is about self-empowerment..

Most people get caught in procrastination, avoidance, confusion, vacillation, indecisiveness, disorientation, disassociation and inability to take action. Then they beat themselves up for not seeing that they could accomplish what they set out to do. Unfortunately, they are driven by the programs in their database in the Subconscious Mind. Until you clear the program you set up to fail, you cannot get to success; ninety-five per cent of the population do not feel they are entitled to money or abundance. It takes work to release all the programs affecting our self-images.

When we have no resistance blocking us, we can proceed to our goal. It starts with desire, intention, commitment, discipline and the courage to follow through. When we get a few victories in our success files, we can see that it is very easy when there are no limiting programs.

Your Body is Talking, Are You Listening?

Chapter 10

Beliefs and Cause/Effect

Our lives are run by beliefs, concepts, interpretations and attitudes that create programs. *In utero* interpretations (recorded and locked into the cellular structure before we are born) will create beliefs that, if acted on, will become programs that control the balance of our lives, unless they are released.

Then, after we were born, if our parents continued to treat us in a manner similar to the *in utero* sensory input we had already interpreted and recorded in our cellular memories, we validated those interpretations as true. As a result, they became beliefs that set up our life-patterns. When we were born, there were no beliefs in our minds; we created them all from the moment we entered the physical body.

When we first take a new computer out of the box, it comes with just an operating system. This is analogous to the body's autonomic nervous system and chemistry that springs from our parents' genetics. Then we begin to add data and programs from a variety of sources: copying from the previous computer (a past life); borrowing from friends and relatives (imprinting from our caregivers); and downloading from the Internet (interpreting our life experiences).

Over the years, our hard drives become cluttered, so periodically we need to go through all our old programs and data, and purge whatever no longer serves us in the present. Let's look at some of the things that may be cluttering up our personal "hard drives."As we have seen, one of the most devastating beliefs we carry is: "I need to suffer."

This can come from past-life karma we carry forward into this life, or it can come from childhood where we picked it up from a dysfunctional family pattern (and from the false belief that we are born in sin). It can come from religious beliefs and cultural/societal models. If we were abused as a child, having no other model to go on, we assumed that abuse was simply the way life is—which itself became a belief that we will perpetuate into the next generation ... and so the cycle goes on and on, unless broken by a parent not on autopilot.

If we had no love-model present in childhood, we might have interpreted abuse as love, since it was the only form of attention we received. Suppose we made a mistake and someone disciplined us for it, or we accepted that we had done a dumb or stupid thing and put ourselves down for it, or someone else berated us. We could then accept *as a fact* the belief that we had no value, and that lack of self-worth still drives us today, even in adulthood. Why? Because we've never purged our "hard drives."

We can choose to forgive ourselves and the other people involved, *but we did not know that as a child.* If we do not forgive, and do not recognize that we can love ourselves and release ourselves from our mistakes (real or imagined), then we will set up the belief and program that "I need to suffer for my mistake." Unless we recognize that our belief systems are in error, the beliefs and programs will continue to haunt us throughout adulthood. Worse yet, each time we put ourselves down, the program and belief increase in intensity, first to, "I really need to suffer," and then to, "I really must need to suffer."

The extreme, of course, is "I need to die for what I have done," or the "crucifixion complex." (Is this an isolated phenomenon? Among my clientele, a staggering ninety-eight per cent have this belief and program to some degree, from mild to crippling.)

The question is: "How do we stop this from happening?" Detecting karma from past lives is difficult, unless you can read the past-life records. Even then, it's hard to read your own records accurately. However, once detected, simply erasing and deleting the program and belief will end their influence.

Seldom do we act in ways that are not controlled by a belief, program or habit pattern. Our interpretations of our experience, along with our interpretations of other people's interpretations, will create beliefs and record them in our database. Our minds are very literal, and use any repeated activities or actions to project that we will be treated the same way in the future.

Another source of erroneous beliefs you accept are those so-called authority figures, whose words can program your mind just by listening to them talking to you or explaining something. Anyone you accept as more knowledgeable than you are on a subject—be it a car mechanic, a medical doctor or a rocket scientist—becomes an authority figure to you, and your mind will accept their opinions as correct, which then creates a belief. At this point, if you react or feel threatened by the belief, it can be transferred to a program (see Figure 2).

When we were children, our parents set up much of our belief systems by the way they cared for and treated us. Conversations we overheard with no real importance to us could set up beliefs that would play out later in life. Childhood events can make serious imprints on our minds.

For example, a client who was 120 pounds overweight had tried all the available weight-loss programs, yet she could not lose any weight. In fact, she had actually gained weight on diets, but could maintain her weight with a normal diet.

We found the cause rooted in a discussion she had overheard when she was eight years old. Her grandfather was extolling the virtues of being fat, because it had saved him from dying of starvation in a POW camp during WWI. She had taken that statement in as a belief, which had tied onto a program about not being loved (which also causes a person to turn to food as a substitute for love). We needed to remove and delete the program, "*I need to be fat to survive.*"

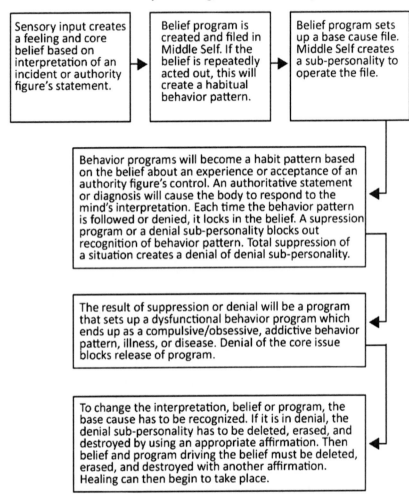

Sensory input creates a feeling and core belief based on interpretation of an incident or authority figure's statement.

Belief program is created and filed in Middle Self. If the belief is repeatedly acted out, this will create a habitual behavior pattern.

Belief program sets up a base cause file. Middle Self creates a sub-personality to operate the file.

Behavior programs will become a habit pattern based on the belief about an experience or acceptance of an authority figure's control. An authoritative statement or diagnosis will cause the body to respond to the mind's interpretation. Each time the behavior pattern is followed or denied, it locks in the belief. A supression program or a denial sub-personality blocks out recognition of behavior pattern. Total suppression of a situation creates a denial of denial sub-personality.

The result of suppression or denial will be a program that sets up a dysfunctional behavior program which ends up as a compulsive/obsessive, addictive behavior pattern, illness, or disease. Denial of the core issue blocks release of program.

To change the interpretation, belief or program, the base cause has to be recognized. If it is in denial, the denial sub-personality has to be deleted, erased, and destroyed by using an appropriate affirmation. Then belief and program driving the belief must be deleted, erased, and destroyed with another affirmation. Healing can then begin to take place.

Figure 2: How a Belief is Created

The fear of death, viewing obesity as a way to avoid death, and the feeling of rejection had coupled up to create a program that said, "If I am not fat, I will die!" We cleared all the programs about rejection and the need to be fat, and reinstalled the love program.

Your Body is Talking, Are You Listening?

She then began to lose weight at a rate of ten pounds a week for a month, then at a lower rate. In a year, she was back to normal weight and on a normal diet. (We have to be careful of the language we use, too. Our minds may be very sensitive to the words "lose weight," since it may read it as 'failure'—'losing instead of 'winning.' It may be better to use "reduce" or "decrease" it.)

A young woman made an appointment to see me after she had seen a doctor who had diagnosed her with breast cancer. They said the tumor was so large they'd have to do a mastectomy. She asked me if there was any way we could remove the tumor. "Yes, we can," I replied, "but first we have to understand why you created it."

She was confused. "I don't know what would have done this, as I don't have any of the behavior patterns you say that create cancer."

She was right. Not one of the situations or programs that create cancer were present in her mind. However, as we questioned further using muscle testing, we found one that her mother had died when she was eight years old. At the family gathering, her father and other members of the family had said, "We have to be extra careful with our girls, since three women have died from breast cancer. It must be hereditary in our family."

All three of the others had died at forty years of age, and she had just turned . . . forty! When we checked for causes we hit it right on. She believed she would get cancer at forty years of age. Her family had programmed her, and she had not even known it had happened.

We cleared the cancer in less than fifteen minutes. She asked me to check for the tumor, and it kind of shocked me, as I am not an M.D. "Go ahead and check," she said. I did, and it was totally gone. Of course, she received the standard response from the doctor: *I don't believe it. You will have to come to the office and be checked.* "If you will do it without charging me," she replied, "I will do it. I know I am clear of the cancer."

They could not find any tumor. No treatment or surgery had been performed, yet the tumor was gone. How do you say spontaneous remission about this one? The tumor was just gone. "It is gone!" she exclaimed.

One of the most troubling cultural myths that has no truth concerns hereditary dysfunction, illness or disease being carried from generation to generation. It is the *belief* that is passed on to the children by the parents, not the *condition*. The belief controls the illness, disease or condition, and the more the family talks about the hereditary condition, the deeper the belief becomes imbedded in the family-members' minds. In my work with countless clients, we have released the whole disease syndrome by affirmations, acknowledging the situation and forgiving the family member(s) from whom they accepted the erroneous belief.

As an example of this syndrome, a person with a serious case of diabetes came to see me after a lecture, and asked, "If my diabetes is a belief, why did it manifest when I was forty-two, when I haven't had an outbreak since I was sixteen?" When we found a catalyst or activator from childhood that came up to reinstall the condition, a simple affirmation was enough to eliminate the diabetes forever.

If such a "disease program" is in the mind, it will reoccur whenever the catalyst or trigger is re-experienced unless the programs are cleared. The belief delivered the payoff in the past, and it will do so again if you have not overcome the emotional condition and cleared the program that created the belief.

A belief in hereditary disease can be passed on through beliefs. For example, a client asked, "Can we determine whether I'm carrying the gene or DNA program for a rare heart disease that both my father and son died from?"

The answer was, "Yes," so we accessed their karmic records and found out the cause of death—a belief in hereditary heart disease that had been carried in the family for generations. Their medical doctors had deemed them incurable because nothing seemed to halt the deterioration of the men's heart conditions. This was because there really was no disease to cure; they had both died from the inherited belief that they had heart disease. We removed the false belief, so that she would no longer be affected by it. The doctors could not understand how this genetic code could just disappear.

A belief will become a program if it sits in your database long enough for it to become a *habit pattern*. If the habit pattern becomes well-enough established, then a Middle Self's program manager will create a program, adopt that program and lock it in. If we sell out our power to Middle Self and are on autopilot, this can also create a sub-personality in the Conscious Mind. If we do not want to deal with the experience or the trauma, we will bury the whole thing in a denial file. If we then choose to forget it and avoid it totally, we put it into a "denial-of-denial" file.

Most of this programming goes on beneath our conscious knowledge. The less we employ Conscious Mind, and the more we rely on Artificial Intelligence, the deeper we go into autopilot. As a result, more feelings, emotions, beliefs and programs become suppressed and buried, to the point that we end up denying that they even exist. In this case, any effort we make to find the programs or release the emotions will fail, because the belief tells us that they don't even exist in conscious awareness. Our mind sets up a denial file that locks up the belief and program so that we cannot access it.

We interpret all sensory input. If the input is a feeling, you understand its context and it does not threaten you, then you will deal with it and let it go. However, suppose that as a child you were walking down the street, and a large dog suddenly barked at you and chased you. You felt threatened, ran out into the busy traffic, and were almost hit by a car.

Your parents' criticism for putting yourself in harm's way might have led you to berate yourself with, "That was a dumb thing to do." A feeling of rejection mounted and it might have triggered an asthma attack. Then, every time the catalyst situation arises (you hear a dog bark), you react as if the whole rejection feeling is happening again. As a result, whenever you hear a dog bark (the catalyst), you have an asthma attack.

One of my clients had a severe allergy to the goldenrod flower. She couldn't understand why until we found that, during the time of year when the goldenrod was in full bloom, her mother had often chased her around her backyard and repeatedly beaten her up in an angry rage. So the scent of goldenrod became tied into her belief of unworthiness as a catalyst, and triggered the allergic reaction whenever it was in bloom.

A chiropractor recommended another woman to me because he could not find the cause of her allergy to grass. An allergy specialist had run extensive tests but could find nothing. Anytime this client would slip or trip in high grass in a field near her house, she'd develop a red rash all over her body, and her face would swell up and turn red. This condition would take two weeks to clear up, and nothing would hasten the process.

Covered in a red rash and with a swollen face, she arrived for the session. When we began testing, we found that it had started at age three. When she had been born, her mother had transferred all her attention to her, which caused her three-year-old brother to feel rejected. The father had not stepped in and supported the son, who had then felt abandoned.

When she had been three and her brother six, the two siblings had played together in high grass behind their house. He would sneak up on her and beat her up, claiming he was "just playing." Her mother had never disciplined him for this, so the daughter had built in the belief, "Boys (and later, men) will mistreat me."

Of course, this belief had governed her choice of men for relationships. Twice during an abusive marriage, on their walks together, her husband had beaten her up in high grass. Following their divorce, the allergy reaction had started. Her literal interpretation was that she would be beaten up if she fell down in high grass.

We cleared all the beliefs about the fear of being abused by men, plus all the anger at her mother and brother, as well as the fear of intimacy. This ended the allergic reaction to high grass. By the end of the session, all the rash and swelling had disappeared.

With many of my clients, their doctors have diagnosed an illness, and that illness has turned into a disease. When a belief drives an illness, there can be no medical cure. Ultimately, a belief embedded in the mind can actually kill you, with medicine helpless to stop the disease. We must find the program that is driving the condition, and clear it.

A friend who is also a nurse told me a baffling story: "I provide home care for housebound patients who don't need to be hospitalized. One of my patients was getting increasingly weak, and could no longer get out of bed. Finally, he was unable to write or hold anything. The doctor hospitalized him for tests and concluded that there was nothing wrong with the man's body. Inexplicably, it was deteriorating, and the patient just wanted to die.

When the wife learned that her husband was close to death, she too got sick, and died within a month. To my amazement, the day his wife died, he started recovering; within a week, he walked out of the hospital, totally healed. The doctor is completely baffled.

"How could this happen? Was this spontaneous remission? He did not have a discernible illness or disease. So what happened?"

"This was not a miracle," I told my friend. "There was no life-threatening illness or accident to recover from. And no one facilitated his healing, because the doctor and nurses had given him up for dead. The answer was that he was trying to escape his wife's covert control and codependency, and the only way he could do this was to die. She had been controlling his life to the extent that he believed that he could not evade her control, nor could he stand up to her, so death was his only escape. But with her husband's death imminent, she realized that she would no longer be able to control him, so she

125

became frustrated and died herself. Once his wife could no longer control him, he decided that there was no need to die, so he recovered, with no ill effects from the ordeal."

"The odd thing is," the nurse replied, "he was unable to communicate with anybody at the time, and no one had told him about his wife's death. So how did he know she was dead?"

I reminded her that our minds do not just work in a linear time-frame, on the physical level only. They have amazing abilities to access information we don't think we have available to us. She told me that the husband had started to become more aware and awake, right around the time his wife passed over. He had been close to death, yet somehow he'd gotten the message that he was now free of the cause of his impending death, so he just walked back into life.

He soon left the hospital, with no indications that he'd been only days from death. (This had also happened to my father, but he had not gotten the message that he had to reclaim his personal power and take responsibility, so he had crossed over.)

An obvious question is, "If the belief is somehow erased, does recovery happen every time?" I have found the answer to be "Yes" at least 95 percent of the time, *if you erase the belief and concept.* (If the client is doubtful or skeptical, then that skepticism must first be released.)

With many clients, I have cleared the causes and the core issues, yet the dysfunction remains. Why is this? You can believe in what we're doing at a conscious level, but *all three minds* must be in agreement and aligned with the goal.

The next step has to be a *knowing*—not just a belief or faith —to cause the final healing to happen. Both belief and faith are fear-based, as you are assuming something only *might* happen. If it fails, then you can blame the process or the practitioner. In other words, you're hedging your bets. The real cause is doubt and fear. It is an inside job. No one creates your reality for you; you do it all. For any path or addiction you choose, all we need do is find the belief that's driving it, release it and it is gone.

Beliefs can be passed on to a person or a group, and if enough people accept a belief, it will become a reality for the group. One of the more bizarre beliefs I run into is that our chakras have a "mind" and can think rational thoughts. My understanding is that chakras are non-physical energy centers, connected to the various endocrine glands and organs, and located in the mental and emotional energy fields. They do pick up and transmit feelings, and put them out as an energy that has to be interpreted.

That the heart chakra can make rational decisions is a myth, yet many people believe it, as shown by the figure of speech, "My heart is not in it." (All you are really are saying is that you consciously do not want to do something.) Also, many people view the mind as an unfeeling enemy, so they say, "You must come from the heart level." However, sensitive feeling people who are in control of their minds can make effective decisions.

I have found many people who feel they must come from "the heart," yet they are not in control of their feelings. Also, most of them are codependent and have a poor handle on life. But then again, I have also talked with people who just have a different concept on how feelings are processed. Once more, our beliefs control how we interpret a given situation.

Feelings can be very deceptive if you're the type to jump to conclusions or have problems dealing with conflict. When you feel attacked, your first defense is to attack or defend. This is known as the "fight or flight syndrome"—the belief that your only options are to take action and fight, or run for your life.

A good example of this came at a retreat I once attended. We had scheduled locations to hold our lectures, but when I arrived at the space I had chosen, I discovered that the group that had booked the space before me was still there, and had no intention of moving. As the leader haughtily asserted, "I thought the space was available to me all day," and he then promptly ignored me.

A man whom we will call Jeff (and who I assumed to be one of the retreat leaders) also intervened. "Your anger is making people feel bad," he told me. "You can make other arrangements, because we can't move all these children when they're having such fun. Do you want to deprive them of this?"

In the end, I had to cancel my lecture, because there was no other location at such short notice. The next day I attended a workshop at which this fellow Jeff was also present, so I mentioned the previous day's incident to the class. Jeff immediately went into reaction, defending his behavior, so the workshop leader decided to role-play the incident, as a teaching example.

As Jeff and I replayed the encounter, the leader pointed out to Jeff his habit of becoming defensive and seeking to control other people by using guilt. "You seek to diminish others and make them feel that they're the aggressor and that they're wrong. You choose not to deal with other people's feelings or needs, but place your own needs ahead of theirs. Your group should have signed up for more time but you didn't, so you should have recognized your responsibility to the next presenter, rather than trying to make him feel wrong."

The role-playing did not give Jeff the outcome he wanted, so he brought up another incident about his own children, which turned out equally disappointing for him. From the discussion, we learned about Jeff's belief that he must appear to be a good, supportive person, in order to protect his feelings. If he felt bad, he believed he was not acceptable as a person.

With his children, he wanted to seem a good father, but when he couldn't get them to do what he wanted, he believed that they were making him look bad. He was controlled by outer appearances and sought to manipulate how others saw him. When he could not control a situation, he went on the defensive, which aggravated the situation. In the case of his children, he became defensive and removed them from the view of others, so that they wouldn't judge him to be a bad father.

Outer-directed people believe that they must always appear acceptable to others. Inner-directed people are not concerned with what others think of them. In Jeff's case, we saw clearly that beliefs about how he appeared to others totally controlled his behavior. (If he had understood the lessons being presented to him, he might have shifted the behavior, but I doubt that that we got through to him, since his programs stemmed from childhood and were deeply locked into his mind.)

Clients often tell me, "I have a block in my throat or fifth chakra. Why is this happening?" It starts with a belief and a feeling, which is transferred to the emotional field. If we react to the feeling, then it will manifest in the body as, say, a sore throat. To deal with it, we must listen to what the body is telling us.

If we get the lesson, or the action we must take, the sore throat will disappear. Our minds will always place a feeling on all sensory input, based on the programs already in the files. What we do or don't do with this sensory input governs how we will respond or react to it, and the feeling that we have from it.

Harold Saxon Burr, an English medical researcher in the 1930s, found what he called "L fields" (the auric or energy field). By using his clairvoyant/clairaudient abilities to get the message before it appeared in the body, he found that he could diagnose illness and disease, up to two weeks before it actually manifested in the body. He was often able to help his patients release a condition before it even appeared in the physical body. The body talks at many different levels; the challenge is to decipher the message.

Mind control is more prevalent than ever. At every level of our society, we are bombarded by controlling messages, and must be vigilant about all the sensory input coming to us, as our mind records everything it picks up. We must detect and cancel all information that does not support our life paths.

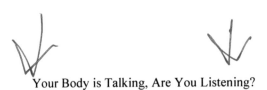

The best way to this is to be alert and observant and, when we encounter something we don't want to take in, to say to ourselves, "Cancel. Cancel," or, "This is not my issue."

Never argue with the input, as it will set you up in a defensive mode and activate your adrenaline, putting you into fight-or-flight mode. People may inadvertently say things to us that they do not realize will cause harm, so do not blame them. We must forgive and accept them the way they are.

Our childhood beliefs and programs will control us until they are erased, deleted and released. We should be especially wary of authority figures; anyone can be an authority figure if your mind so defines them, such as when someone knows more about a subject that you do. You will give your power away to them

We must also eliminate and remove all the autopilot sub-personalities that are driven by the need to control, manipulate, resent, or blame, by using anger and fear stored in our beliefs, programs and habit patterns. We must be careful regarding what beliefs we accept and how they apply in our life; if we let them, they can control us totally.

In the last two years, we have discovered that when we remove split and multiple personalities we might not be removing all of them. We have found program-specific multiple personalities that can control a specific situation or program in our life.

A good example was a man I demonstrated with at a lecture. He had a severe stuttering conflict, to the point where he had a difficult time speaking in public locations. He could speak one-to-one, but when there was a group, he stuttered so badly he did not want to speak in public. When we removed one of the multiple personalities, he stopped stuttering. This was five years ago; he has not stuttered since. When we looked for the base cause and core issue, we found it was his father, who was an overbearing man who had yelled at his son all the time. He could not do anything right for his father.

Cancel, Cancel This is not my issue.

Summary

As we can see, beliefs, attitudes, perceptions and interpretations control our life. We have to be really careful what we pick up from what people are saying around us. They do not even have to be speaking directly to us; all we have to do is listen to their conversation. TV and radio can also program us: there is a lot of subliminal programming inserted below our level of sound recognition.

There are many ways computers can program us from all the videos and audios we watch and listen to. You Tube and all the other video programs can have subliminal information in the background. Even the visible information can cause programming we are not aware of. Effective use of Neurolinguistic Programming can set up programming (a system to control language). There are methods to use hypnosis that can used without a person's awareness.

It is really is a battle for our minds. We have to be very careful and protective of what we listen to and watch. Even that is not enough, as our minds pick up information intuitively from meta communication (unspoken information it picks up from people).

Our minds can retrieve information we are not aware of that comes from past, present and future time lines which were programmed in the past. Childhood programming can pop up from denial files which were suppressed when we did not want to deal with the feelings and perceptions we had at the time.

It is a good practice to do a clearing and purging of programs, beliefs and patterns that are not essential for operation of our life. If we have skeletons in our closets, they may start rattling at some future date, causing illness or some behavior pattern to pop up out of nowhere

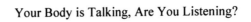

Chapter 11

Meta-Communication: How You Project Your Self Image

Meta-Communication is the ultimate form of body language. Our bodies project our thoughts, feelings and attitudes all around us without our knowledge. Your body is talking, but are you listening? Did you know that who you are precedes you everywhere you go? You project out to everyone you meet, exactly how you feel about yourself. If others are observant, they will be able to form an impression of how you feel about yourself before you say a word.

You may think you can put on a front and fool people about who you are, but your mind always betrays you when you try to put on a cover. It always tells the truth, even if you live in an illusion or delude yourself into thinking you can hide or block other people from seeing who you are or how you feel. An intuitive person can observe exactly how you feel about yourself. Your mind projects the basic interpretation of your self image, self-worth and self-confidence to those intuitive enough to pick it up.

This is one of the most important features of your mind that must be mastered, and the only way to do it is to release all the feelings that defeat you. To do this, you have to work through the childhood feelings that cause you to feel you are not all right. This is described elsewhere in this book, so suffice to say that one of the major programs that blocks us from achieving any end is, "*I am not entitled to....*"

133

This block applies to anything that we want in life, and the mere act of wanting something guarantees that you will not get it. You will deny yourself money, fame, success, acceptance, functional relationships, the ideal position or job and many other things, because you feel you are not entitled to whatever it may be. *You cannot want and have at the same time.*

Suppose you apply for a loan to buy a house, a car or any large-value item, and are turned down. You cannot see why: You dressed the proper way, and did all the right things, yet were turned down. A friend goes in to get the same loan. He or she is not dressed in "banker's clothes," doesn't have your income or your credit rating, yet gets the loan. Why, you ask?

It actually has nothing to do with how you presented yourself externally. You are presenting yourself to a person who has to feel comfortable with your trustworthiness. The meta-communication that you transmit influences the loan officer's decision more than any other "credentials" you can present. It's not how you look that matters, but how you present yourself on an inner level that counts. You may complain, "That's unfair; how can this happen?" and wonder, "What can I do about this?"

It's all about recovery of your self-worth, and the letting go of fear, control and manipulation. It's about being willing and able to forgive everyone in your life, about not harboring blame or resentment, about not projecting "victim" in your meta-communication. The person who exudes self-confidence, self-worth and self-esteem is interpreted by other people as being a more trustworthy person. The self-image is projecting a competent effective person. Generally he or she is more ethical and will follow through with the responsibilities taken on.

The person who lacks these qualities will generally project an "I'm not all right; I'm not entitled to ..." attitude that is clearly evident to people who have to evaluate other people for a living. Quite often people with low self-esteem will make poor decisions in how they handle their lives.

Twenty years ago, if I had to purchase something, due to my earlier programming I would unerringly choose a vendor who would take advantage of me, or a product that was guaranteed to fail. It was as though I was signaling, "I'm a sucker who will let you take advantage of me!" It must have been written all over me. Unfortunately, we attract other people to validate how we feel about ourselves and teach us a lesson. I got angry at myself when I discovered what I was doing, but I kept on doing it until I finally woke up to the fact that I was creating it all.

When we take our personal power back, begin to operate from high self-esteem, and validate ourselves, people will no longer take advantage of us. If we set ourselves up as doormats, people will obligingly walk all over us. When I recovered my self-worth, -confidence and -esteem, I stopped projecting this negative image. Suddenly, people changed their attitude about me, yet they did not know they had done so. People started helping me instead of ripping me off. I had become a different person, and walked into another life.

We unknowingly project our self-image to whomever will listen. What you say or do makes no difference unless you work on your innermost feelings about who you are at a deep level. Most people have denial sub-personalities covering and suppressing who they really are, so they have no way of uncovering the cause. Getting in contact with the programs that are defeating us takes committed, disciplined work. Most people run on autopilot, unwilling to spend time or money to get to the cause and clear it.

Most of my clients who claim to be working on spiritual growth have no idea what their meta-communication is projecting out to other people, regardless of what they say about themselves. New York University's Department of Psychology conducted one of the most definitive studies on meta-communication. In conjunction with the New York Police Department, fifty men and women convicted of robbery, molestation, rape, attack and many other crimes were asked to study people picked at random—many of whom had already been victims of some sort—and select those they would most likely choose as victims.

Not surprisingly, only the former victims were chosen, those who had been attacked in the past. Furthermore, the "victims" selected most frequently had been attacked many times before. The psychological profiles of the victims and non-victims revealed great differences in self-worth and good feelings about themselves.

Prior to 1981, if I got stuck with a defective product, I would say, "That is a lesson, and I should let go and release it." But after I had a new interpretation, the next time I had to take a product back and get credit for it—a defective screen door—I accepted the responsibility to reclaim my power. I had a new attitude, too. My intent was not to get a credit or refund, but to make a point.

When the clerk realized that I was neither blaming nor being a victim, she quickly gave me a credit. I didn't attack her or the company, even though she volunteered that they'd had many doors returned. The important thing was that I was not complaining or attacking; I had no need to control or manipulate. She recognized that because I wasn't playing the victim and yelling at her, she didn't have to protect herself and could allow herself the vulnerability to admit this was a defective product that they no longer carried. My meta-communication allowed her to respond positively to my request, and the outcome was mutually beneficial.

When you take responsibility for your actions and stand up for yourself, people will take notice and help you. This has happened many times, even when someone refuses to repair or accept a product back. Admittedly, it doesn't always work, and I have had to threaten to resort to small claims court a few times. Our "denial" sub-personalities often set us up and steer us away from the very situations that would help us. Our "justifier" sub-personality will convince us that we did the right thing. We will follow its path, not knowing that we lost our way, until we reach the point of pain (physical or emotional).

Even though we have not broken through their barriers of denial, clients will offer excuses to justify why they are not seeing me anymore. I clearly see the meta-communication, yet I cannot break through their denial for them, unless they decide that they want to. Many clients truly desire to break through, but their minds have been so programmed to operate in a certain way that they have to really discipline themselves to watch every thought and statement.

The only way out is to get into recovery, take responsibility, and let go of all blame, control and manipulation. Control is the biggest addiction there is, and most of us use it covertly and overtly. Being able to blame someone else for taking advantage of you creates a comfortable sense of security.

WE RELEASE IT WITH UNCONDITIONAL LOVE AND FORGIVNESS

Chapter 12

The History of Energy Psychology & Energy Medicine

Neuro/Cellular Repatterning (N/CR)™ is a new field of practice within Energy Psychology and Energy Medicine that uses as its basic modalities love and forgiveness—the only two modalities that will cause healing. N/CR will be one of the healing modalities of the future, because it holds the promise of healing any dysfunction, emotional/mental problem, illness or disease, without pain, drugs or surgery.

All diseases, illnesses and breakdowns (emotional or physical) are dysfunctional behavior patterns, but we don't need to know what the dysfunction is, nor must we name or diagnose it. All we need to know is what created it, and then we release it. By accepting the situation or the person who created the fear, rejection or anger, we release it with unconditional love and forgiveness. With this new awareness, I finally found the solution. Delusion, denial and inability to take responsibility for our lives are the blocks to total healing.

Psychoneuroimmunology was the result of the practice of Energy Psychology and Energy Medicine. We had described N/CR as a somatic psychotherapy process, yet we have found it encompasses many formats. We can track any dysfunction, situation or malfunction in a person's life and locate the exact age or date when that conflict happened. Sometimes we can track it down to the exact hour, who participated and what was said that caused the misinterpretation or belief that created a dysfunctional program.

When I started developing this process, it was a very effective modality. Little did I know that over the next twenty-five years, it would progress to where it is now. It seemed as if I was both the laboratory and the researcher. If I could clear the issue or program from myself, we would find a client who had the same situation or condition. My challenge to people who attended my seminars, lectures or read my books was, "You present or name the condition and we will find the root cause and the core issue."

The more we found, the broader our scope became. We have found that there is no form of affliction, dysfunction or condition that can stop us. We can locate the cause of any illness, disease, behavioral dysfunction or condition that blocks or limits a person from attaining total and complete wellness, peace, happiness, harmony, joy, unconditional love and financial abundance.

If you do not deal with the programs locked in your mind from past lives and childhood experiences, they will eventually win you over and crash your life. We are entitled to peace, happiness, harmony, joy, unconditional love, acceptance and abundance.

We assumed that healing was a mechanical process. If you release the cellular memory and/or the beliefs, the pain or the cause will be released, because release signals to the mind that the program has been deleted. We have discovered that this does not always work, since programs that are locked into the mind may be in different locations. We might get the surface location, which will release the immediate situation, but it also can be hidden in denial or denial-of-denial.

Middle Self can also create activator viruses (similar to those in computers) that can activate with a crisis situation, a statement, or an interplay from sensory input. When they activate, they create the whole program over again, which installs all the same files we had assumed we'd released. It was very disappointing to find the program come back when you thought it had been cleared.

Most alternative healing processes will clear up situations and pain, etc., but I have found that most of them work only on symptoms, not on the cause. Some claim to be working on the cause, but few can pragmatically document the results. Some can point to a few miracles, but is it across the board?

Placebo healing takes place all the time—it is not the therapist who heals anyone, but the individual who heals himself. If the client believes in your process and knows it will work, it will work—and you have a miracle. But does that mean we accomplished it?

N/CR has been through double-blind test studies, and emerged with flying colors once we discovered that therapy work is like peeling an onion: one layer leads to another layer. It is not a quick fix or a one-time hit, but a matter of releasing the layers as they come up.

Many times our minds will lock in layers, in many locations in various operating systems within it, and these will not be revealed until we clear each layer and get down to the base cause or core issue. If we have a lesson that the mind senses we must learn, it will not release illness, disease or pain until we recognize and release that lesson. When we come to full awareness of the lesson, and release, love and forgive ourselves, the pain will be released.

This indicates a need to be clear with your purpose and to release all of the emotional garbage that could cause you to lose your center. The more we get on purpose and become unattached to what *should be*, the more we can live in the now moment. Releasing illusion and denial are paramount. You can only see what you believe, which put you into a Catch-22 if you feel you must see it to believe it. This will keep you in denial- of- denial, spinning with no direction.

When we understand the power the Subconscious Mind has to disable our immune systems, we will recognize how disease is created. If you analyze the Subconscious Mind as a computer, you will see that it can only do the tasks that have been programmed into it. If you have false beliefs or are living in denial of these beliefs, then you have no control over the computer.

In computer terms, the body and mind are the hardware. The software is the programs installed w i t h in the mind. The Instinctual Mind is just that: if you go into survival-mode, it takes over. It has no ability to reason, process or make rational decisions. The Conscious Mind is the programmer, and it can also hold false beliefs and concepts of which you are unaware. If you do not question these beliefs, they will run your life. (The Conscious Mind must be on track all the time. If you walk out and go on autopilot, the Middle Self and the Subconscious Mind will take over, because somebody has to be at the wheel.)

N/CR is an eclectic process that came from my desire to find a process that would actually cause healing to take place during client sessions. I was not satisfied with releasing pain or emotions in a cathartic release, only to have them return a few days later. Often, we feel we have actually released the problem, but, in my experience, if you give the practitioner authority, you will do almost anything he wants you to do. (For example, all hypnosis is self-hypnosis and is self-induced.)

You must give the therapist permission to do what he is doing with you. In fact, we are being hypnotized all the time by TV, radio, magazines, newspapers or anyone seeming to be in authority. We allow what we read, hear or receive into our Conscious and Subconscious Minds t o program us and create our belief system. The t h e r a p i s t 's challenge is to de-hypnotize people, so they awaken and take responsibility for their lives.

We have experienced miracles with hundreds of people. Spontaneous releases, w i t h in minutes, of diseases, emotional dysfunctions or genetic defects were amazing to us, yet some clients did not respond very well and the dysfunctions would return. At this point, we realized that *we* were not doing it; we were not "healers" or therapists. We were only there to teach people how to love themselves and receive love. If they could make that shift in consciousness, permanent healing would result. We could not change the holographic image that clients held about themselves; we could only help them make the spiritual shift, causing the healing. If they could not shift, then the healing process would only give them a temporary release.

We have found that N/CR will work in spite of clients, because we are not working with the Conscious Mind. As a result we have been able to duplicate the process 95 percent of the time with different people.

Since we know we are the scriptwriter, producer and director of all the shows in our lives, we ask Middle Self to let clients come out from the wings and take center stage. Now that they are the leads in their plays, it will cooperate with them. This is accomplished by talking to the Middle Self with an affirmation and making peace with it. We let it know that it is an important part of the team, and that the client does not want to take away its power or destroy it.

It is not the modality that causes healing to happen. Many therapies, both allopathic and alternative, have claimed provable visible healings, but they cannot explain why remission happens, or how to reduplicate the process with any regularity. I have discovered that the key is the effectiveness of the practitioner to get in touch with a client's feeling self.

You must set up a trust, so the clients feel that you care and love them—this is what allows the healing to take place. Healing is governed by only one law: the law of LOVE, and it works every time. (My study with *A Course in Miracles* formed part of the base for this assertion. It is also documented in Dolores Kregar's book, *The Healing Touch*.)

We now understand how the process works and we can explain it in scientific terms. Psychiatrists, doctors, psychologists, practitioners and lecturers have recognized the need to release negative emotions, yet few have accessed a controlled process which will get to the core issue.

For more than five years after we discovered the body/mind connection, we were unable to accurately describe how N/CR worked, yet we had to come up with an acceptable scientific explanation for people in the medical field attending our workshops. The results have shown that each practitioner achieves virtually the same results.

Fear appears on the left side, anger on the right side of the body. All rejection deposits along the spine, and we found sixty individual locations for other specific emotional dysfunctional programs. So many doctors and medical researchers have given us the answers to the puzzle of healing that it will take time to decipher them. (A 1993 article in *Discovery Magazine*, "A Bug in The System" claimed that scientists had discovered the causes of the disease syndrome, but they had no cure, prognosis or way to correct it. They have labeled it a "genetic defect.")

In fact, cellular breakdown is caused by the cell's mitochondria losing its ability to process and absorb nutrients. The cellular structure begins to collapse from lack of food, and begins to malfunction. Their interpretation is the cells are dying and will cause whatever diagnosis they hang on it. This fills in the missing link in understanding why healing works with N/CR. We erase the cellular memories of rejection, lack of love, etc., and help the cell to recover its original blueprint. Then it begins to rebuild new healthy cells.

With counseling, physical therapy and most all alternative therapies, you can remove the energy that is causing the pain or discomfort. But, if you do not locate the root cause, healing will be a simple symptomatic release. We have just masked the problem until the same catalyst or stimulus reappears and causes the energy to build up again, reactivating the disease or dysfunctional emotional program. With N/CR we locate the core issue uncovering the Subconscious Mind's program. When an experience is filed, it creates a record and program with energy.

It makes small chemical changes in the body. Each program records how we reacted and handled the incident the first time. Each time we encounter this situation in the future, we build more patterns with instructions on how we will handle similar situations again. Eventually these chemical changes will cause a physical breakdown in the body. (This explained why my body had been breaking down: conventional methods could not get to the base cause or the core issue.)

Your Body is Talking, Are You Listening?

To release the dysfunctional emotion and the program, we must understand the cause, and the reason you reacted to it the way you did. Now that we understand the dialogue your Subconscious Mind is having with your body, we can release it. When we have accomplished that, we then can erase the program's instructions, destroy the patterns and file the record, pattern and program in the history section of Subconscious Mind's archives. At this point, the energy is released and the behavior program is no longer accessible to you. (Of course, if you have been getting a lot of mileage out of the soap opera, you can always create a new one.)

At the physical level, the cellular memory is released, which allows the muscle to return to its original form. The short circuit in the meridian that caused the muscle to go into contraction from the emotional trauma is released. At the same the time, the patterns, the neuro-pathways created from the emotional experience, are released and erased. The original program for the muscles now takes over again and the pain is gone.

In the case of a life-threatening dysfunctional program, the same process happens. The endocrine system has its original programs restored, so the immune system can rebuild the "T" cell and leukocyte counts to destroy the dysfunctional invading cells. All the physical programs are controlled by the mind's computer (Subconscious Mind). The body is a hologram, so we must work with all levels at the same time: physical, mental, emotional, and spiritual.

If we work on the physical body without understanding the root cause in the mind, the treatment will only be symptomatic and temporary. If the emotional/spiritual levels are not addressed, the problem will eventually recur in the same or another location in the body. N/CR will access the root cause because it requires practitioners to get in contact with the feeling self. By doing so, we can listen to information in the Subconscious Mind, which has been deposited in muscles/acupuncture points by the client's mind.

Practitioners use acupuncture points for a switch to turn on the video/audio and allow the mind to bring the picture and

experience up. This is where the similarity with other therapy processes stops. Since practitioners are able to listen to body/mind and go directly to the base cause, we get a clear understanding of what is causing the dysfunction. We describe the situation that caused the dysfunction, and then use an affirmation that the client repeats, thus permanently releasing the blockage. (My experience with Science of Mind has helped me to understand and develop the affirmation part of N/CR. This is the key part to releasing and filing the record, program and pattern. N/CR is continually evolving, and we constantly upgrade the process as we verify the results.)

The focus of most therapy today, regardless of the modality, is on releasing or suppressing the symptoms of ailments and diseases; unfortunately, that will not heal the body. Most practitioners expect the end result of their treatments to be some form of remission, cure or healing; again, as stated above, if you do not access the root cause, such treatment will only be temporary and symptomatic.

The body will always tell the truth, no matter what we believe or even if we choose not to believe it. We always find that fear, anger and rejection are the base causes, yet we are always trying to blame some outside incident, person or virus. The mind can create any disease it chooses; the only process that heals is *love*. With N/CR, we are allowing clients a safe space to learn how to love themselves and release the blockages in their bodies. In doing this, you will free yourself to receive the basic needs of all people—love, acceptance, approval and alrightness—that produce self-esteem and self-worth.

Your body is your mind. As a result, all negative experiences are locked into your body and will cause emotional reactions until they are recognized and released. Many people recognize the need to release emotional/physical memory, but few achieve results. *All disease, illness and dysfunctional emotional behavior patterns are directly caused by the lack of ability to accept oneself as alright and give and receive love! We can heal anything with love.* To reverse the negative process, we must understand unconditional love and accept its relationship to healing.

After I discovered the process twenty-five years ago, I was describing it as Structural Repatterning™. I had spent 20 years wandering through working allopathic doctors and then studying all the alternatives to allopathic medicine, looking for a cure for my own physical problems. I was not able to find one person who could understand my problem or alleviate my pain. I thought nutrition might be the key, but found it was only part of the solution. When I discovered the power of the mind, I realized it was not what you put in your mouth but what your mind accepts as truth that matters.

At this point I was investigating nutrition. This caused me to look for a healing modality that could get to the base cause of dysfunctions without having to spend hours trying to dig out the cause from a person who was unable to understand it in the first place. Most people don't know what their minds have stored, let alone understand it.

I did not at that time connect my physical pain to emotional dysfunctional programs within my mind. I thought all physical problems had only physical origins—at least that's what the doctors told me. Yet they were not able to understand why my spine was deteriorating. I was told that if it did not stop, I would end up in a wheelchair, but they found no specific cause.

I decided that psychology might have the answer. In my training, conventional psychology seemed to be satisfied to blame all ailments, either on someone else or on an unknown factor. I could not accept that we had to be victims of another person's reaction.

I also did not know that my body was continually running a dialogue with me. If I had listened, it would have revealed the causes to me. In my subsequent training with Paul Solomon, we approached psychology from a holistic spiritual aspect, a very different slant from my original training. This did answer some of my questions, helping me understand the dialogue, but it did not heal my body.

In a workshop with Ronald Beesley, I was able to understand how the body stores the memory and the basics of removing it. With this knowledge, I had the tools to integrate spiritual psychology with body/mind therapy. This became the missing link I incorporated into N/CR as the basis for my counseling. Even though I finally found the missing link in 1982, it took me another 20 years to complete the process we have now.

Physical dysfunctions reveal themselves, but not their causes. Emotional and mental pain are intangible, which makes locating and working with it difficult. I was unaware that my belief system had suppressed emotional programs that were causing my physical problem.

Most people had no understanding or awareness of this syndrome until John Bradshaw made his entry on TV with the "dysfunctional family" programs. In my training, Fritz Perles and Virginia Satir approached this with different semantics, but it was the same syndrome. AA started the 12-Step Program but it did not become accepted until Codependency Anonymous, Adult Children of Alcoholics and many others came along.

When I started in psychology and hypnosis, we were told that the Subconscious Mind was where all the power was, and that ego was located within it; ego was the enemy that we had to control. In fact, most people accepted the notion that ego and Subconscious Mind had 88 percent control of our minds, while Conscious Mind had only the remaining 12 percent.

I have discovered that it's the total opposite; Conscious Mind and Inner Conscious Mind have full control. Subconscious Mind is just a database for our memories, while ego is a mere file manager located in Middle Self. It has no control over anything, nor does it hold an agenda to control us, or anyone else. We also discovered four operating systems that are not in alignment with each other, each of which can and will sabotage us all the time. We found that it was very simple to reprogram all these mind's operating systems and change any dysfunction behavior. As we went along, we discovered many programs we could clear with general affirmations, since everybody had these conditions active in their minds.

The affirmations in this book originated from my work with my clients. I set up a series of standard affirmations to use with every person so that we could speed up the process. This was possible once we found that everybody had basically the same types of programs present. With this method, we can now reprogram any dysfunctional behavior, illness or disease, or any program blocking abundance, success, peace, happiness, harmony and joy.

We have discovered that most people are operating from a multiple personality that is totally separate from their true selves. This personality self controls our lives, yet we don't even know who it is. It is very simple to heal the separation from self and recover our lost selves, yet we do not know we are separated; ninety-five per cent of my clients are operating from multiple personalities, what people often term "a lost soul" or "splintered spirit."

Neither term is accurate. Our souls and spirit are watching us, ready to guide us when we decide to listen. When we recover our lost selves, true self is able to emerge. We can get back on track to success, peace, happiness, harmony, joy, unconditional love and abundance in our life. Until we do, we will sabotage ourselves.

You can use left- brain analytical concepts to become successful if you use your will and push hard enough, using the proper mechanical systems and processes to become successful, but there is a catch: Are you willing to confront the issues in your life and take responsibility? Few people are, but those who do control the world.

This is the basic process of Energy Psychology for clearing the path to begin healing. Energy Psychology is the emotional release pattern to clear operational programs, whereas Energy Medicine is the second step to releasing the energy from the cellular memory programs in the acupuncture points along the meridian systems. Since the body is the mind, both Energy Psychology and Energy Medicine are intertwined. One does not work without the other.

We are removing all the negative, self-defeating software that limits or blocks a person's path to empowerment, self-worth, self-confidence, reclaiming of personal power and self-esteem. When we remove or rewrite all the operating systems and backup files our minds depend on for safety and security, Inner Conscious Mind can cause a relapse if it does not feel comfortable with the new path. When we attempt to remove inner Conscious Mind it will put up a fight. It has had control of our minds since we were children. It is not ready to give up that control.

When we first developed this process twenty years ago, we had accepted the concept that ego and Subconscious Mind had over eighty per cent of the control. We have since discovered this is simply not true; Conscious Mind and Middle Selves retain all the control.

The question is, **what percentage of the whole are *we* in control of?** Usually not very much. As you release and rewrite all the operating systems in Middle Self, you will recognize the awesome power and control they have had over your behavior.

Most people became lost in childhood, splintered and separated from who they really were; due to fear and traumatic experiences, they may have escaped into Magical Child to avoid the feelings of fear, pain, rejection and abandonment. When we separate from our true selves (Spirit and Soul), Conscious Mind splits into three separate operating systems. Conscious Mind (where we should be operating from) shuts down, activating Inner Conscious Mind and multiple personality selves.

When we escape, somebody has to run the show, so our minds set up split and multiple personality selves who run our lives on autopilot through artificial intelligence, outside our control. Since we are separated from our true selves, we are not even aware that we have no control over our minds and bodies.

As a result, the personality selves run our lives, since we have separated from true self and are not present. Some people shut down completely and live in an emotionless mode of survival, with no feelings. They shut themselves off from life so they will not feel pain.

Most people will disagree that we are lost and struggling in survival, yet it is documented in our research. The challenge is to get back to our true clear selves, and erase the separation within ourselves. Until April, 2003, it was a hit-and-miss situation: if we could not get the Conscious Mind to cooperate, we were unable to clear the separation. (Since *this book* was revised and republished in January, 2003, this information is not in it.)

Discovering that multiple personalities were taking up residence in the Conscious Mind solved the puzzle, and gave us the keys to how the mind operates. Split and multiple personalities are essential tools in the challenge of correcting human behavior.

We have avoided this subject in the past, as we considered it an area for mental health professionals. Mental dysfunction was a realm very few people understood. However, we now have the key to correcting every level of a person's life that is malfunctioning. The trick is to convince clients to take responsibility and clear their separation from self. The magic of taking control of one's life is something we cannot force upon a person.

The problem is that fear will overpower and prevent a person from taking control and reclaiming his personal power. Each person is responsible to take this step, him- or herself. We can show you where the blocks are that cause the breakdown and separation, but we cannot remove them unless you make the decision and follow through, with the intent of taking responsibility to release the separation from self.

When we ran into Conscious Controlling Mind we thought we had found the cause for why people were out of control. Then, over the next fifteen years, we discovered Irrational Conscious Mind. All these mind-controllers were just ways Inner Conscious Mind played games with us and let us think we were in control, though it was still controlling our minds.

In 2012 I discovered how much control it held over us (after I had had a major battle with it in January of 2011). I decided we have to remove it so we can take total control over our minds. It was a difficult task but I accomplished it, and it really has made a major difference in my life and those of others with whom I have worked.

There are many payoffs in clinging to illness, disease and all the myriad malfunctions that cause chronic fatigue, depression, mental dysfunction and other debilitations our minds provide. Many people struggle and suffer, assuming that this is the way it's going to be, never realizing they are creating their own life paths.

We all are entitled to peace, happiness, harmony, joy, unconditional love and acceptance. We are also entitled to an abundance of success and wealth in everything we do. Very few people are able to recognize this and claim their abundance and prosperity.

As with peeling an onion, we find layers of consciousness covering layers below them, and we must clear each plateau before we get to the next one. The same goes for past lives. Sometimes we cannot get to a past life until all the layers involving prior past lives are cleared.

Past- life karma will create fear of approaching a particular situation, so we avoid it but don't understand why. Multiple personalities and the three saboteurs control and block us so we cannot even access the files. If we could get through all the barriers and doors that block us from achieving total abundance in our life, we could have it all, effortlessly.

In some sessions, a client may just slog along, session after session, with very slow change. Yet, another client, with the same indications, might fly and accomplish twice or three times as much. It all depends on the client's willingness to change and the ability to take off the blinders. There may be people you cannot help at all because, quite often, their body feels like a turtle shell. They will tell you they have no sensitivity at all. You hold an acupuncture point and they cannot even feel it. (You *may* be able to break down the fear by using intuitive sensing and going through the session as if it were normal, even though it feels that you are getting nowhere; if so, the next session may actually be normal.

Many people describe N/CR as magic because it releases pain on the spot without any manipulation or force. However, every step in N/CR practice is explainable and requires no psychic healing or laying on of hands, because we can describe exactly what responses the minds are recording and what effect the work is having on the bodies.

It is not magic, hypnosis, hands-on healing or energy work as most people describe it themselves. It is based on a computer model, basically working with computer programming. Affirmations are the software we use to correct the corrupted programs and rewrite them.

Changing the programming changes the cellular structure, all the way down to the genetic and DNA levels. Thoughts and feelings affect the body, locking in an energy component that changes the structure, weakening the muscles and the organs of the body. A simple affirmation will signal the mind to let go of the locked-in energy and begin healing the body at a cellular level, changing the DNA structure. The resulting effect is described as Energy Medicine.

When we put a finger on the acupuncture point and couple it with an affirmation, cellular memory is released. Quite often the point will be painful, but only while the pressure is applied. An acupuncture point is like a switch that turns on the VCR in the Subconscious Mind and selects the tape applicable to the point on which we are working. As the program, pattern and image come up, we can sense what it is and receive feedback similar to thought processing. If the incident has considerable impact, the picture may also be projected, and it's like watching a movie on TV. At this point, we describe it to the client and then discuss it. Using the appropriate affirmation will release the program. Sometimes we get an incomplete release, so the pain persists. In this case, we continue with similar affirmations.

Most people feel that they must have all the affirmations written out, so they can use them properly. I used to feel that

INTROS TWO — Psychics

way, too, but my experience has shown that people who have the confidence in themselves will be able to let their minds create the affirmation appropriate for their situations and applications.

In the same way, clients will often question how they can access their clairvoyant abilities. (Psychic ability is not the same as clairvoyant ability. Psychics process information through the solar plexus, which can color or place their own feelings into the reading. Clairvoyance uses our intuitive ability which goes outside the normal realm to obtain more accurate information.)

Our process is very simple to learn, yet many people make it complicated and feel they cannot practice it as it was laid out. As a result, they water d o w n the technique, so it will not be so threatening to them. In N/CR, the practitioner cannot escape his/her own issues in the therapy process. In most schools of thought or therapy modalities, you can easily escape your own issues by directing the process away from your own issues. Until you are willing to claim your personal power and confront all the issues in your life, they will continue to pop up in client sessions.

In N/CR, you cannot avoid any of your issues, because so many clients will mirror back your limitations. When we become aware of the issue, we can become detached so that we can use will to consciously keep control of the situation. I have noticed that when I work an issue completely through, I become non-attached to any triggers that used to set me off in the past. When the issue is worked out, I no longer get tested, because the people who created the challenges are either no longer in my life or are not responding the same way.

Many of us think our lives are working well until we run into the wall of resentment, anger or fear we have been stuffing or suppressing. We cannot blame anybody, as we knew what we were getting into when we took on a body.

Since I have been in recovery, I have recovered my lost self and the flight plan. I do not feel that I must search for meaning in life anymore. I can also look at the process of healing in a different light now: You do not have to be sick to ᴋɴᴏ.. you are not in wellness.

N/CR is not for everybody, because it puts your issues right in your face. When we release all the mind's back-up programs, there is no place to hide. You must look at them straight on. If you are not ready to face them, you will find a reason to discount the therapist or the process, or justify the issue (even though there is no justification of any issue). You want to either clear it or live with it. When you clear an issue, it no longer causes any response or reaction.

The intent of N/CR is to desensitize a person, rewrite the dysfunctional software in the mind, install new programs and release the cellular memory that causes the dysfunctional behavior. When we accept "what is," life becomes much more comfortable. There is no need to judge, control, justify, criticize or try to make other people meet our expectations of the situation. If the behavior is not to our liking, we say so with "I" statements. ("You" statements trigger an immediate reaction to protect or justify the self.)

In the past, many people viewed the N/CR process as almost mechanical. You release this program by holding the proper acupuncture point and repeat the affirmation applicable to the situation, and it clears the pain. Very little discussion went on during a session. Since the therapist was running the session, some clients felt they had little input. This was true in a way.

I now recognize that clients want some time to respond to what we are releasing. If it is something they're not aware of, they may want to talk about it. I now direct the session, but I no longer control it. There is a need for training in Energy Psychology, so that practitioners can guide a client in the right direction in the transformational process and provide direction within that process. (That is now part of the training in workshops.)

In the spring of 1993, we found a block that I did not understand, because I did not yet realize the power of the Instinctual Mind. We have since discovered that the Instinctual Mind becomes operative only when a person gives up in life, or has had a traumatic experience; the Instinctual Mind then installs *"I want to die"* programs that will stay in the file until they are removed. (Medical and brain researchers describe this as the Limbic Mind. According to them, it is an animal/reptilian-like mind. Once I got a handle on it, I found it easy to deal with.)

The Instinctual Mind works from programming only. It is the "survival self," and it views every action in a survival mode, but just change the programming and uninstall its operating system and instructions, and it will comply. It cannot make rational decisions or understand any commands other than its programming. It works through the Conscious Mind rather than the Subconscious one, although i t can act with the Subconscious Mind in a survival mode.

Since the events of September 11, 2001, this has all changed. Now, 99 out of 100 people have been pushed into survival mode by the disaster. In the first months (for some, even years) after the tragedy, many people could not deal with the trauma, which pushed them beyond their ability to handle stress. Ten years and more later, this has eased off, yet many people are still in survival. (Those who are not still in survival do see it as terrorism, and they know who set this up.)

I also discovered the powers of the Conscious Mind and will power. With enough will power, the Conscious Mind can overcome the Subconscious Mind's programs. It will take enormous energy and the person will feel burned out, but it can be done. This is why some people with life-threatening diseases live against all odds. We use Neuro-Kinesiology as a directional device a person can use to track down the situation in the beginning of a session. We have found it to be a useful tool in locating and reprogramming concepts and beliefs, especially ones that have no programs tied to them.

When I studied with Dr. John Diamond in the 1970s, I did some work with Behavioral Kinesiology, which I found interesting but did not include in N/CR until years later. We have now refined it into a more effective form of Kinesiology. In 1991, I incorporated the testing for electrical polarity reversals as part of the testing, because I found that a polarity reversal causes all answers received using kinesiology to be reversed: *Yes* will appear as *No* and *No* as *Yes*. When we clear this, the testing reverts back to normal. In the 1970s, I learned a simple Chinese process and included it in the process beginning in 1979; however, I did not use it until I recognized that we need to normalize polarity to get right answers with Behavioral Kinesiology.

With the effects of walking out of the body becoming more common now, I have had to find a remedy for this. In 1992, I put together a new affirmation to pull people back into their bodies. A client who couldn't stay in her body when I was working with her helped me create the affirmation to pull a person back in.

When you confront something during sessions that clients do not want to deal with, they will mentally leave, something we term "graying out." Clients sense this when you make them aware of their reactions. Eventually this becomes easy for clients to recognize, and saying the affirmation will pull them right back into the body.

The purpose of Energy Psychology is to locate the blocks and limitations that cause breakdowns in the body and mind, so we can release the energy driving the illness or disease, and the dysfunctional habit patterns. Energy Medicine releases the cellular memory that is locked into the acupuncture points, along the meridians in the muscles and fascia tissue of the body. It can also get locked into organs in the body, which causes breakdowns in those organs and the endocrine system.

Most people live in survival, fear, resentment and anger. Our intention is to get 100-percent control back, so we can function as the spiritual beings we are. We were intended to operate in wholeness, but if we are separated, splintered and blocked out from our true selves, we are lost. With the improved method we can do that now. When we reclaim our power, we set an intention and goal to be consistent with our commitments to follow through.

You also may be tested by your inner teacher, to see if you have taken control over your life. Temptations will be presented to you, in order to test your ability to see if you will fall back into the old pattern. If you pass the test and retain your personal power, you will not be tested again. On the other hand, if you fail the test, it will throw you back into survival. We can create the same patterns over again and fall back into survival, which activates Instinctual Mind files. If this happens, it will shut down file and program manager operating systems.

It will also shut off the love program. This may reactivate personality selves, Inner Conscious Mind and shadow selves. If this happens, read the Instinctual Mind affirmation and check that file and program manager systems have been reactivated. Check the other files to make sure nothing has been reinstalled. This must be done at the beginning of each session. The intent is to clear all the programs and multiple and sub-personalities, and reclaim our personal power.

With neuro-kinesiology, you are getting the information from the person through a muscle reaction instead of using your own intuition. Quite often when working with a client, you will get more accurate answers with muscle-testing because you will not be filtering it through your own mind, which could color the answers if you have strong beliefs, interpretations or feelings about the subject in question.

Control sub-personalities may interpret letting go as giving up their power. You may have to assure Middle Self that it is not losing anything, but is instead gaining new power because you are reclaiming your personal power. Inner Conscious mind really likes the fact it could control your life, and it feels threatened because it has to give up control. If that happens, then all sub-personalities must be deleted from the file before you can claim control.

This is a process that takes training and experience, so you will must practice this process. The most important factor is being clear of outside or inside influences. You can control the answers very easy if you do not want to do a particular task or if you are unaware that there is resistance in your Conscious Mind.

We have found two new aspects of the mind we were not aware of in the past. Conscious Mind has two divisions:

- Conscious Rational Mind; and
- Inner Conscious Mind (existing in autopilot).

Middle Self has an Inner operating system, too. Both of them seem to be the autopilot function and many times will resist change if they feel you will not follow through with your commitment and discipline yourself to make the change. They can reinstall programs very easily without your knowledge.

This does not mean that sub-personalities will never be reinstalled, since your Conscious Mind can recreate a new set anytime you shirk the responsibility to follow through with the decisions you have chosen to act upon. Your mind does not like unfinished answers or sentences, or incomplete actions or commitments.

Do not say you are going to do something unless you intend to follow through. If you do not follow through, your mind will assume you did not want to act on the decision you made. If you do not take action, your mind has to close that program. This closure will create a sub-personality and a program about not wanting to take action.

If it happens often enough, avoider, confuser, procrastinator, disorientor and disorganizer sub-personalities get installed, along with a "not wanting to take responsibility" sub-personality. It can go on and on if you get into indecision and back away from taking action on the path you were choosing to take responsibility for. Any time you make a commitment that you do not follow through with, it creates a program that is interpreted as, "I am not willing to take control of my life." If this happens over a number of years, your Instinctual Self will interpret this as, "I want to die."

Your mind will not leave any loose ends unattended, and has to have closure on every thought, statement or action you take. Even if you start a sentence without finishing it, will complete the sentence for you. So every thought and action you create must be completed or your mind will finish it and file it. It is on 24/7 and is a very good housekeeper, but it may not complete the file the way you would have done.

A program creates a multiple personality and will drive that personality self to get the desired result. If self-rejection is carried to the final stage, it will create a life-threatening illness. There may be disease specific multiple personalities that were created with the disease or dysfunctional program or belief. A disease, illness or dysfunction cannot exist in the body without a program to drive it. There must be some activating force to break down the immune system or cause stress on the adrenals or the endocrine system.

Any form of negative thought or action will start an immediate breakdown in the immune and the endocrine systems. Receptor sites on the leukocytes are notified in microseconds by the neuropeptides. This begins a physical deterioration of the immune and endocrine systems, which in turn causes the beginning of illness and disease as the immune system function is compromised and fewer T-cells and leukocytes are produced.

When releasing programs, make sure that you check for the multiple personalities that could be enabling them. Each time you clear a time-line or operating file, it may activate another series that has been set to be brought up in position from a back-up file or a denial file. When clearing karmic files, check for gatekeepers, guards and saboteurs that can be connected with the files. They will try to block release of the files. They can be cleared in the same way as attached spirit beings.

If a person degenerates or sets up *I want to die* programs, the control of the mind/body shifts to the Instinctual Mind. Programs can set up in this mind when this takes place. Any conflict in the mind about *fear of dying* and *I want to die* will set up sub-personalities in the Survival Self (Middle Self). This conflict is the main cause of Alzheimer's disease: these two programs cause an Alzheimer's file to be created, which must be cleared before the person begins the backward slide or it becomes very difficult to stop.

When clearing, you must clear all denial and denial-of-denial programs and multiple personalities. You can bring them up by asking with kinesiology if this program is a belief and then a reality. If it comes up positive on both, then ask Higher Self to go through all the veils, shields and illusions into the back-up files, time-line files, denial and denial-of-denial files, bringing all the hidden files to the surface to reveal the true answers.

If it continues to come up positive, you have a program locked into the physical body. If the reality question comes up weak, then you have a denial. Check for them and clear them from all files. In cases where there has been trauma, it will create time-lines that can be in denial, also. They can also be in autopilot, denial or denial-of-denial.

We must also check for reactivator, recreator, regenerator, reduplicator and reinstaller programs or viruses that will create the same program again and again. These will be attached to individual programs so you must check each program for this each time you clear the program and sub-personality.

We have also found another program that can recreate sub-personalities and programs. Similar to a computer virus, this program only functions when activated by a word, an activity, a feeling or an emotion. It will activate a program that will run its course and then close down. If you do not catch it during its operational cycle, it disappears.

The results or effects of its activity will remain, but we could not find out how this situation was created until we discovered how to ask the proper questions to reveal it. We found another virus that acts in the same as a regenerator, which we described as an activator virus. It can create or activate existing programs that may be dormant, such as an allergy. (This is the reason we go through such an extensive process of releasing, deleting and destroying dysfunctional software programs.)

The number of sub-personalities and programs that reoccur over time reveals our progress in handling our life path. Once we clear all the sub-personalities, some will be recreated depending upon our ability to handle the situations that come up in our life. When we are able to handle all situations without losing center (not needing to be right, be in power and control or give our power away, while following through with all our intentions and commitments), our minds will not install sub-personalities. Anger or resentment will open emotional doors, so programs and sub-personalities will be installed. The ideal is to get to a point where no sub-personalities are installed. When this occurs, you will have 100 percent control over your life.

Each time we conduct a session, w e must check to make sure Inner Conscious mind has not found a way to sneak in. If they keep recurring, we need to find out why a person is not taking full responsibility for his or her life. You may find that they just do not want to take control or discipline themselves. We have found very few first-time clients who are actually in control of their lives. Many will claim to be, based on all the seminars, workshops, training and therapy they have participated in or taken, but in most cases, little has changed. However, we must be careful not to judge or criticize what people have done in the past. They did the best they could with the tools and awareness they had at the time.

Taking responsibility is a very big issue in everyone's life. We said we had some answers in the past, but we could not actually describe how you take responsibility in your life. We can now, as we have found all the programs, beliefs and sub-personalities that block a person. One of the major blocks is plain laziness.

When we have cleared all the blocks, it comes down to the individual's desire, which is controlled by Conscious Mind. If clients do not *want* to apply personal control and become self-actualized, there is nothing we can do as practitioners to change that situation. We can ask all the questions we want and receive many answers, but are they the correct answers? Highly unlikely if we are not clear of the controllers in our minds.

Since the last printing of this manual we have discovered a massive amount of information about how the mind controls our lives. We thought we had the answer when we found the Magical Child Syndrome but it was only the tip of the iceberg. The discovery of Inner Conscious Mind and the personality selves opened the door to how the mind controls us.

Finding the violent birth experience opened another door to why we lose our self-esteem and self-worth. In the past we had assumed when people fell back and could not maintain their control and retain their personal power, it was their fault for not disciplining themselves to stay on top of their mind control. We have found that is not the case. There is a battle going on in our minds to stop us from taking control. Personality selves will recreate sub-personalities and programs, with the help of Middle Self to maintain control.

Now that we can remove all the back-up programs, as well as the virus recreation and reinstaller programs that the mind uses to maintain control, it be co mes v e r y c l ea r when a person is not taking responsibility. People will fall back into survival when incidents come up that they cannot handle, or that threaten them. It can be as simple as a thought that you are unsure of how to handle a situation. S omeone may also be negative toward you, and you accept what they say as an attack or view of what is blocking you from taking control in your life. We can locate the incident and track it down, to the day and hour.

The mind assumes everything is happening now, and it cannot recognize the past unless you describe the incident as happening in the past. Therefore, when talking about past experiences, you must speak in third person and use past tense, or your mind will assume the incident is happening now, and will attempt to protect you. Resistance can be very hard to overcome, as can getting out of the rut of autopilot. Also, procrastination will throw you into survival. To break a habit or a pattern, sometimes we must use the 21-day writing affirmation to burn in the concept until the mind gives in and allows us to take control of our lives.

We do not judge where a person is on the individual path; the body/mind will reveal that to us. The path a person decides to take is totally up to that person. All we can provide is guidance and the software to rewrite our life scripts. N/CR cannot force people to take control over their lives.

We are releasing the imbedded cellular memory from past experiences. Each cell has a memory of the perfect image of how it can regenerate itself. If there is no dysfunctional negative overlay of emotional energy blocking, all cellular structures will regenerate perfectly from the blueprint each time the cells are rebuilt. (I have seen many miracles with clients, but was unsure of how it actually took place.)

There is hope. Recovery is possible in every case. The only catch is the desire to take control and discipline yourself to do what it takes. I am a walking example of a miracle. In this book I document many case histories of people who literally shifted their beliefs and were healed in minutes.

Others took days, some even years, depending on the willingness to let go of attachments to the causes and core issues that had manifested the dysfunction. All of them are the same; *The root cause in any dysfunction of the body or the mind is anger, fear or rejection, which results in lack of love.* When the connection to Source is restored, love can begin to heal the body/mind.

Control is the most widespread addiction we have today. It is insidious in the way we react to it, both as therapists and clients. If you are not in recovery, it is not an issue. Many people in recovery do not recognize it as an issue, either. If we have an expectation of how a program or meeting should proceed, or how a person should respond, we seek to control.

As therapists, we are only able to guide and help clients understand the causes and core issues that are causing the dysfunction in their lives. The biggest challenge comes if they cannot receive love, or love themselves. If love does not exist in a person's reality, how does he or she recover self-esteem and self-worth, let alone heal themselves? When we separate from our Source, we shut off the presence of God within.

Chapter 13

N/CR: A Self-Healing Process?

We would like to think we can heal ourselves, but after thirty years in the healing field, I know very few who have successfully managed to sidestep the mind's games. Many clients who claim to have cleared these issues themselves have attended a workshop or two , learned a few self-healing techniques ... and bingo, they think they can heal themselves.

I cannot say they can't, because I have seen many people who have healed themselves. But when we actually access the issues, we find that very few have cleared all the issues in their lives. At a conscious level, their minds accept and assume that they have healed themselves, so a belief is set up that they have cleared themselves of the issues. When we check at the reality level, though, Subconscious Mind disagrees.

In this work, we have found that Kinesiology (Muscle testing), using only the arm (or whatever muscle group we use), will always indicate Conscious Mind's opinion on the subject. It always wants to be right, so we will always get an affirmative answer. If an Authority sub-personality is active, then Conscious Mind will give your power away to the tester; he or she can get whatever answer he or she wants, unless we use the truth/reality test. We must ask whether this is a belief or reality. As we have described in earlier chapters, you must have the client put the hand over the solar plexus or navel to get a correct answer. In this way, you are asking the Subconscious Mind, which will give you the correct answer. Few people listen to their bodies (or their minds), so they do not know or understand what is causing the breakdowns in their bodies.

If they did, we would not have so many deranged, emotionally imbalanced, dysfunctional or sick people in our world. If people were aware of what their behaviors cause, we would also have fewer abused children, crimes and wars.

How about those who have studied alternative healing, are on a path to transformation, and are committed to working out their issues? I have found that more than seventy-five per cent are in denial of many of the issues blocking their progress. What of the many teachers, shamans and therapists who claim to help people out of their past and create new paths to transformation? Are they clear enough in their own paths do so?

Pattern Release Process

This section indicates how to access and release beliefs, programs and sub-personalities:

Symptom :   Mental, emotional or physical pain, depression,
               illness, etc. (obvious or assumed cause).

Record :   Base cause, actual interpretation of situation,
               Subconscious Mind's recording of reaction,
               activity or situation.

Program: Core issue, Subconscious Mind's or Middle Self's
               sub-personality instructions recorded in the
               computer (how I will handle this situation next
               time).

Pattern: Habitual reaction, the illusion of how I have
               handled the situation in the past whenever the
               stimulus arose (addiction, control, justification,
               denial, authority, distortion, dishonesty,
               delusion).

Those who can access this information can work with N/CR themselves, but few people are clear enough to do so. Sometimes, the programs are so strong that they're right on the surface so anyone can recognize them and release them, but most of the time, they're deeply hidden or in denial, and the deeper they are, the harder it is to locate and access them. Even some clairvoyants and clairaudients cannot read their own book.

Yes, I healed many of my blocks myself, but I could not get to the deeply-buried issues. Ironically, they came up when I was working with my clients and had to deal with them in a session. By putting myself in the affirmation with the client, I was able to release many of my own programs.

You may be able to release or relieve a symptom yourself, and achieve remission or release of pain, but this will not cause healing to take place. You are simply manipulating the energy tied up in the neurological pathway, meridian, muscle, organ or tissue. If you do not release the base cause and the core issue, the instructions will eventually cause the pattern to reassert itself when a crisis issue arises in your life.

The Conscious Mind can set up a belief, and the soul can understand the process, but if the Subconscious Mind does not release the record from the files and lock up the operating instructions in the archives, the instructions will cause the computer to restore the program. It will continue to do so until the pattern/program/record is recognized, filed and released with love and forgiveness. Then, the original cell imprint can begin operating again, healing all the dysfunctional parts of the cell.

The immune system can then regenerate, which allows the T-cells and leukocytes to resume their work. To activate the body's healing ability, the body must be able to access the original blueprint. When the programs are lifted from cell-memory, the body/mind will be able to heal the disease and/or emotional dysfunction.

After twenty five years of practice with N/CR, I can access almost anything and rewrite the program, thus healing it myself, but with programs and sub-personalities in denial-of-denial, I still need a practitioner to help me. However, if I cannot locate the cause, I do not get caught up in pride. My desire is to be as clear as quickly as possible, so I am not going to get trapped in the need to be in control or to manipulate the situation so I can look good.

I have no need to have someone validate me for how effective I am at healing myself or my clients. Being a know-it-all, being in control, having to be an authority figure, arrogance and resistance do not get us anywhere. I often find these qualities in self-proclaimed "enlightened" people, yet they are unaware of these traits because they are held in denial. True seekers, on the other hand, shine out in their clarity.

The next section provides a format for setting up a session and the use of affirmations. The basis of all this work is to rewrite the software in the mind and redirect the manner in which the mind processes information.

The Neuro/Cellular Reprogramming Session

Please note that this brief description does not equip anyone to perform a full treatment session. Neuro-kinesiology is described in separate booklet for those who want to study N/CR process in depth. A manual for N/CR is also available for those who plan to take the training. The cost is $97.00, which will be credited and applied to the cost for a session. The basic processes use behavioral kinesiology (muscle testing) and do not require the practitioner to be clairvoyant, but it helps.

The electrical polarity of the client's body must be balanced before we can begin a session. We are an electromagnetic mechanism, and must have our electrical polarity balanced in order to operate effectively. If it is reversed, we cannot get accurate answers. Most people's polarity is out of synch due to the stress and fear prevalent in today's world.

The purpose of N/CR is to remove defective software from the mind by deleting, erasing and destroying it. Once done, we install a new program or reinstate the original program that was blocked out and written over. This is done using an affirmation. The therapist cannot install programs on behalf of clients; clients must install the program themselves by repeating the affirmation after the therapist. This installs the program in the computer. The therapist must be observant and listen carefully when a client is repeating the affirmation so that every word is in the right sequence.

A client who skips a word or phrase indicates resistance, a heavy control program, or a sub-personality blocking the issue.

The affirmations are specifically worded so as to release an old program or install a new one. Every word the mind takes in can have an effect on you. To ask questions accurately, put one hand on the client's forearm and ask the client to place the hand over the solar plexus (third chakra). This accesses the Subconscious Mind rather than the Conscious mind.

The Use of Behavioral Kinesiology (Muscle Testing)

Basic Kinesiology checks

Two important tools of N/CR are the use of affirmations and Kinesiology. These two modalities give us the means to locate the files in the body/mind. My original training in Kinesiology was with Dr. John Diamond, the originator of Behavioral Kinesiology (BK). His unique methods reveal what the inner mind is holding. This is how he described BK at the time. "I did not understand in the beginning why, when using Kinesiology, putting my hand over my abdomen gave an answer that always seemed to be more accurate than arm- testing alone."

In my work, I have found this to be true one hundred per cent of the time, but I narrowed the location down to the solar plexus. I no longer check with the arm only (unless I am demonstrating how the two minds differ in their answers). Why do people who work with muscle testing use a process that is only marginally effective? Because they do not know that there is a more effective way. Diamond clearly knew that we received better answers in 1978. We have proven, without a doubt, that when you do not put your hand on the Solar Plexus when you test, you do not get accurate answers. You will find that you get totally different answers when you use the arm only.

When you find the client's arm is like an iron bar and will not go down with any question or pressure, there is something controlling the client's neurological system. This could turn out to be a contest of wills; more often, it is the work of controlling sub-personalities or entity/being possession. You will have to clear those entities before you can begin any work.

There are many descriptions of Kinesiology. Everybody seems to put their own prefix on it to describe their individual process. We use "Behavioral" because we are asking the body to tap into the programs in the mind. It does this through the muscles' response through the neurological system. In actuality, all muscle testing works in this manner no matter what prefix you use.

The mind is telling you what its response is through a neuro-synapse reaction. All muscle response is controlled by the mind. When you ask the question, it accesses the computer's database and reveals the answers. If you ask it to check a product to see if the client needs a particular nutrient, the mind will check the body and report back the answers. There are only three ways it can communicate: through intuitive projection, neuro-synapses or neuro-peptides.

I developed this process over the last 15 years. I found that I could pick up the answers without any outside means, but many people did not believe what I was telling them so I decided I needed to develop a system to validate more definitively what I was describing. I used my Behavioral Kinesiology training to develop my new method and we found a new avenue to help people answer questions without having to use their intuitive or clairvoyant abilities.

We found that if we directed the mind to ask the question of the right source, then we could access anything, including the Akashic Record. Clarity is of the utmost importance when using muscle testing, and there are many ways to use it. First and foremost, however, the practitioner must be clear. You can use your mind's awesome abilities to talk to your own body or to God with the Kinesiology process just as easily as with any other technique.

You can use any set of muscles that will give you an "up and down" action or an "open/closed" indication. Using fingers, you can hold your thumb and middle finger together and try to pull them apart. Using an arm or a leg, you ask the person to resist your pushing or pulling. If you are unable to get accurate answers with Kinesiology, find a practitioner experienced in clearing, in order to clear the client of outside forces so that you can get accurate answers.

When beginning to work with a client, always set the paradigm so you will know what is "yes" and "no." Generally "yes" is a strong response and "no" is a weak response, but some clients may respond differently. Ask, "Give me a 'yes' and give me a 'no.' " Test twice to make sure you have the right response. If you have been doing muscle testing for many years, you have an indigenous program that sets the basic parameters before you start so you do not have to do any testing. Your basic parameters will be followed by the client.

In using Behavioral Kinesiology, you will use one hand on the client's wrist. Ask them to hold the hand over the belly-button area. If you ask a question using the arm only, you will be accessing beliefs held in the Conscious Mind, which may not be accurate. Always check to see if the Conscious Mind has a different viewpoint when you begin to do this work, so that you can experience the difference.

To check Subconscious Mind, put one hand over the solar plexus or third chakra when testing. This will give the Subconscious Mind's viewpoint on the subject. It is always accurate, unless you have outside interference.

Most forms of Kinesiology suggest that you use light pressure. This may work most of the time; occasionally, varying pressure must be used due to control by sub-personalities, attached beings or resistance from some program in the mind. Recognizing all the indications that are presented takes practice.

If you begin to test a client whose arm will not move with any questions, make sure you are not having a muscle battle with a strong person. Explain, "This is not a contest to see if you can stop me from pushing your arm down." It may take some practice to find just the right amount of resistance to get the three minds to work with the muscles and give accurate readings. If the arm will not go down under normal pressure, you have outside influence. The attached astral beings must be cleared before continuing or they will continue to disrupt accuracy.

You may also notice that, at times, the arm will hold, then break and go down. This indicates that the answer would be positive if the person was clear of intervening influences. Finding the controller may take some work, but it must be found or the answers will not be accurate. Sometimes a sub-personality is the cause but, most of the time, it is a hidden attached being.

When you are asking questions of the Subconscious Mind, accuracy could be compromised by information suppressed in the time-lines, back-up files, denial or denial-of-denial files. The time-line files are written in the year when a traumatic or negative experience happened, and the mind does not want to deal with it. The mind drops it into denial so you do not have to deal with it again.

If a lesson has been brought up to deal with and you refuse to acknowledge the lesson, it will be put in denial-of-denial, locked up and will not come up again. It may also have been linked to an autopilot file. If a controller sub-personality was using the program at the time, when it was suppressed on the denial file, the autopilot was also suppressed with it. These must be removed or they will control a person's life.

When all these tests are made, you can be reasonably sure that you can directly contact Higher Self and the Subconscious Mind. If you want to go on-line with the Akashic Internet, then simply connect the phone lines by asking your Higher Self and the Highest Source of your being to connect you. You then can ask questions that are not body-based.

If you choose to use a pendulum, you may run into interference from astral entities, or from entities within yourself or the client. (They can control pendulums without you even knowing it.) It will appear that the answers are correct, but other forces are actually in control. We have experienced this many times over the past twenty years. Because they are heavier, brass pendulums seem to be influenced less. (There are many excellent books in print on pendulums and dowsing. We recommend

David Allen Schultz's *Improve Your Life Through Dowsing*, which is available through Personal Transformation Press.)

As with Kinesiology, we must first establish a protocol as to how the pendulum is going to swing. Ask your mind to give you the directions for yes and no. Remember the pendulum is just an extension of your mind, and you are projecting the answer out to the pendulum instead of getting it clairvoyantly or through your intuition. Ask it to indicate a "no" and a "yes." The swing will be your guide. Most people will get different to- and-fro and back-and-forth swings or circles. Practice to see what your "yes" and "no" action will be. As you work with the pendulum, you will find there are more answers in addition to yes and no (doubtful, not known, etc.)

Behavioral Kinesiology uses the same principle. You are getting the information from the client through a muscle reaction, instead of using your own intuition. Quite often when working with a client, you will get more accurate answers with muscle testing because you will not be filtering it through your mind (that could color the answers if you have strong beliefs, interpretations or feelings about the subject in question).

When we have cleared all outside forces, we must next set up a reasonable understanding with Middle Self that it is not the Source or the phone operator for the Presence of God. Many sub-personalities would like to be in that position, and may well try to convince you of that. In that case, you will be channeling your Middle Self. This will happen when you do not clear it. When you get Middle Self to understand that you sold your power out to all the saboteurs when you were a child due to the need for survival, it will begin to work with you.

Control sub-personalities may interpret letting go as giving up their power. You may have been able to assure Middle Self that it is not losing anything but gaining a new ally, because you are reclaiming your personal power. It may glory in the fact that it can manipulate you. If that happens, then all multiple personalities must be deleted from the file before you can claim control. This takes training and experience, so you will have practice this process.

Unfortunately, eliminating sub-personalities does not mean that they are gone forever, because your Conscious Mind can recreate a new set whenever you do not take responsibility to follow through with the decisions you have decided to take action on. Your mind does not like unfinished answers, sentences, actions or commitments you have made. Do not say you are going to do something unless you intend to follow through. If you do not follow through, your mind will assume you did not want to move forward on the decision you made.

If you do not take action, your mind has to close that program, so it creates closure by creating a sub-personality and a program about not wanting to take action on that subject. If it happens often enough, then avoider, confuser, procrastinator, disorientor and disorganizer sub-personalities get installed, along with a "not wanting to take responsibility" sub- personality. The list can go on and on, if you get into indecision and back away from acting on a choice you have made. Any time you make a commitment and do not follow through, a program is created that is interpreted as "I am not willing to take control of my life."

If this happens for a number of years, your Instinctual Self will interpret this as if you want to die. Your mind cannot leave any loose ends unattended; every thought, statement or action you take must have closure; if you start a sentence, Conscious Mind will complete it for you. So every thought and action you create has to be completed or your mind will finish it and file it. It is a very good housekeeper, but it may not complete the task as you would have done.

A program creates a sub-personality and will drive it to get the desired result. If self-rejection is carried to the final stage, it will create a life-threatening illness. There may be disease- specific sub-personalities that were created with the disease, dysfunctional program or belief. A disease, illness or dysfunction cannot exist in the body without a program to drive it. There must be some activating force to break down the immune system or cause stress on the adrenals or the endocrine system.

Any form of negative thought or action will start an immediate breakdown in the immune and endocrine systems.

Receptor sites on the leukocytes are notified by the neuro-peptides in microseconds, which begins a physical deterioration of both systems, which in turn causes the beginning of illness and disease, as the immune system function is compromised and fewer T-cells and leukocytes are produced.

When releasing programs, make sure that you check for the sub-personalities that could be enabling them. Each time you clear a time-line or operating file, it may activate another series that has been set up to be restored from a back-up file or a denial file. With "I want to die" programs, control of the mind/body shifts to the Instinctual Mind. When this happens, programs can be set up in this mind. If there is a conflict in the mind about "I'm afraid to die" and "I want to die," it will set up sub-personalities in the Survival Self, which is part of the Middle Self. This conflict is the main cause of Alzheimer's disease. The two programs cause an Alzheimer's file to be created. This must be cleared before the person begins the backward slide or it will be difficult to stop.

When clearing, you must clear all denial and denial-of-denial programs and sub-personalities. You can bring them up by asking with Kinesiology, "Is this program a belief?" and, "Is this program a reality?" If both are positive, ask Holographic Mind to go through all the veils, shields and illusions in the back-up, time-line, denial and denial-of-denial files, bringing all those hidden files to the surface to reveal the truth.

If the answers continue to come up positive, you have a program that is locked into the physical body. If the "reality" answer comes up weak, then you have a denial. Check for denials and clear them from all files. In cases where the client has been in traumatic situations, time-lines may be in denial files, also. They can also be in autopilot and in denial or denial-of-denial files. We must also check for reactivator, recreator and regenerator viruses that will create the same program, again and again. These will be attached to individual programs so you must check each program for this each time you clear the program and sub-personality.

We have recently found another program that can recreate sub-personalities and programs. Similar to a computer virus, this program only functions when activated by a word, an activity, a feeling or an emotion. It will activate a program that will run its course and then close down. If you do not catch it during its operational cycle, it disappears. The results or effects of its activity will remain, but we cannot find out how this situation was created until we ask the proper questions to reveal it. We also found another virus that acts the same as a regenerator, which we term an "activator" virus. It can create or activate an existing program that may be dormant. Each time you clear, the sub-personalities will reveal how clients are doing in taking responsibility for their lives. Each time they get into a situation where they do not handle it properly and make it a win-win situation, then Middle Self and Conscious Mind will install controller and many other sub-personalities that apply to the situation where the client lost control or did not take total responsibility.

When we are able to handle all situations without losing center—needing to be right, in power and control, giving our power away, or not following through with all our intentions and commitments—our minds will not install those sub-personalities. Anger or resentment will open emotional doors, allowing the programs and sub-personalities to be installed. The ideal is to get to a point where no sub-personalities are reinstalled. When this occurs, you will have 100 percent control over your life.

Each time we conduct a session, we check to see if File and Program Managers are working. If not, we have them read steps nine and ten and in the session manual (a separate book). Very few people are actually in control of their lives. Many *claim* to be, based on all the seminars, workshops and therapies they have taken, but, in most cases, little has changed.

Taking responsibility is a key issue in everyone's life. Although we had some answers in the past, we could not actually describe how one actually takes responsibility. Now we can, having found all the programs, beliefs and sub-personalities that block a person's ability. (One of the major blocks is plain laziness.) Once we have cleared all the blocks, it is then a matter of the client's *desire*, which is controlled by his or her Conscious Mind. With clients who do not want to apply themselves and step in and become self-actualized, there is nothing we can do as practitioners to change that situation. We do not judge where clients are on their individual paths. The body/mind reveals that to us. N/CR cannot force them to take control over their lives.

Steps Practitioners Must Take Before Beginning Sessions

One of the major mistakes practitioners make is to step into the therapy process without first clearing themselves. Practitioners who want to sell you supplements, herbs or drugs, or want to prove their point that you need what they are demonstrating to you, can do this easily; all people have an authority-figure program that gives their power away to people who may know more than they do about a subject. We will accept their opinions, which they can prove to us with muscle testing. (There is an affirmation to clear the authority program in the session manual.)

The tester must be clear of Middle Self control and the need to be right. There are many sub-personalities that will control your ability to use any form of a divination process. The main ones are the Controller, Authority and Manipulator. They always want to be right. An authority figure can manipulate the test results by the mere fact that the client will give personal power away to the tester. (This is very common in the medical field.)

If testers are not clear, they will get a desired result to sell the client their process or product, or to validate themselves. Testers driven by a sub-personality will not get accurate results. They must release the controlling sub-personality and reclaim their personal power. Outside forces can also impose controls on the effectiveness of testers. They must be clear of attached beings before beginning sessions, or the beings attached to the practitioner will jump over to the client.

177

In doing this clearing process, testers may run into control or interference by attached beings. If this happens, they must clear the entities before going further. There can also be interference if clients will not identify with the name they are using, and testers should test for name recognition. If the arm goes weak on using a particular name, test to see which name is causing the difficulty. Quite often, women will have a negative response to a married name, if they are now divorced or separated from their husbands. Sometimes, clients can also have a negative reaction to the family name if they had a traumatic childhood. Choose a name that tests positive before testing, and test again.

If after considerable testing for name recognition, the tester is unable to test with muscle testing because the arm will not move, there is either a power struggle with Middle Self's sub-personalities or an outside force. It could be that the client does not know how much resistance to put up during Kinesiology, or that a control sub-personality is trying to control. Quite often we find a possessive being has stepped in, taken over and is controlling the muscle test. If this is the case, test for entity attachment and clear cords and entities. We have an indigenous program that gives away our personal power to authority figures. It was an acceptable program during childhood so we would obey our parents, but it has no value as an adult. This must be cleared, too (see Steps in Sessions below).

Steps that must be followed prior to testing

1. *Ground yourself* and *balance your polarity*: This needs to be done only once a day and may be done upon awakening in the morning. This can be done with the wrist-holding process as it provides all the that is needed (see Steps in Sessions). *Do not put shields, robes of color or energy around yourself to protect yourself.* If you do, you will reflect back all the energy and anything you have removed from the person, stopping the effect of healing.

2. *Clear yourself of any attached beings* before beginning a session or you will drop them on a client. Conversely, if

you are not protected, clients will drop them on you. One of the major problems we have is passing out in a session caused by entities that will use the client's mental power to knock you out.

3. *Set your paradigm:* Mentally ask the client to give you a "yes" and a "no." Most people will respond with a "no" as weak or down. "Yes" will be strong, or up. Using the fingers (client tries to keep thumb and middle finger together), closed fingers is usually "yes" and weak or open is "no."

With the finger method, you can test yourself. The tester can set the paradigm in any manner desired; we prefer "yes" as the arm tests strong, and "no" as the arm cannot resist pressure and becomes weak. Have the client hold the arm up, and test to make sure it holds up against resistance. Ask the client to say first and last name while you are holding pressure on the arm, and have him/her continue saying the name until it gets weak and goes down. This tests for control by a control/authority sub-personality. (Testers can use this test on either clients or themselves.)

The most important person to test is the practitioner who is doing the testing. Many times, the tester has received inaccurate answers from me when muscle testing me and wondered why. It is because I know what I am doing and can control the answers; if the client's sub-personalities are in control, you will not be able to test very effectively.

You may want to wait a few minutes and retest to see if Middle Self is playing games. If it is, the arm will resist again. Retest again until the arm becomes weak. The arm may not go down at all. If this happens, then the person cannot function as a tester and get valid results due to control. You must be in a clear space to do effective muscle testing.

One the most troubling issues we find concerns clients who attend the workshops and then begin practicing on others without first working on their own issues. We cannot avoid our own issues, yet we have found that half of the attendees will not get into recovery. Therapists must be working on their own issues regularly with another therapist, as practitioners must be in recovery working with their own issues all the time. N/CR brings them up, and they will interfere with the process when working with a client.

If you do not want to work with your own issues, you will slide the client out of the tight space you put yourself in when they come up. You may even pass out during the session if you do not want to face the issue. This can happen to both the client and the practitioner. Sometimes it can happen simultaneously.

Chapter 14

How the Mind Functions

Our minds are tools for transformation provided that we use them properly. Contrary to popular belief, there is more to our minds than brain researchers have found. Some psychologists divide the mind into the Conscious and Unconscious minds. Others refer to the Subconscious Mind, which is the appropriate description because it is far from the dictionary description of the word "unconscious." It is on 24/7 and records in its database every form of sensory input that we allow in. The key word is "allowed," because if we are at the "keyboard" of our computer and in control of its programming, we can control the information that is being recorded. If we are not in control of the process, autopilot records in the database anything that the mind picks up.

It is like a funnel with a big sponge at the bottom that absorbs everything you hear, see or feel. The awesome power of the mind can run your life without your consent, since it operates very effectively without your input, so understanding how it functions is critical. In fact, the most important part of any therapy or healing process is understanding how the mind functions because it controls all functions of the body. Earlier chapters have skimmed this subject, and this chapter examines what we have found in our research. The mind has four basic operating systems, or four levels of cognition, each with specific duties to perform:

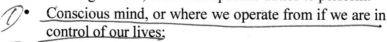

1) • Conscious mind, or where we operate from if we are in control of our lives;

2) • Middle Self, or the program manager;

- File manager, or Ego;
- Subconscious Mind, the data storage or memory;
- Higher Self, managing how our mind rates operates.

The challenge is to get all four levels aligned with each other so they have the same objectives and same priorities to accomplish our goals in life. But seldom do I find people with all four systems aligned and operating together.

Historically, what we have thought of as "Ego" has been totally off-base. Until 1992, I was accusing my Ego of fouling up my life and controlling my behavior. I threatened to replace it with a new Ego until, one day, when a student of N/CR was working with me, my left shoulder began to hurt so much that I could not pick anything up or even hold the steering wheel in my car.

My physical therapist, Frank Hughes, who had helped me in the early years of my recovery, said it was the old bursitis acting up again. He proceeded to break up the calcium deposits locked in the muscles. His treatment was very painful, but it resulted in more movement in my shoulder. What he was doing was breaking up the locked-in programs in the muscle fascia and the acupuncture meridians. Even though he was able to loosen it up, it always locked back up again in a week or so. (I had to continue having treatments, and each time it was a little less locked up.)

The next morning, however, I awoke with such excruciating pain that I could not move my arm. My shoulder was locked in a position with my arm at my side. I could bend my elbow but any movement of my shoulder was so painful that I had to cancel that day's appointments. I consulted Chris, one of my practitioners, and we tried everything we could to find the program responsible, but to no avail. Because we could find no other source, we thought Ego was holding onto a program and blocking the information so we could not release the pain. This proved to be false, but we did not know it at the time, so we proceeded to fight with Ego, and got nowhere.

I have not taken medication of any sort since childhood and had declined painkillers when I had back pain ten years earlier, but this shoulder pain was beyond my ability to handle it. I also had to see clients the following day. Chris suggested I take a pain remedy, which did help me to function and work with the clients scheduled for the following day.

Two days later, with four practitioners working with me, we found that the source was my fear of talking with my mother, and telling her the truth of how I felt about my childhood. But, when a lesson is up and you're on the two-yard line in your life drama, nothing will work until you deal with the cause. You cannot avoid the lesson when you're at the end of the line. I had been avoiding discussing the issues from my childhood with my mother for thirty years. Since she was ninety years of age, I did not want to upset her, but I had to deal with the issue. I know I had to clear with her before she passed on out of this life. It turned out to be a highly charged emotional meeting, with intense emotions surfacing, but we were able to clear up many issues and release the shoulder pain.

Discovering that the Ego was not the controlling factor in our minds was a major shift in my healing approach and understanding of how the mind functions. Until 1992, I was after Ego, because the traditional belief in psychology and in many cultures painted Ego as the enemy. I had followed *A Course In Miracles* since 1977 so, for me, Ego was the formidable driving force that kept us separate from God and ourselves. I had been sponsoring a *Course In Miracles* group and decided it was time to pass it on to someone else in the group, because my views were now at odds with the course's teachings.

My concepts all changed in 1993, when I found that we were up against a saboteur that we could not control. With the help of the practitioners I was training, we spent a long time working on this driving force in the mind, that seemed to control our behavior. I was amazed to find that it was not Ego at all. Ego had nothing to do with control, nor did it even *want* to control any part of us. It was just the file manager for our Subconscious Mind.

Ego *per se* does not run our lives; it is only the secretary, librarian and memory retrieval system. The conventional concept of it as "the enemy" is totally false. (Of course, if you beat it up, it will defend itself but, if you make friends with it, it will serve you well.) There really is no "enemy" in our minds, or so I thought at the time. Even though it seems at times that our minds are working against us, I did not know who was running the show.

The parts of our minds that could most closely be described as "enemy" are our controller sub-personalities (shadow selves, manipulator, judger, authority, self-righteous, perfectionist, justifier, inner critic and critical parent). These "critics within" are our major adversaries; they can act in what we call ego-like habit patterns, and we must accept that *we* have allowed all the programs, habit patterns and self-talkers to be programmed into our minds. That we create it all can be a hard pill to swallow. Nobody did it to us!

Life is like a crossword puzzle, in which the blacked out squares are karma that we must take care of at some point. The open squares represent free choice in which *we do only what we want to do, no matter how we made the decision. We have a choice every minute of each day to take responsibility for our actions.*

The Middle Self

The concept of Middle Self has been in the Hawaiian culture for thousands of years, but the missionaries suppressed native philosophy about the mind, so it is not generally known or accepted by Western psychology. The Christian missionaries destroyed all written material but, fortunately, the information was handed down orally, so this valuable knowledge was preserved. Proving that Middle Self's sub-personalities, and not Ego, are the controllers has taken me almost ten years, and most people still will not accept the concept. Most are unaware of how these sub-personalities function, so they hold onto the old Ego concept. Ego is nothing more than an operating system in our Middle Self.

Its basic role is to transfer data back and forth between Subconscious and Conscious Minds, and it can be reprogrammed very easily.

Few people are aware that, every minute of every day, their mind has an ongoing dialogue with itself. As the previous day's sensory input is filed away, it accesses related data in the files in your Subconscious Mind. It never sleeps; it is on duty 24/7. Shadow selves are the chatter and crosstalk that goes on in our minds when we try to quiet them.

We have many voices going on in the Middle Self all the time. It is our responsibility to take control and silence the crosstalk and inner chatter that goes on there. They are the negative aspect of the mind that drags us into anger, rage and resentment. They also set up grudges and resentments. Shadow selves can be eliminated with an affirmation, as they are also an operating system in the Middle Self.

At this point, I have not been able to get any of the major speakers on the subjects of self-help, psychology, alternative medicine or energy medicine to accept my concepts about Ego as File Manager. In the past, hearing these so-called experts blame Ego or describe behavior as "egotistic" would irritate me, because I knew it was not true. I have finally accepted that, at some point in the future, my views will prevail and, until then, I will just be satisfied with helping and training people in Energy Medicine and Energy Psychology.

In my research, I ran into a barrier to getting all the programs cleared. We would release all the programs the Subconscious Mind was holding on a particular emotional pattern, get Ego into alignment, and reach consensus with the Conscious Mind's intentions, yet we were not getting a total release. The situation would resurface or create a new set of breakdowns. We finally discovered the source of the conflict: Middle Self.

When I discovered that Ego was not the villain that was fouling up our lives, I also found that all the activities in our minds are controlled by operating systems. This was a major find because I had been sabotaging myself quite often, but I

185

could not seem to stop it. Then I discovered that the operating systems were not working in my best interests, and that they could be reprogrammed to align with my life goals and priorities.

In the past, I had assumed that Conscious Mind was Middle Self, from my study of the Hawaiian description of the mind. The more I researched into how to rewrite the operating systems, however, I recognized there was more to Middle Self than the Kahuna concepts had described. I discovered that Middle Self consists of several components (see Figure 3):

- *Conscious Rational Mind*, the functional aspect, the "keyboard" where you, the conscious self, program and control your life.
- *Conscious Mind Operating files,* The operating files that run your life on a day-to-day basis when you are in control of your mind's activities. (If you are not in control, your mind goes on autopilot and Artificial Intelligence in the Inner Middle Self.)
- *Autopilot*, which can run your life without your control through Artificial Intelligence and all the sub- personalities in Middle Self's files. When people go on autopilot, they give their power away to a sub- personality that they have created to escape from some situation or experience.
- *Middle Self*, with Control and Manipulator sub-personalities, will control all your behavior if you have given away your personal power and control to autopilot. Artificial Intelligence (AI) is an operating system that operates through the inner mind's operating systems, and it will control your life along with autopilot when you default on your attempt to regain control and take your power back. It has an exact duplicate set of the file operating programs in the Conscious Mind, so it can run our lives without our support.
- *Survival Self/Instinctual Mind,* which operates out of the limbic part of the brain. Some people describe it as the animal or reptilian mind. Brain researchers theorize that this is the oldest part of the brain. I

feel this could be inaccurate, since its actions interleave with those of the Inner Middle Self, which operates from beliefs, concepts, interpretations and attitudes. These, if acted on over time, will create programs and patterns. It also has a set of sub-personalities for each concept or belief. These two are not active unless one goes into survival from a life-threatening illness.

HIGH SELF

Connection to GOD Self. Akashic Record Telephone Operator
Connection to Source Mind and the Hall of Records

MIDDLE SELF

Conscious Rational Mind
Program Manager
File Manager (Ego)
Auto Pilot (Justifier, Judger, Control,
Manipulator sub-personalities, Survival Self)

LOWER SELF

Subconscious Mind

Figure 3: The Middle Self

Autopilot and Artificial Intelligence may do a fine job of guiding you through your day if there are no crises or confrontations where you have to make decisions, but if a situation occurs that requires decisive action, someone has to make that decision.

Middle Self bases its action on how you have handled the situation in the past. It scans the files and, if no program exists, the committee will take whatever action best promotes its survival. If you are in a situation that, at a conscious level, you consider beneficial to you, but your committee of sub-personalities views as threatening, it will try to sabotage you.

Autopilot.

If you are not in total control of your life, your Middle Self committee will try to stop any threat to its power, due to Inner Conscious Mind being in control. If you give it the message that you are claiming your personal power and taking responsibility for your life, it will readily relinquish its power to you. (However, it won't trust you at first, so you will have to prove yourself.) If you have defaulted on attempts to reclaim your personal power and take control of your life, Artificial Intelligence, which operates out of Inner Conscious Mind, will have taken over control of your life with autopilot. At this point, you will need to demonstrate your intention and commitment, or AI will not give up control very easy if you have previously defaulted in many attempts to take control of your life.

Here is a case in point: A new client came to my lecture and was impressed with my description of how you could change your life path. During the appointment she made, she affirmed that she was fully committed to changing her life. However, I did not realize that she was merely a collector of ideas and concepts, and would try them but never follow through. After a few minutes into the session, she said she was getting sick to her stomach. She dashed to the bathroom four times to dump the contents of her stomach.

She asked if I had another appointment available later in the day. I did, so she went home and returned that evening looking very wrung out, wrapped up in a blanket and carrying a hot water bottle. "I went to bed and tried to sleep," she said, "but I couldn't. All day, I went from chills to sweats, heaved my insides out until I feel like I am raw inside and consumed with fear. Why is this happening to me? I didn't do anything I know of to bring this on."

I asked her, "Did you use or work with any of the processes or programs you learned in seminars and workshops you attended?"

Your Body is Talking, Are You Listening?

"I tried, but couldn't follow through with them. They were too difficult, and did not make sense to me."

My response was brief: "You're like many people who cannot discipline themselves to apply what they have learned in the seminars. Unfortunately, your mind will help you assimilate the information but, if you don't apply it, then autopilot takes over again. If that happens four or five times, Inner Conscious then takes over, and it does not let go of control easily."

By the time she had turned eight years old, Inner Conscious mind had taken over totally, so she had no control over her life at all, but didn't know it until she came to me for a session. Unwinding the web of control programs took some doing, because we had to negotiate at length with Inner Conscious Mind so that it would give up control. We finally did get it to relinquish control, so she could reclaim her personal power and take control of her life. She disciplined herself to follow through with what we had laid out for her, and she was able to get on the path back to peace, happiness, harmony and joy with unconditional love in her life. (If I had known then what I know now it would have been a much easier path to go down.)

To harness the awesome power of the mind, we must take control over it. This power is available on demand, but first you must get your committee aligned with your goals and purposes, otherwise it will sabotage you. If, in the past, you have given it free reign or sold out your power to it, you must reclaim it.

The first task is to make friends with your Conscious (rational) Mind, and with your Middle Self and its sub-personality committees. The affirmation and the process to make friends with Middle Self and File Manager is the first step. (I am not now as concerned with Sub-Personalities as I was when I found them 20 years ago. I have found it is more important to remove the Multiple Personalities, and to clear the corrupted programs from both Conscious and Subconscious minds.)

Then you have to take your power back from the three saboteurs. Inner Conscious Mind will be the most difficult one to remove and delete its operating system. It took over when you were two years old and sees itself as your savior. Next, you give them a structured format with parameters to follow, and most of the time, you can get them to work with you. The more you have separated yourself from controlling your life (say, by being a victim), the longer the path to reclaim control of your world.

There is a payoff in each path we take, usually in the form of getting attention or as a substitute for love. We all want to be loved, validated and accepted, and the number-one priority of your Middle Self subcommittee is being validated and loved. It therefore views any concentrated form of attention as love, whether it is physical or emotional kindness and caring, or abuse. It will accept anything as a substitute for love, other than outright rejection. The actual form does not seem to matter, as long as other people acknowledge that we make a difference in their lives. Depending on its interpretation of the available options, Middle Self may choose victim or survivor.

To people who have been abused, this analysis may seem callous. Yet unless they accept that they set up the abusive situation based on the lessons they needed to learn, and that they perpetuate the situation until they "get" the lesson, it will continue to control their lives. To come to this point, they must recognize that when they reclaim their personal power and stop blaming others for their plight, they can pull out of victim consciousness. The final lesson is to love and forgive those who abused them. It is very hard to accept that you must forgive those who hurt you, but the lesson is not released until you do.

For many years, I have worked with people who have installed Magical Child Syndrome (MCS) due to a traumatic experience in childhood. I had assumed that it happened to a few people, but wasn't a widespread phenomenon. (At least I described it as a phenomenon in the past.) It apparently has to do with one's perception and interpretation of the event. In some cases, I was sure that MCS was present, but it was not. In yet other cases, MCS *was* operating, despite the absence of a traumatic event.

I have now found that we cannot make value judgments about a person's circumstances. Since 2002, I have begun to test for MCS in everyone because of a couple of cases that showed up despite lack of trauma. I have since found that many of my clients have MCS. The following cases show how our mind reacts to perceived trauma.

My first session with a medical practitioner was eye-opening. As we began, he was unable to repeat the affirmations properly, missing or leaving out and mispronouncing words, and asking me to explain things he should have known about, being in the medical field. I checked his hearing but that turned out to be perfect. Then I asked him, "Can you hear me okay?"

He replied, "Not all the time."

I checked many causes of his selective deafness until I came up with MCS as the source. It turns out that, at eight years old, his emotional development had been stalled. His comprehension factor checked out at only fifty per cent, thus clearly revealing the problem. In future sessions, we were able to bring his comprehension up to speed as we cleared his emotional traumas.

MCS is activated or triggered when people want to avoid mental/emotional or physical pain that is being directed toward them. The personality self walks out and releases conscious control. At this point, Middle Self must decide what action to take. It may create a split or multiple personality to take over if the situation lasts more than a few hours, or it can put the body/mind and sub-personalities in control until the personality self returns.

Any time a similar situation occurs, a catalyst is set up in the mind to cause the personality self to exit and launch MCS to take over. This is similar to blacking out or passing out, except that the body/mind continues to function normally. This will leave blank spots in conscious memory similar to amnesia even though the Subconscious Mind's database is recording all sensory input. (I have worked with many who I knew were working out of MCS, some of whose situations are described in the Case Histories in Appendix A.)

The main challenge is to understand how your mind operates. Your Subconscious Mind is simply the computer's database that makes no rational decisions, and cannot "think

Your Body is Talking, Are You Listening?

out situations." What we call the autonomic nervous system is actually a set of indigenous programs in the Subconscious Mind that automatically control t h e organs, the endocrine system and the cellular functions of the body. It uses programming already in the files to tell all the cellular computers how to control the body's organs and the endocrine system. Because it controls your endocrine and immune systems functions, in effect, your mind controls your resistance to disease.

Recent research with psychoneuroimmunology has shown that any negative sensory input to the mind will cause a depressive reaction on the whole body. Information is sent out via neuropeptides in microseconds when negative thoughts, feelings, actions or sensory input are experienced. The level of severity of the input will govern the extent of the depressive effect on the body. The immune and endocrine systems take the major hit from negative stress. The more we work against the negative programs filed in our data files, the higher the stress level on the body, and harder our adrenals must work to keep us up to speed.

Fear activates the negative action and draws our whole system down, depressing the immune system and quickly depleting adrenal function. Research has shown that there are receptors on all organs and glands, which indicates that our bodies are "network computers."

The main roadblock in this research is that, while some practitioners understand the effect, few understand the theory of Energy Medicine and Energy Psychology that can be used to release the causes of breakdowns in the body. When the mind is freed from the limitations of the negative programs, the body will heal itself.

There are many examples of this. One that few people who understand is the concept behind grieving. When a loved one dies, we are upset about our loss, especially if we didn't have closure before the person died, so we hold onto the attachment. Furthermore, any disputes over the assets of the deceased person can prolong our grief, because we're holding onto to the fact that we have lost something. The sub- personalities that the personality self uses to control us are actually behind all this.

COMPASSIONATE DETACHED

The root issue is one of taking responsibility and reclaiming our personal power. If we are not complete and whole in our selves, we have given our power away to the situation and can hold onto our grief for years, because we feel that we have lost something we cannot identify.

We will also try to control those around us, in order to generate support for our depression. If they are empathizers and rescuers, we will draw them down, too, because they will feel obliged to support our need. If they do not stay with us and support us, we will even make them feel guilty. The longer we hold onto our grief, the more it depresses our endocrine system, as it tries to keep us buoyed up and stop us from sinking further into depression. The problem is that the negative sensory input from our feelings depresses the endocrine system further, draining it to the point that it has no more reserves to call on, so we go into chronic clinical depression.

I call myself a "compassionate detached," in that I don't get into other people's needs, as there is no payoff for me in rescuing people. This may seem callous to some, because we're all taught that we should help people in need. When my father passed on, I knew why he was walking out of life. I was detached from any loss and let him go, with no grief at all. I was more concerned about my son's reaction since they had a tight bond, yet we all let him go with no adverse reaction. When my wife's father died, followed by her mother six months later, we handled our response well—three parents dying in the same year, yet it had no adverse reaction our family. Avoiding being a savior takes great willpower. Because our minds are holding onto programs that draw us into the payoff, we are prone to falling into traps. If we have a guilt program or belief that tells us that we must not abandon someone in a state of need, we will hold onto the notion that we are helping, when we're actually just enabling that person to hold onto loss
and depression.

Our payoff is that we get validation and acceptance by sticking with them. We feel that we're doing the right thing, because "they need our help." (If we're balanced in our own needs, we won't enable them to continue in their depression, confusion, disorientation and feelings of futility. We'll know that those in grief do not want you telling them what they need to do.)

You must also ask yourself if you want to drag yourself down with them. As we've stated before, your mind is not always rational in its decisions, so it may react to the stimulus as if you're sharing the loss, which will eventually drag you down, too.

My sense is that, following a loss, we need to have a "pity party," let go of our feelings, and then address our fears and needs. If we do that, then we will not need to continue playing out the soap opera we call our lives. The longer we play out our tragedy, the more ingrained the soap-opera script becomes locked into our mind.

Codependent victims often perpetuate an activity to control the person from whom they are drawing their support. They have an ulterior motive in their control, so they use covert control to avoid the issue they want to control. Our minds can be quite devious in their needs and how they get the payoff. Most people who are in this situation are controlled by autopilot and from the Inner Conscious Mind and Middle Self.

Most of the mind's inner dialogue goes on without our conscious recognition, yet is faithfully stored in your computer's files. Now, any sensory input can compromise the function of the original program, and if sensory input or emotional trauma overloads a file, your body starts talking to you through little pains. If you don't listen to these, they can grow into a more serious dysfunction.

The first message may be just a whisper. The next one will be a pain or a malfunction such as an illness. If you do not get that one, the next may be more serious, up to and including a life-threatening disease. Most people do not see this progression creeping up on them, and generate a landslide of business for doctors, who try to treat the symptom. Unfortunately, the symptom has nothing at all to do with the program or the action of the sub-personality responsible.

Traditionally, we used to assume that "self-talk" was Ego and Subconscious Mind carrying on an internal discourse or making observations and judgments about the outside world. I see now that the Middle Self's sub-personalities are in constant dialogue, which includes accessing information from the Subconscious Mind's database. (They request information from Ego, but Ego is very seldom in on the dialogue.) When we see how the mind operates, we become aware of the awesome power of the mind to run and control our lives. For optimum functioning, we must get all sections of our minds into alignment. When we get Middle Self and Lower Self to integrate with Higher Self, we can really make progress.

The major challenge we have is recovering our true selves and eliminating the personality self. I have found very few people who have found their true selves and can function in them. We lost our true identities in childhood and defaulted to personality selves, due to all the negative programming that was affecting us. Inner Conscious Mind took over and left us standing on the sideline to watch.

As a result very few children ever know who they really are. When personality self takes over, we lose our identities as all the Middle Self's operating systems take control of our lives. To get back to true self, we must delete all the operating systems that the sub and multiple personalities function from, and then delete all the sub-personality files. This takes discipline and committed intention, as we will tend to fall back into habit patterns that will reinstall the sub-personality operating systems, even if we have deleted and removed all the programs in a therapy session.

We must be vigilant and monitor our feelings and thoughts, along with the sensory input that is presented to us at all times. We cannot afford negative input at any time. Most people do not know what is required to take responsibility, and the remainder do not want to put in the effort to discipline themselves. Evaluating the situation from an objective standpoint is difficult if illusion or denial is in control.

The major fallacy in medicine is that we can use drugs or surgery on a symptom. Sometimes it may work, but the doctors I have discussed this with say that their success-level is about thirty per cent. It is interesting to note that in double-blind tests, the placebo effect has a fifty-four per cent overall success record, almost double that of drugs or surgery.

As an example, about three years ago, a man we'll call Jeff made an appointment after he had heard my lecture. He had seen me once before and told me, "The release work you did with me didn't work, and I still have severe back pains that are transmitting down to my foot. The doctors have said the only treatment available is surgery, but I refuse to go that route because the location of the supposed pinched nerve is right next to my spinal column." Since botched back surgery is a frequent cause of paralysis, he had refused that avenue.

The doctors then put an electric stimulator under his skin located near the nerve, allowing him to adjust the level of stimulation to relieve the pain. However, even the stimulator stopped being effective, so, having exhausted every avenue for treatment Jeff came back to me, because his first treatment had provided at least some relief. He had so resisted letting go of his programs that we had made little more progress, but he had found some relief, so he decided to keep coming to see me. In the last session, we had had a breakthrough and found the core issue.

His main problem was that he wanted someone else to do his healing for him. The basis of Energy Medicine is that clients must take responsibility for their own healing processes. I can show them the way, but I cannot do it for them. We spent a whole session releasing the victim programs, so that he could see where he was on the path to healing himself. All back pain is caused by self-rejection, but Jeff's case also involved a refusal to take responsibility and an unwillingness to speak his mind. He told people what they wanted to hear so that he would not feel rejected and abandoned.

As with most of my clients, Jeff's problems started in childhood with a very dysfunctional family but his mind had put all the beliefs, attitudes, programs and feelings into denial-of-denial, so he had no recollection of his childhood. His life was controlled by Magical Child Syndrome and autopilot, as many are. Since he refused to take responsibility for his condition,

Inner Conscious Mind was controlling his life. His wife was a duplicate of his mother so he had to deal with that, too. Now that we have cleared most of the childhood trauma, Jeff is finally making good progress. The next step is to work on his resistance to getting clear with the issues with his wife.

I was working with another man, who was having a many conflicts in his life; he had been divorced twice and was drawing dysfunctional relationships which were not working. When we cleared all the split and multiple personalities, he became more successful in his practice as a dentist and with relationships. He took a trip to see his first wife, and his children who were now in their twenties. When he walked into the house he did not recognize anything, even though he had lived in this house for ten years. He did not even recognize his ex-wife.)He had seen the children when they were younger so he recognized them.) He even asked her, "We were married"?

When he returned home, he contacted me and asked, "Are multiple personalities blocking my past that much that I cannot even remember my ex-wife?" Apparently, the trauma of the divorce had caused him to exit into a multiple personality that already had been created when he was a child. Years of memories were blocked out when he deleted all the multiple personalities he had been living in for most of his life.

The Operation of the Mind

As Figures 4.1 and 4.2 show, the process begins with the receipt of sensory input, be it a sound, sight, smell or touch. However, the stimulus can also be a thought or memory, meta-communication, information from higher sources, and new thought forms. Figure 4.1 shows how the mind routes information. Figure 4.2 (in two parts) shows the results of the reactions and responses.

When the Conscious Mind records sensory input, it decides how it will react or respond, interprets how it feels about the incoming information, and places a feeling on it. It will either take responsibility and route that information to the Conscious

Rational Mind, or make no decision and pass it on to Inner Conscious Mind and Middle Self. If we are making our own decisions on how to handle the situation, Middle Self routes the information to Ego (file manager), which files it in Subconscious Mind's database. Ego can retrieve information from our database and return it to Conscious Mind for future use.

As we can see by Figure 4.1, if we do not take responsibility, sensory input takes a totally different route through our mind. If we choose not to be in control, Inner Conscious Mind runs our life quite well. The problem with this, however, is that we have no control about what action it takes. When there are people we are rejecting or avoiding, sometimes we cannot remember what happened. It is like amnesia, since we are operating out of a total different personality self. It can cause a myriad of illnesses and diseases to act out our fear or anger. I have seen dysfunctional programs disappear when we clear Multiple Personalities.

When we clear all the multiple personalities and negative habit patterns, we can get control back. It takes some work to get the flow of information to run through our minds without being detoured through the sub-personalities. Figure 4.1 shows how the mind routes the sensory input through the operating systems, and Figure 4.2 shows how the mind responds or reacts to the sensory input, and the effects it has on our behavior.

1. **Sensory Input** (visual, auditory, physical feeling, meta-communication, and information from higher sources) and new thought forms (creative, inventive and intuitive), plus processing dialogue (negative or positive thought forms, flashbacks, memories, misinterpretations) are fed to the Middle Self.

2. **Middle Self** interprets the perceived information, processing it through the Conscious Rational Mind or autopilot sub- personalities. (Middle Self and Subconscious Mind search for programs of past reactions or responses, and the operational program controls Reaction/Response.)

3. **Assignment of Feeling** determines what action to take. At this point, you have two choices: reaction or response. Your choice is based on past beliefs or perceived effects from installed programs.

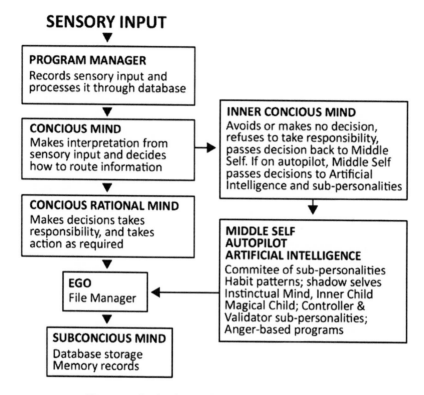

Figure 4.1: Outline of How the Mind Operates

4. A ***Catalyst*** causes loss of control, pushing you into fear/anger, degenerating into emotional reaction and giving away your personal power.

5. ***Unconscious Decisions*** are made in an instant, based on the catalyst as to which action to take (fight or flight).

6. ***Emotional Reaction***, offering no choice/decision, resulting in either:

    a.) Flight/avoidance. Run away from feeling;

    b.) Fight/confrontation. Defensive, blowup out of control;

    c.) Defense of action. Justification of action, denial of eelings;

    d.) No reaction: total avoidance with repression of
        feeling/emotion;

e.) Either denial or waking up to the lesson and reviewing the situation that causes the reaction.

7. ***Denial/Justification***: Falling back into the illusion of the past denial as a victim, justifying behavior as the only responsible reaction we could take. At this point, illusion and denial may form a denial-of-denial sub-personality, If this happens, the cause of the behavior is totally suppressed as if it does not exist. We can then assume that our reaction was an accurate truthful way to handle the situation.

8. ***Recycle Lesson***: At this point, you may review your behavior and ask yourself, "Do I want to feel/react this way now and in the future?" If you can do this, you can recycle the lesson.

9. ***Recognition of Denial***:

    a) Review behavior you deem as ineffective;
    b) Recognize the effect of the lesson;
    c) Move into recovery and erase the ineffective programand remove the sub-personality driving the program;
    d) Remove denial-of-denial sub-personalities if you can recognize them;
    e) Change the negative justifying reactions to positive responses;
    f) Rewrite a new program and install it in the files;
    g) Recognize that you create all lessons, so that you can shift from victim to cause;
    h) Love and forgive yourself for allowing this to happen.

10. ***Choice/Decision***: When we recognize this decision point, we have about 30 seconds to detach from the emotion and respond in an effective way. State, "I choose to step out of denial, illusion and justification. I will not act out, repress, justify, manipulate, try to control or judge another's behavior."

11. ***Response***: If we are not able to detach from the emotion immediately, we will go into recycle. If we can respond effectively and positively, we review the possible avenues and responses to handle the situation with acceptance, forgiveness and unconditional love. At this point, we can detach from the emotion and avoid separation from self.

12. **Denial Reaction** will take over due to our inability to maintain and control our response. Loss of control will push us into the emotion. We recycle the lesson again.

13. **Detachment**: Hallmarks of successful detachment are the ability to recognize the feeling with a new viewpoint and interpretation, and honestly say to ourselves:

a) This is not an attack on my self-worth or who I am.
b) I do not have or need authority/control over anybody.
c) I can respond in a positive manner, to every feeling or situation and all people at all times.
d) I am all right under all conditions, in all circumstances, in all situations and at all times.
e) My self-esteem and self-worth are unaffected by this experience.
f) I can respond with love, kindness and forgiveness at all times.

14. **Transformation**: This occurs when we can recognize that we do not need control or authority at any time. We will not be attacked at any time, nor do we have to defend ourselves or attack back. When we release fear, anger, control, authority, judgment and justification, we have made it through the transfiguration, and unconditional love, peace, happiness, harmony and joy is our entitlement.

Split Personalities

Sub-personalities are the driving force behind habit patterns. If you follow a certain action, belief or interpretation often enough, it will become a habit pattern. Habit patterns become programs which that control your life. If you deny that you are following that pattern it will continue to set up a program even though you deny it.

NEW SENSORY INPUT (Visual, auditory, touch)	NEW THOUGHT FORMS (Creative/inventive theory)

NO CONTROL

PROCESSING DIALOGUE
(Negative/positive thoughts,
Memories, Misinterpretations)
▼
INTERPRETATION
Processing through the
Subconcious Mind for past
reactions or responses
▼
ASSIGNMENT OF FEELING ———
Determine belief based action of
percieved effect on you. Make instant
decision and follow to final result
▼
CATALYST
Fear/anger rises. Give away
personal power. Loss of control
leads to an emotional reaction,
denial of self and into illusion
▼
NO CHOICE/NO DECISION
Review handling of reactions to similar
situations. Act out victim feeling
of no control. Feeling is based in fear
of threat, rejection abandonment,
jealousy, anger, loss of control, etc.
▼
EMOTIONAL REACTION
• Flight = fear, run, from feeling
• Fight = anger, defense/blowup
• Justification/defensivness
• No reaction, repress feelings
▼
DENIAL/JUSTIFICATION
Failure back into illusion of past
denial, assuming/justifying that
your behavior is an accurate,
truthful way to handle situations,
The lesson will return.
▼
RECYCLE LESSON
Do I want to feel/react this
way now and in the future?

EFFECTIVE DECISION

CHOICE/DECISIONS
I choose to snap out of denial
illusion & justification. I will not
act out, repress, react or control.
I have 30 seconds to reconize
the anger/fear, detach from the
emotion or go into recycle
▼
RESPOND EFFECTIVELY
You review the possible avenues
and responses to handle the
situation with acceptance, love,
and forgiveness. You detach from
potential emotion immediately.
▼
DETACHMENT
1. I don't have or need to
   have authority or control
   over anyone
2. I am not threatened. I don't
   need to attack, be attacked,
   or defend myself in any way.
3. I can respond in a positive
   way to every feeling & person.
4. I always respond with love,
   kindness and forgiveness.
5. I am alright under all
   situations. My self-esteem,
   self-worth are not affected
   by this.
▼
TRANSFORMATION
Unconditional love, peace,
harmony, happiness and joy.
Release of fear, control
judgement and justification

Figure 4-2: Operation of the Mind

If you persist in denying the program that the pattern created, you may become totally separated from yourself and move into denial of denial. If you disassociate from yourself at times of great stress, you become a multiple personality. At this point, the sub-personalities become who you are, as you become totally separated from self.

Most people with this dysfunction are labeled as psychotic or schizophrenic, a condition that may result in a possessive spirit walking in and taking over. At this point, people can leave for short times (a few minutes to hours), but sometimes, people leave for many years, with no recollection of what they have done or where they have been. This demonstrates the awesome power of the mind to operate without our approval or direction.

All mental dysfunction is caused by a choice by the mind to create another world to run away from some traumatic experience. Almost all dysfunction of this type starts with a childhood experience. The child will escape into an imaginary world that he or she sets up to avoid pain. I refer to this as "escaping into the Magical Child," which is controlled by the inner child sub-personality. This will be carried through life until it is released.

I have worked with many people who "disappear" in a sense. They are physically in the same body but they lose track of time. When they get back in their body they cannot account for days, and sometimes months or years. If we can unwind the programs and experiences, we can bring the original personality back. People can also disappear when they go on autopilot and give their power away to another created multiple personality that was created to escape from some situation or experience. Middle Self sub-personalities can set up autopilot operating systems in the Conscious Rational Mind and, as a result, our life is run without our consent or control.

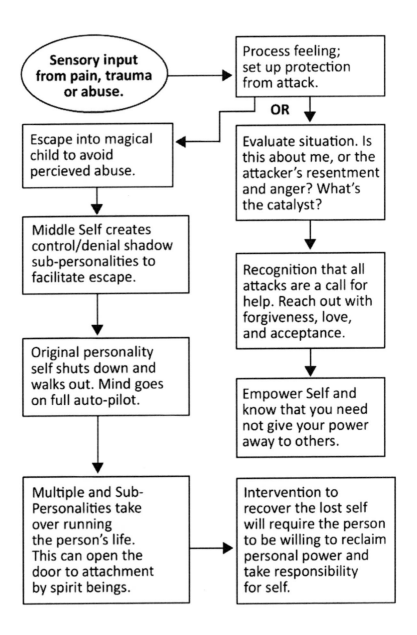

Figure 5: Creation of a Split and Multiple Personality

Figure 5 portrays the formation of a split personality:

1. Sensory input from a trauma, pain, situation or any form of abuse will cause a person to escape into a magical child
2. Middle Self creates a multiple personality to accommodate the escape.
3. Person goes on autopilot or has been on autopilot at times. This evolves into multiple personalities that control the mind's functioning. The person and the original personality self shut down. Multiple personalities are a series of sub-personalities running a person's life.
4. Multiple personality disorder and schizophrenia are generally caused by an attached spirit being taking over, becoming another personality self.

Sometimes I have been able to pull clients back and remove all the multiple personalities if they want to do so; often, however, they have made the choice to die, and do not want to come back. I have found sometimes that they are angry, and force other people to take care of them.

Parental Legacy
In well-balanced people, the levels of the mind are tightly integrated, but they may operate separately due to separation in childhood. Few people have parents who direct and support their children to become creative thinkers and support the development of their self-esteem and self-worth. Self-confidence comes from proper direction, which gives a child the feeling of making the right decisions. Most children do not feel they are all right and acceptable, so they reject themselves and do not have confidence in their actions. Parents unwittingly program their children for failure by being critical and putting them down.

Most of the time, parents are unaware of their own programs which cause them to compete with their children and make them feel they can never match up to the parents' desires. The biggest villains in this behavior pattern are the controller and manipulator sub-personalities—everything has to be done their way or it's not acceptable.

Lower Self or Subconscious Mind has its agenda to keep your behavior balanced. I used to believe that Ego ran our life when we did not take control, but it does not have that power at all, although blaming it is a popular pastime. Middle Self creates individual selves (sub-personalities) that cause more separation and fragmentation.

If you were abused by a parent or a partner, you can choose to hold onto the anger, fear and self-rejection. Alternatively, you can face the denial and illusion, and then let it go. Are there any tools in your life that will help you to release the illusion and open the door to peace, happiness, harmony, and joy with financial abundance and unconditional love? Have you tried them and do they work? *The challenge is to recognize the lesson—that no one can hurt you; only you can.*

Following a traumatic situation, what causes you to feel emotions about the trauma? It is your interpretation and belief about the situation; your mind creates the feeling, and you or your sub-personalities give it a definition. You choose to either accept and let go of the situation, or to go into emotional trauma. How deep and intense is your choice? Granted as children, we were unable to understand the consequences of how our parents treated us. But what about the children that seem to overcome almost insurmountable odds and successfully make it out of abusive families without the scars of emotional trauma? It all has to do with our viewpoint and how we respond.

An electrical current flows unimpeded through a thick copper wire, but if we run the same current through a fine wire, the wire will glow hot and may burn out. This is because the fine wire has greater resistance to the current—its ability to conduct electricity is less than the thick wire. Similarly, physical or emotional pain stems from energy meeting resistance in a meridian that is somehow blocked. Suppose you fall down and hurt yourself. The pain you feel is real, and most people would claim that the pain cannot be released immediately.

However, it is evident that pain reactions are mind-induced. Many people undergo major surgery in China with no anesthesia other than acupuncture. Others use hypnosis, which through autosuggestion, suppresses pain during surgery. Countless other examples demonstrate the awesome power of the mind when used properly.

Aging, too, is a state of mind, a belief that we buy into completely. Society and the healthcare and insurance industries tell us that we have increased our longevity to seventy-five plus years. However, in Tibet, the life span is 125 or older in some cases. Tibetans are isolated from Western culture and medicine. They have no stress. Family units are close. The nuclear family is intact and there is no fight for equality that causes competition. Everyone is accepted as equal. They are also vegetarians for the most part. Their water has a high mineral content. Even those over one hundred get plenty of exercise. They have no air pollution, and they are not bombarded by insurance company mortality statistics.

Our bodies give us wake up calls all the time, but are we awake to the message? The first time, it may just be a whisper to get you to notice, then maybe a bump with pain attached. If that doesn't work, it may arrange a car wreck to get your attention. Your body will get more aggressive each time, and sustained denial and avoidance will eventually result in illness, disease or some other form of body or mind dysfunction. You can recognize the message, but first you may have to overcome denial.

If you are in denial, you may be using an addictive or dysfunctional behavior pattern to maintain control over other people, in an effort to extract their conditional love and acceptance. No one has to suffer, however. Peace, happiness, harmony, joy and unconditional love are our birthright, but most of us get love in odd and dysfunctional ways, since, during childhood, we were improperly programmed about what love is.

As children, if we interpret any focused attention as love, we may continue to do that as adults, and wonder why our lives do not give us what we want. Twelve-step recovery programs often

207

trade one addiction for another. Addiction indicates that you're overdoing it and getting too much of something you don't want. Some people say they are addicted to love, but how can you become addicted to something that most people do not get enough of? Can that really be true about love? I don't think so. To me, it is relationship addiction, based on the fear of being alone.

You will follow the path and act according to the contents of your programs and their files. However, based on sheer willpower, people do successfully countermand their files and programs. But it's hard on the body/mind, however, because you create a double-bind.

When your mind's program tells you, "You cannot do this particular task," but you do it anyway, it takes a lot of energy, drains your adrenal glands, and wears you out. It is much easier to clear and release the programs, so that your life can flow, instead of bumping into boulders in your path.

The more stress we place on ourselves, and the more we speed up to stay with the pace of life, the more pressure we place on our minds and bodies. Our body/minds should function at a frequency of 25-to-35 Hz, yet most people operate between 9000 and 9500 Hz, which strains the adrenal glands.

As the frequency increases, increased adrenaline production serves as an antidote to the "happy" brain chemicals— serotonin, interluken, interferon, etc. As a result, we can burn out and go into adrenal insufficiency, which in turn can cause chronic fatigue syndrome, Epstein-Barr syndrome and chronic depression. (See Appendix C for a description of the Body/Mind StressBlocker that will bring down the frequency and cause accelerated healing of the body.)

Summary of How the Mind Works

My research into how the mind receives and processes information, and the effects on the body, has found many variables, because people interpret sensory input differently. In my seminars, I hear many family members discuss their childhoods among themselves and exclaim, "I know we're from the same family, but it seems that we were raised by different parents, because I didn't experience what you are describing." People can also be victims or survivors. Survivors view life with a generally positive outlook, whereas victims usually have a negative viewpoint as one of those women did.

When negative sensory input comes our way, we have just thirty seconds to decide how we're going to handle it (again, see Figure 6). We have to decide how we are going to respond or react to the input. If we can reject negative input, it will not affect us (as you can see in the diagram).

The brain is not the only part of the body with the ability to think. Every cell has a limited ability to make decisions based on input by neuropeptides and cytokinins. Every organ and gland has receptors that communicate with the brain's switching network, and evaluate all sensory input as it comes in for interpretation and application.

The brain's switching network consults your mind's database for files from the past and decides how you will react or respond, based on how you reacted in the past. Your mind interprets the feeling, which in turn causes a chemical reaction or response in the body at all levels. A positive feeling creates a positive response that sends supportive information to the cells, organs and glands, which in turn strengthens and builds health and wellness and a feeling of well-being. This feeling causes the release of "happy" brain chemicals: interlukins, seratonin, interferon, and L-Dopa, which in turn causes a feeling of peace, happiness, harmony and joy.

Negative feelings, on the other hand, cause a chain reaction, shutting down the happy chemicals and sending negative reactions through the neuropeptides and cytokinins to the body at every level, which begins to suppress, depress and breakdown cellular structures in every cell, organ and gland. If the mind senses attack, it sets up a fight-or-flight syndrome.

The immune and endocrine systems try to build a defense, but are limited because they cannot counteract the negative thought-form reaction that's being circulated throughout the body. The adrenals begin to pump all the time, creating adrenal overload as they try to support the body. The mind signals fear and stress, which cause the body to go into adrenal exhaustion trying to counteract the stress. If this continues to the point of adrenal exhaustion, it will cause depression.

If the Magical Child Syndrome is active and is triggered or activated, the personality self will shut down the Conscious Mind and disappear. Very seldom does one notice this happening, as it is all internal and begins within microseconds after the input is sensed. There is one exception to this reaction: those who are strong enough and have the willpower to stay in control can ward off the downer reaction for years.

Eventually, though, the body will break down and the mind will crash the operating system with traumatic results, as the person will crash with depression or a serious illness. We can't keep warding off the results of negative attitudes, feelings and sensory input. No matter how we defend ourselves, we will eventually break down.

In some situations, people cannot accept positive support because they have never experienced unconditional love and acceptance. They interpret the support as an attempt to control or manipulate them, so they reject it, which results in the reaction going negative, with the above reactions. All they have ever received was conditional love, which had strings attached.

These reactions are the basis of psychoneuroimmunology. We must stop negative thought patterns, avoiding negative input at all costs, as it sets up patterns that are perpetuated in the mind every time we encounter the same triggers, catalysts, and activators. Each time the reaction happens, it creates a deeper rut in the file, so it becomes easier to fall into the same pattern. We cannot afford negative thoughts or sensory input, a these are the basis of all illness, disease and dysfunctional behavior. (A later chapter will reveal how to stop this cycle.)

There are two avenues for processing sensory input and information:

- Right-brain dominant people use their creative minds, which visualizes in pictures so these people can process a series of information in one pass. The right brain is a multi-tracking digital processor that works at very high speed.

- Left-brain dominant people are logical/ linear/ analog processors. They can only process one item or concept at a time. (With training, some people can become bicameral, using both sides of the brain.)

Since I am a right-brain processor, I sometimes get into trouble in conversations because left-brain people have difficulty following me, as I can talk about two subjects at the same time, changing the subject and running one subject into the next, without explaining what I'm doing. The person I'm talking to thinks I am still on the same subject and gets confused, unable to understand that I've moved on. Or I can bring up a subject about which we spoke in the past, yet the other person now has no recall of the subject and does not know what I'm talking about. (Even after I remind them, they often can't remember.)

Left- brain processors must search their databases to access information. If they have blocked memories, they will not be able to find the information at all. Right-brain digital processors access this information quickly, often with photographic memories so they can hold and access a tremendous amount of information in micro-seconds. (Not all right-brain people use this aspect of their minds, although it is available to them.)

My photographic memory is a real asset, as it records everything we talk about, including the client's reactions to the session and all the programs we worked on. At later sessions, even a year later, I can recall exactly the details of all previous sessions.

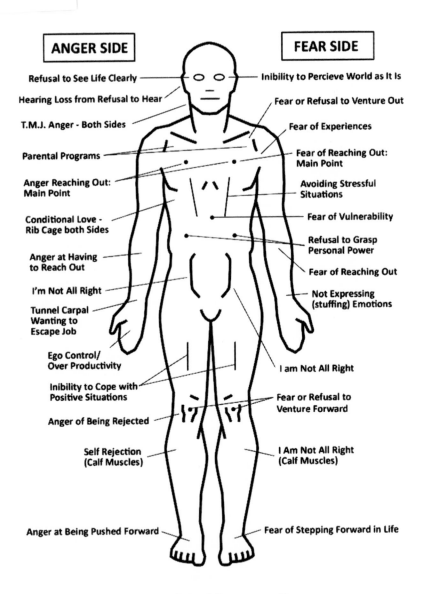

ANGER SIDE

Refusal to See Life Clearly

Hearing Loss from Refusal to Hear

T.M.J. Anger - Both Sides

Parental Programs

Anger Reaching Out:
Main Point

Conditional Love -
Rib Cage both Sides

Anger at Having
to Reach Out

I'm Not All Right

Tunnel Carpal
Wanting to
Escape Job

Ego Control/
Over Productivity

Inibility to Cope with
Positive Situations

Anger of Being Rejected

Self Rejection
(Calf Muscles)

Anger at Being Pushed Forward

FEAR SIDE

Inibility to Percieve World as It Is

Fear or Refusal to Venture Out

Fear of Experiences

Fear of Reaching Out:
Main Point

Avoiding Stressful
Situations

Fear of Vulnerability

Refusal to Grasp
Personal Power

Fear of Reaching Out

Not Expressing
(stuffing) Emotions

I am Not All Right

Fear or Refusal to
Venture Forward

I Am Not All Right
(Calf Muscles)

Fear of Stepping Forward in Life

Figure 6: Stored Programs, Front

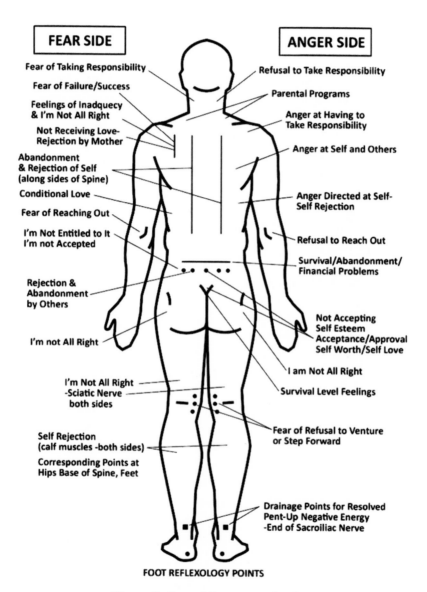

FEAR SIDE

ANGER SIDE

Fear of Taking Responsibility

Fear of Failure/Success

Feelings of Inadquecy & I'm Not All Right

Not Receiving Love- Rejection by Mother

Abandonment & Rejection of Self (along sides of Spine)

Conditional Love

Fear of Reaching Out

I'm Not Entitled to It I'm not Accepted

Rejection & Abandonment by Others

I'm not All Right

I'm Not All Right -Sciatic Nerve both sides

Self Rejection (calf muscles -both sides)

Corresponding Points at Hips Base of Spine, Feet

Refusal to Take Responsibility

Parental Programs

Anger at Having to Take Responsibility

Anger at Self and Others

Anger Directed at Self- Self Rejection

Refusal to Reach Out

Survival/Abandonment/ Financial Problems

Not Accepting Self Esteem Acceptance/Approval Self Worth/Self Love

I am Not All Right

Survival Level Feelings

Fear of Refusal to Venture or Step Forward

Drainage Points for Resolved Pent-Up Negative Energy -End of Sacroiliac Nerve

FOOT REFLEXOLOGY POINTS

Figure 7: Stored Programs, Back

How the Body Stores Programs Locked in Cellular Memory

Figures six and seven show front and back "body maps" respectively, of where in the body various programs are stored. Each point on these maps is an acupuncture point. When emotional reactions occur and are recorded in the mind, then they are sent to these cellular memory locations. Each time they are deposited to the cellular memory database, they build up until they cause pain at this location.

Seldom can you release this pain with drugs or manipulation, because the programs that hold them in place must also be addressed. To release the program, all we need do is find the cause and core issue, repeat an affirmation to forgive, and then accept the situation as cleared. The pain will be released. These cellular memory programs start recording *in utero*. As early as the first trimester, the fetus begins recording in its cellular memory how the mother and those around her feel about her being pregnant. After birth, the cellular memory is transformed into programs that will continue to build, based on how the child is treated by its primary caregivers.

When a program has an emotional charge to a situation, the mind deposits it in a specific location in the body. Locating these acupuncture points has been a twenty-year research project. When I located a specific emotional reaction, I also found that all similar syndromes or reactions were stored in the same place. If this showed up in twenty or more clients, I added it to the body map. Everyone, male or female, stores the programs in the same locations.

Some healers claim they can remove the pain associated with the program by many different methods, but I have yet to see long-lasting results. Many of my clients who have seen alternative practitioners tell me that the pain, illness, or dysfunctional pattern was relieved, yet it later returned. I have found that if the program is not removed from all files, it will reactivate when the same catalyst triggers it. Our minds back up all their files daily while we sleep, and our dreams are often windows into this back-up process. As the two figures show, fear is stored on the left side of the body; anger on the right, with rejection along the spine. In fact, we have uncovered sixty individual locations for specific other emotional, dysfunctional programs.

Summary

This is an overview of how our minds function. I am writing a new book which will be a more definitive look at the subject. Many psychologists and medical researchers look at the mind as a part of the brain. My own research, along with that of many others, perceives the brain as a switching network, more of a central-processing center for our minds, which direct the brain's functions. In my new book, " Your Mind Is Your Savior Or Your Enemy," I lay out how your mind can become your support system—for success or for failure—and the methods for programming it to broadcast an effective self image that supports you in your life.

Your Body is Talking, Are You Listening?

Chapter 15

Sub-Personalities and Multiple Personalities: Origins and Effects

In the beginning of my research on how the mind functions, I was unaware of any form of control, outside of habit patterns and what I had read about the function of the brain and the neurological system. Of course, I had known about sub-personalities from my college psychology classes, but it was no big deal, since no one put much value on sub-personalities.

I never knew they had so much influence in our lives until 1989, when I began to realize how they functioned, but the full impact did not come until 1992, when I discovered that Ego was not the villain. The discovery of personality self and the committee of sub-personalities opened a new concept in how the mind functioned.

In my college studies of Transactional Analysis, we worked with the five basic sub-personalities: Inner Child, Critical Parent, Survivor Self, Inner Adult, and Inner Self. These sub-personalities are the group that is in our mind's files from birth. They can have a major effect on your life and, if you operate on autopilot or give your power away to any of them, they will function *as you* and *for you*, projecting their agendas on your actions.

Over the years, we have discovered the personality self is composed of more than seventy-five sub-personalities, along with all the mind's operating systems that drive them.

Your Body is Talking, Are You Listening?

We have also added another sub-personality to the basic five: discovering the Shadow Self was another major breakthrough, for we had discovered the sub-personality that creates much of the conflict in our lives.

Shadow Self works through and with Critical Parent, and focuses on criticism, negativity, anger, resentment, blame and rage, because it likes to stir up trouble, conflict and argument. (Shadow Self is the creator of compulsive/obsessive behavior patterns. It is also the cross-talker chattering in the backs of our minds when we want to be quiet.)

For many years, I had assumed that Ego was the enemy that sabotages our lives, but when I learned about the myriad sub-personality selves and their agendas, I changed my views. I know now that instead of trying to vanquish Ego, we must make friends with it, and erase the operating systems from which the controlling sub-personalities derive their power.

This is one of the most important finds we made in developing Neuro/Cellular Repatterning. (Few people are aware of this concept or want to accept it, so several other chapters in this book will repeat it for emphasis.)

Quite often, when I explain my concept about Ego, people say, "That sounds reasonable. I can accept that." Then, ten minutes later, they fall right back into the old Ego theory. I have had to make peace about this issue with myself, so I do not force the issue or jump on people who do not understand the new theory, and stick to the old concept that *Ego* causes our behavior problems. When we discovered that the mind is not limited to the basic five sub-personalities, we discovered that the Personality Self really runs our life, with its committee of seventy-five or more sub-personalities, each acting out a specific behavior trait.

As we dug deeper into this, we discovered that Personality Self that people have traditionally labeled Ego is self-righteous self. As we expanded our knowledge of the concept, we found that we could change clients' personality traits, which changed their life paths. People who were considered self-centered and egotistic would become more compassionate and supportive. Those who were non-assertive would move to a more assertive position and reclaim their personal power.

Over time, we were able to show people how to reconstruct their personality so they would be more effective in their life. This is the goal of psychology, but it does not work very well. It certainly didn't work for me, so I gave it up and began to search for a new approach. The process of Voice Dialogue, developed by Hal Stone, Ph.D., introduced us to "disowned selves." It uses three chairs, one each for the positive and negative aspects of self, and a third in the center for the inner self (the balanced self who will generally tell the truth.)

I was working with Stone's son, Joshua, at the time, and it seemed to be a very workable concept, as we had helped quite a few clients with the process. (Having since discovered how the mind is really controlled—by sub-personalities, multiple personalities, and the three saboteurs and possessive beings—I now wonder exactly who we were talking to sometimes.) As the pattern unfolded, I began to discover who we had been talking to during Voice Dialogue. I just did not know who was talking at the time. Hal Stone described many of them as disowned selves with whom we had to make peace. My feeling was that I wanted to erase these disowned selves and delete them from the files, but I found that we first had to get in contact with the programs running them, and then clear them.

As we were able to rewrite the scripts we live by, we found we could change the person's direction in life, by simply deleting the program, erasing the multiple and sub-personalities and their operating systems, and installing new programs to replace the dysfunctional one. This will then change the client's basic behavior pattern. Negative habit patterns disappear as clients reclaim their personal power and become responsible for their own life paths.

The five basic sub-personalities are indigenous to our minds. This means that they cannot be deleted or destroyed, even though I would like to have done so many times. We must train the basic sub-personalities to work with us, and give us back control.

As children, we needed their help to navigate through life but, as we grew up and learned to deal with life, they should fade into the background. However, they do not "fade away" when people do not take their personal power back from them, preferring to relinquish responsibility for their life.

In the past, sub-personalities were believed to be located in the Subconscious Mind; in fact, they reside in the Middle Self and function autonomously, almost as a separate mind. It was also thought that the five were driven by Ego, which spawned the term "egotistical" since they do, at times, display what most people mean by the term "egotistical behavior."

However, this is erroneous, because Ego has no driving force that would cause it to act egotistically, nor can it recreate a sub-personality trait driven by the controller, justifier, self-righteous, competitor, confronter, know-it-all, manipulator, authority and judger sub-personalities. The only part of t h e mind that can create a sub-personality is Middle self, which serves as Program Manager (see Figure 8).

When people are on autopilot, the sub-personalities run the body/mind on their own, having no real connection with Ego at all. The more we evaluated Ego, we found it to be simply a file manager for the database in Subconscious Mind's computer, serving as librarian, secretary and file clerk. When we stopped confronting Ego as an adversary, it became friendly and helpful.

We also discovered an interesting phenomenon: people's memories started getting better, proving that Ego was the file clerk for our memories. As we delved into this unknown area of the mind, we found that the makeup of the mind was as orderly and smooth-running as a computer running an operating system and programs that could be reprogrammed.

We believed that Middle self was the area of the mind in which sub-personalities operated; at least, that was our impression until we ran into autopilot, which has sub-personalities that created when we let autopilot run our lives and refuse to take responsibility.

Although it resides in Middle self, autopilot operates from the Conscious mind working through Artificial Intelligence. We found many sub-personalities, each driving a particular emotion or behavioral habit pattern. We also found that sub-personalities can drive beliefs, interpretations, feelings and programs. The more we evaluated the personality self, the more we found that all emotional behavior is caused by sub-personalities. Programs cause emotional behavior, but they must have sub-personalities to act out the emotional behavior.

People often blame the inner child for unruly behavior, and then deny that they have control over it. Many people in twelve-step recovery groups, such as Codependents Anonymous, separate out the inner child as "not them" and then blame it for their emotional behavior. But inner child *is* part of us, and we must get it to grow up and stop acting like a victim.

The degree to which it will fight for control depends on how much power we have given to it. Most of the time, it is not working on its own but through the Magical Child syndrome.

Survivor self sees its role as protecting you, so it will sabotage you if it feels you are going the wrong direction. Critical Parent berates you for not doing an effective job, so that you reject yourself. Critical parent is the most active in children because they feel they do not match up (due to rejection and parental expectations) and it spares no effort in validating any perceived shortcomings.

As you grow up, you create the judger, controller, justifier, manipulator, competitor, avoider and myriad anger- and- fear selves that run your life. Each time you run into a problem you cannot handle, your mind searches the database and may create another sub-personality to deal with it.

```
┌─────────────────────────────────────┐
│ Any action we take to control,      │
│ judge, blame, justify, manipulate,  │
│ or give away our power and          │
│ become a victim, such as any        │
│ anger or fear-based emotion.        │
└─────────────────────────────────────┘
```

```
┌──────────────────────────────┐
│ A base sub-personality is    │
│ created when we take a       │
│ certain controlling action   │
│ over a period of time.       │
└──────────────────────────────┘
```

```
┌──────────────────────────────┐
│ A denial sub-personality     │
│ is created when we justify   │
│ and denythat we have         │
│ taken any action over a      │
│ period of time               │
└──────────────────────────────┘
```

```
┌──────────────────────────────┐
│ This sub-personality         │
│ is caused by habitual        │
│ patterns that are            │
│ created by a belief or       │
│ a program that is part       │
│ of the operating system      │
└──────────────────────────────┘
```

```
┌──────────────────────────────┐
│ When we suppress the         │
│ feeling or the behavior      │
│ and are not aware that       │
│ we are denying it, it will   │
│ shift into denial of denial. │
│ At this point, it does not   │
│ exist in our reality at all. │
│ We continue the behavior     │
│ even though we're            │
│ unaware of it.               │
└──────────────────────────────┘
```

```
┌──────────────────────────────┐
│ If we are not aware          │
│ of the behavior and          │
│ continue to operate          │
│ from the program,            │
│ Middle Self will shift       │
│ to auto-pilot.               │
└──────────────────────────────┘
```

Figure 8: Creation of a Sub-Personality

If you encounter a habit pattern that you don't want to deal with, and choose to delude yourself, your denial creates a denial sub-personality to justify your behavior and cover it up, so that you don't even understand what you are running away from. If you try to suppress the pattern totally, the sub-personality will create a "denial of denial" sub-personality to bury it completely. You will not even recognize the behavior pattern, yet it is clearly visible to other people.

This cascade effect was one of the most significant causes of separation from self. When separation from self begins to take hold, an inner shadow sub-personality blocks the person from understanding this phenomena. The more we go into denial of separation from self, more inner shadow sub-personalities are created. I have removed up to thirty-five inner shadow sub-personalities that were feeding negative self-talk to a client.

Dysfunctional programs and patterns often have a backup sub-personality. If these are not addressed, they will create a new program or belief to drive them. We once believed that we simply had to get to the core issue and the base cause. Now we realize that we must also check for sub-personalities. That's not all, each sub-personality has denial sub-personalities, with a backup for each.

The hardest sub-personalities to locate are the "denial-of-denial" ones. Unless you're willing to face the truth and go for it, dropping all of the illusions you operate from, and face the situations you are able to deal with, you cannot get to these denial sub-personalities. They are there for the very purpose of denial, so you will be blocked, making even just locating them very hard.

If you feel you have handled the situation (when, in fact, all you did was suppress or release the feeling with a cathartic emotional discharge), then you put the issue into denial. The issue continues to be active except that it is suppressed and no longer accessible by your Conscious mind.

If the issue surfaces again and you do not clear it, then it goes into a "no perception of denial- of-denial" file. The more we deny behavior patterns and issues, the more we tell Middle self that we do not want to take responsibility. This causes Middle self to refer the issue to autopilot, which in turn creates more sub-personalities to handle our lives. We have found that most people have little control over their lives. I used to believe that autopilot was not an effective part of clients' minds, so I would erase the operating system and assume it was gone. At the time, I did not realize how little control people had over their life, so when I erased the operating system, my clients would often pass out because I had crashed their Middle self's operating system. It was then that I decided we should make friends with Middle self and find an affirmation to reinstall a new operating system.

When we did that, everything went much more smoothly. In the past, I had released sub-personalities and assumed that we were finished with them. To my surprise, clients would return for the next session with the exact same sub-personalities reinstalled, and sometimes with *more* than they had left with the last time. This was a disappointment to both of us. When we began to look at this in depth, we found that people could recreate and install the same sub-personalities if they didn't change their habit patterns. This was based on their beliefs that governed situations in their lives. The sub-personalities that are present for each session indicate clients' weaknesses. This lets us understand the blocks they have in their path.

The sub-personalities and programs that reoccur indicate where their issues are located and where they lose control or give their power away. When people decide to take responsibility and reclaim their personal power, Middle self will stop creating sub-personalities, and autopilot and Artificial Intelligence will cease interfering to control the situation

Believing that we had released all of the body-based programs, the beliefs, the core issues, and the base cause, we wondered why a program we had released would often resurface. When we discovered the denial and denial-of-denial sub-personalities, we found that they could re-establish a habit pattern and the programs that run it. If any part of the file is not erased, it can be recreated and reactivated. The result is that, even though we've cleared all beliefs and the programs, the denial sub-personalities can restructure and reactivate an old program.

When we discovered that the mind backs up all files every day, we ran into another challenge. Why were these sub-

personalities recreating themselves when we had removed them. We discovered two reasons.

First, the recreator, regenerator, reactivator, reproducer and reinstaller programs were operating in backup files in a way similar to a computer virus: if we didn't clear them also, they would reinstall the files.

Second, if clients continue the dysfunctional behavior habit pattern, the "virus-like" programs will reinstall the sub-personality that corresponds to the behavior pattern from which they are operating.

We must be vigilant and watch everything we *think*, *say* and *do*, plus we must monitor everything anybody says to us. All sensory input is potential programming unless we are aware and know how to neutralize or cancel any negative or confronting sensory input.

An example of this is a client we'll call Kelly. She was in a failure syndrome, to the point where she couldn't accomplish anything on time. When I started working with her, I was amazed at the number of sub-personalities she had.

This was a few years ago and, at that time, we were counting the number of programs and sub-personalities but once we got into the millions, we could not seem to break them down or erase them. We no longer count them, as it's faster to just refer to *an infinite number* to represent all the sub-personalities and programs.

Every time I saw Kelly for a session, she had recreated over 100,000 sub-personalities, within a month. In one instance, we did treatments two days apart. We cleared her sub- personalities, but then found over 800 Procrastinator sub- personalities in the second session.

We were both frustrated because she was running around in circles and just could not accomplish anything. Only when there was a deadline could she get anything done, and even then only at the last minute.

At this point, I decided on another approach, so I asked her to write out an affirmation in longhand, 21 times a day for 21 days:

"I realize that I am unable to accomplish anything that I set out to do. I am committing myself to take control of my life now. I am 100 percent committed to disciplining myself to take responsibility and follow through with my priorities each day. I am loving myself and forgiving myself for failing to follow through in the past. I am doing that now." I told her we could not do any more sessions until she completed the 21 days. It took Kelly five attempts over six months to complete the 21-day program. Her first try was four days; the second, nine; the third, she lasted 14 days; the fourth, 19.

In this exercise, you must write the affirmation 21 times within a 24-hour period. If you miss one day, you must start over from Day One. When she had dropped out at 19 days, she knew she only had two hours left to finish on that day, but had started watching television, fallen asleep and lost her concentration. Having missed the 24-hour stipulation, she had to start over from Day One again. This time, she made up her mind to discipline herself to make the 21-day program work. She did and it worked.

Once Kelly learned about discipline and commitment, she accomplished more in the next four months than in the previous fifteen years. In her next session, we found very few sub-personalities, which was gratifying to us both. In the following sessions, the sub-personalities were eliminated altogether. A few popped up occasionally in subsequent sessions but she now has taken control of her life, and it is working well.

Since I have been working with the twenty-one-day program, we have seen amazing results with people who have difficulty accomplishing any task. If clients are afraid about something in their life, writing down the affirmation consistently for twenty-one days removes the fear by breaking through the feelings of resistance. This kinesthetic learning process works because we are repeating in our mind as we write the affirmation, and following it with our eyes. I often give clients twenty-one-day program "homework" to break through blocked habit patterns. It works well if they discipline themselves to follow through. As with any change, it is intention, commitment, consistency—and discipline, discipline, discipline!

Recently, we discovered another file that explains why some programs get reinstalled. Whenever I am frustrated in solving a problem, I find that if I just become quiet and listen to my intuition, the answer will simply come to me. I did this one time while sitting in a steam room at my health club (I often meditate in the steam room or sauna).

Suddenly, I realized that we had to look into future time-lines. Many programs can be locked into these future time-lines, along with specific dates when they are to activate or reactivate. This was a major find, because we have now been able to find and clear sub-personalities with programs that we not only put in denial-of-denial, but also put into future time-lines to be dealt with in the future.

If you feel that you have handled a situation when, in fact, all you did was suppress the emotion, you have created "no perception of denial" and the issue effectively no longer exists in your Conscious Mind. As it's suppressed, it will be buried in denial-of-denial, and becomes lost in your mind.

~ ~ ~

We all want to live in peace, happiness, harmony and joy, with an abundance of prosperity and unconditional love, but how many really achieve that? My experience is that less than twenty per cent are satisfied with their lives, while only five per cent are really happy with life as it is, and would not change a thing. Many people will delude themselves into feeling they are happy when, in fact, on checking with their Inner Mind's view of life, we find different answers.

Furthermore, less than ten percent of people love themselves or will allow others to love them. This is because most people want, but are not willing to apply themselves, to have the bounty that intention, commitment and discipline bring when they take responsibility and reclaim their personal power. It's the same old story—it takes a willingness to work through the anxiety so that you can run your life, rather than hand the reins over to autopilot and sub-personalities.

How many people in serious pain are told by their doctor, "You will just have to live with it, or you can take drugs to kill the symptoms"? Even though this statement is not true, most doctors do not know any differently.

They can only practice what they were taught at medical school, without questioning it. The drug companies push drugs as the solution, and the doctors buy into it. A few have seen the truth but not many. Of course, the medical profession is doing the best it can with the tools and knowledge at its disposal, but control and authority sub-personalities block them from new knowledge.

Recently, a doctor told me, "I would like to get out of medical practice because my success rate is so low, but what would I do? I've tried alternative therapies with a little more success, but this doesn't seem to be the answer, either." Well, he found the answer—education—and began a two-step approach with his patients:

- First, he got people to see that there is an alternative to drugs, surgery and living in pain.
- Then he showed them how to modify and change their behavior, which meant he had had to do it himself before he could show others.

His challenge was to shift his practice and make enough money to cover overhead, but that was hard because most of his patients did not want to change their life style or behavior to adapt to his new approach. Most of them wanted him to take responsibility for their health because he was the doctor. They were satisfied to let autopilot and sub-personalities run their life. His decision was to find another source of income to see him

through while he gathered new patients who would adapt to his new approach.

Another doctor friend called me and wanted to rent my motor-home. He was taking a sabbatical to decide what his next move would be. When I met him I was in the wine business. We lost contact over the next twenty years. When I attended a workshop in Monterey, CA, I looked him up, and spent some time talking to him about what had happened over the last twenty years.

His new view of medicine did not fit into the wealthy, upper-class community where his practice was located. His patients took the view that money would buy them health, and they were willing to pay for it. Even though he had a very successful practice in normal allopathic medicine, he no longer wanted to practice in that way. As his patients began to fall away, he decided to take a sabbatical and reevaluate his options.

He closed his practice and wrote to all his patients, saying that he was switching over to a consulting practice out of his home. This would be one-on-one, with a sliding fee-schedule. His intention was to combine office visits with education. To attract new patients, he presented many lectures, but it did not work out. He discovered the same truth that my other doctor friend did: people simply did not want to take responsibility for their health, and would rather be on autopilot, playing the games that money allows for.

What was very interesting in his transition was he had cleared up his own life first. When I did some sessions with his son, he decided he needed to do some, too. I had empowered his son to standup for himself and reclaim his personal power. (This did not fit well with his mother, who was a controller of the first order.)

I then received a call from the doctor. He had decided it was time for him take control over his own life. Over the next few weeks we created fireworks. The result was that his wife, who was deep into denial and refused to acknowledge his new truth-based approach, ended the relationship.

He discovered he could not stay where he was if he wanted to continue in medicine. So he moved to another town that welcomed his new approach to medicine, and established a practice he could live with. He is now happy with his new life. (I find this happens quite often when you evaluate where you are and what your new goals are.)

Our research into the causes of depression has revealed that it's usually controlled by a sub-personality. The base cause is normally separation from self, not wanting to take responsibility, or running away from some situation that you do not want to face. The resulting worry, anxiety, self-pity, grief, confusion, indecision, disorientation, and feelings of futility and/or hopelessness plunges our body into depression.

Most of us are unwilling to detach and let go of what we know, because change is fearful. Quite often, people end up in depression because they refuse to deal with their frustration, disorientation and feelings of futility. The fact that the dollar value of the sale of illegal mind-altering drugs dwarfs any other component of this country's Gross National Product shows us the level of separation from self, which creates depression.

The cause of depression is that, under stress, the body's frequency increases and the adrenal glands release extra adrenaline, which focuses us on "fight or flight." Once the body's need for the excess adrenaline is over, the mind normally signals with a shot of nor-adrenaline, the antidote and neutralizer to the adrenaline. Under continued stress, though, the adrenal glands continue to kick in large amount of adrenaline to keep you functioning. However, you can eventually go into adrenal insufficiency as your body frequency goes up and the brain stops producing chemicals, including the so-called "happy-making" brain chemicals, which further depresses our body's functions.

Your energy is now coming from pure adrenaline rather than normal sources. As this continues, the overworked adrenal glands further slow down production. If they get down to twenty-five per cent of normal function, the body further slows down, until it goes into clinical depression and chronic fatigue syndrome. Usually, a person in depression is in denial, so a denial sub-personality runs the autopilot. It then becomes very difficult to reprogram any dysfunctional patterns.

At this point, you feel as if you're dying, because you're operating at twenty per cent or less of capacity. Chronic fatigue and/or Epstein-Barr syndromes set in, which makes it hard to function physically. As every function in your body slows down, you cannot digest food properly, so you do not get proper nutrition. Doctors cannot always diagnose what is happening, so they give "depression" as the cause and prescribe a legal mind-altering drug. This gives your body a boost and allows the adrenal glands to rest, but the body has no incentive to recover because the drugs are supporting and suppressing the symptom.

~ ~ ~

The ideal body frequency is 35-to-40 Hz (cycles per second). In this range, the body functions at its best and will heal quickly. We have worked with people under stress, whose body is operating as high as 9000-to-9500 Hz. Needless to say, this breaks the body down very quickly. We have also found that rewriting programs and clearing sub-personalities is easier when the body/mind functions at its optimum levels. (The StressBlocker™ is an electronic device that promotes optimum functioning. See Appendix D for details.)

The proper approach is to clear all the sub-personalities and multiple program-specific personalities laid down from birth to current time, and all the issues that created them. The ideal outcome is to clear all the sub-personalities so that clients can take control over their life, and that they no longer create future sub-personalities.

The first task is to locate dysfunctional multiple program driven personalities and find out what's driving them. If it's a program, we must find the base cause and where it's located on the body. Then we must find out what caused the client to react and trigger the chain of events (i.e., the core issue, be it a person or a situation). The next step is to go to the cellular memory and clear programs that control behavior patterns. These programs are locked into the body in one or more acupuncture points. When we clear and release the issue, we can rewrite the operating instructions and clear the sub-personality.

If it is a belief and not a reality, we can rewrite the operating instructions with a simple affirmation that clears both belief and concept. Now that we have the total picture, we are able to totally clear a program without recurrence.

Appendices

A: Case Histories

When I began this work in 1978, I was unaware of the potential of my discoveries. I was amazed that all I had to do was put my hands in the right places, and the acupuncture points I touched on the body acted as an extension of my mind. As if I was watching a video, I saw the very experience that the client was talking about. Quite often, my own experience would merge with the client's experience I was seeing.

To speed up the process, I asked clients, before they came to me, to list the issues with which they wanted to work, and not surprisingly, those issues were exactly what would come up in session. And even though we'd use the very same acupuncture points in subsequent sessions, different issues would come up, as if we were peeling an onion.

I carefully documented my clients' cases, to help us better learn about the mind and the dynamics it operated from. Actual names are not given to protect client confidentiality. (If any reader would like to contact clients directly, I will ask them if they wish to talk about their cases, and have that client contact the reader.)

Many times, all I have done is get the program going and if the client is committed, processing will continue and self-healing takes place. In some cases, we have to work an issue through each week over time. The most important part of the therapy seems to be the desire to let go of the dysfunction and take a new path. If clients are getting mileage out of a dysfunction, I can't do much for them.

It is important to understand that the key to healing is your ability to let go of the illusion that is blocking healing. As you will see in these examples, time to heal is not related to the severity of the dysfunction. Many times, a severe dysfunction will change in minutes, yet others may take years. The following cases discuss the basic dysfunctional program and how it was handled. The most important point to keep in

KEY to Homing – Let Go of the
ILLUSION that is Blocking
the Homing –

Your Body is Talking, Are You Listening?

mind is: <u>How many years did it take to create all the programs?</u>
<u>Do you expect to clear your life path in a few sessions?</u>
We can remove the big stumbling blocks, but the programs
and patterns that have been created from childhood traumas
and fears have to be removed completely. It has taken me over
twenty years to clear my path and I am not finished yet. But by
understanding how the mind operates, along with the sub-
personalities and their denial factors, we can dramatically
curtail the time needed for recovery.

Case #1. At age six, the client had been diagnosed with prism
vision and today wears corrective glasses. Her school assumed
she was learning-disabled, since she had to tilt her head at 45
degrees to see straight. The teachers' misreading of the
situation had effectively destroyed her self-esteem. Doctors
had declared it a genetic defect, and that nothing could be
done other than wear corrective glasses. Although they now
work well, she is a semi-pro skater, and every time she jumps,
her glasses fall off.

In four sessions, we identify the problem as a past-life issue
with the father. Working with both the father and the daughter,
we clear all their karmic contracts. By getting back to the base
cause, we clear the path for the body to alter the DNA pattern
and create perfect sight.

Case #2. The client has breast cancer that suddenly becomes
radical. Because of the speed of growth, her doctors want to
perform a mastectomy. She is a total vegetarian, no eggs or
dairy, and has good relationships with her parents and her
boyfriend. She has no problems at work. She runs twenty
miles a week, does aerobics and rides a bicycle. (A baffling
case, since none of the outside things that cause cancer are
present.)

As we work through her childhood, we find that her mother
had died of breast cancer when she was eight, as did two aunts.
At the funeral, her family members had been talking about
how they must be very careful with their female children,

235

because this must run in the family. Her Middle self accepted the belief and her Subconscious Mind programmed it in. When she turned 40, her mind had a program that she would get breast cancer, so it was manifested in her physical body like a time-bomb.

Once we release the program and the belief, we ask her mind to heal the cancer and erase all the programming. She has no reason to have cancer so it disappears in fifteen minutes. This is done with affirmations only. The client cancels all future doctor appointments.

Case #3. A client has severe pain. We find he was rejected by both parents due to mother's pregnancy prior to marriage. Also, the child was the wrong gender. In his mother/son relationship, he sought out a mother who would love him, and his neediness destroyed the relationship.

We release the pre-birth rejection with all its programs, and then he forgives the parents. Clearing all the childhood self-rejection and the feeling of not being alright opens up new doors to balance. Forgiving involves working through all the childhood trauma and rejection up to the current relationship. The main change is his relationship with self. When that is cleared so that he can love himself, his life turns around and the pain simply vanishes.

Case #4. A female client asks why nothing works in her life. She has had many jobs but always seems to get laid off or fired. She has never had a successful relationship. Severe pain along the spine indicates total self-rejection. We find she has no self-worth, that she feels her value is zero, so why would anyone want to have her as an employee? In exploring her past, we find she was an unexpected "mistake" child who her mother tried to abort. She was treated like an intruder in the family. Her mother tried to delegate caring for her to her older siblings, who did not want to take it on, so even they rejected her. We reclaim her self-worth and self-esteem by forgiving and understanding the parents and loving and forgiving her brothers and sisters.

In clearing the rejection and abandonment, and reclaiming her personal power, we find that she has no program about self-love or receiving love. Once we re-establish balance in her life, she is able to get a good job and form a supportive relationship.

Case #5. A 47-year-old woman has not had a stable relationship in her life. She has been married five times, and all ended with the husband cheating and having affairs. She does not love herself and will not accept love from others. She is not functioning in her body, and her polarity is switched. The first picture I see when looking for the points of pain is one of the father yelling at the mother, "You're giving this child all the attention. I don't get any attention anymore. This child is the center point in your life." The "adult-child" father feels rejected because the mother has to take care of the child and the child competes with the father for the mother's love, while the mother has to straddle the fence to keep peace. The child cannot understand why she gets a lot of attention when the father is not there, but little when he's home. Over about ten sessions, she reclaims her personal power, self-esteem and self-worth.

Case #6. A client introduces me to his friend who stutters so badly that his neurology practice is almost empty. Who wants to see a stuttering neurologist? Apparently not many people. With kinesiology, we find that he started stuttering 15 years ago when his house was burned down. In a past life, he had burned a farmer's barn down in a fit of anger. The karmic lesson came back to roost. We clear the karmic contract and the stuttering stops. He is punishing himself for this lesson. He had already paid the price by losing his house but he is still punishing himself 15 years later. He is so impressed he takes us to dinner, and in the restaurant, he begins to stutter again. I ask him, "Are you having doubts about what we've accomplished?"

He replies, "I'm having a hard time reconciling this situation. I have ten years of college in my specialty and you have no credentials as far as I can see. Yet, none of the neurologists or the speech therapists were able to accomplish anything, but you cleared it all in twenty minutes."

I ask him, "What's more important, credentials or the result? You can see and experience the result of stuttering and what it's done to your life, and now you're free of it."

He agrees, and we finish by repeating the affirmation and asking his Ego and Subconscious Mind to destroy the programs sabotaging his success and lock them up in the archives. That is the end of the stuttering for ever.

Case #7. A women is referred to me because she has flunked the teacher's credential test six times. She feels rejected by the system, and is willing to give up, accept her lot in life, and teach at a substandard level. On checking, we find that her husband continually tells her she's no good at math, so how can she expect to pass the test.

She did have problems with math in school, but her field has no math in it, so that's not the problem. She has a program about giving her power to authority figures. Her husband is an attorney, and she gives her power away to him. (As children, this program is meant to give respect to our parents and obey them, but as adults, it has no value.) We identify her challenge as stopping from giving her power away to authority figures. We release the belief and the program about not being good at math, and reinforce her personal power by erasing the authority-figure program. We write new scripts to take her power back, and know that she can pass the test effortlessly, which she does so on the next try, passing in the 92nd percentile. (In the past, she could not even finish the test in the allotted time.)

What is the difference? Her self-worth and her self-esteem have been recovered. She now sees herself as all right, as a person who has innate value. The "system" had nothing to do with rejecting her; it was her self-rejection and lack of perceived value that caused her failure, as with most people.

Case #8. A client labels her symptoms as Chronic Fatigue Syndrome. On evaluation, I find she's telling herself that she is "sick and tired of this and that" all the time. She is really backing out of life and does not want to participate. All her life, she has taken care of others. Her Middle Self accepts the "sick and tired" statements. Coupled with the caretaker personality, her Ego and Middle Self listen to her constantly telling herself she should stop, so they step in to help as best they can.

When I bring this up to her, she is amazed to learn that our thoughts have power. We release the program about being sick and tired, and reclaim her power to say "no" when people impose on her. The fatigue disappears.

Case #9. A client has severe bursitis, and in working with him, I discover in me a lot of suppressed anger towards my mother. I do not want to accept it, but I find that I have my mother on a pedestal: "You have to respect and accept mothers unconditionally." I uncover denial, but don't know how to handle it at the time.

As we struggle through over fourteen hours of work with eight different practitioners, my left shoulder locks up. My shoulder pain is excruciating, as though a knife has been stuck in my shoulder. After a very painful week, we finally clear it. Now we can walk throughout the same process in a session or two.

Symptoms such as this are about saying how we feel and speaking our truth. Telling people what they want to hear rather than saying what you want to say will only intensify the condition. Most people try to blame it on a pulled muscle.

I have found the pain can be released as soon as we release the feeling of not being alright, and can reclaim our personal power so that we can speak our truth. Once we write a new script, the pain goes away. The lesson is to take our power back and release ourselves from the fear of rejection.

Why the mind chooses a particular dysfunction is unknown. Two people may be in the same situation but manifest different dysfunctions, depending on the core issue. For example, the neurological dysfunction of Multiple Sclerosis (MS), Lou Gehrig Disease (ALS), Muscular Dystrophy (MD) and Parkinson's Disease all operate from the same basic program, yet exhibit different symptoms.

My work with many people with these conditions has met with marginal success. Clients want to escape something in their life path, but if they are willing to face what they are running away from, we can release and heal it. Many times, they are trying to force someone to take care of them, usually stemming from childhood attempts to get recognition by someone.

Neurological dysfunction presents some of the most difficult cases to deal with, as clients are usually in denial of their anger. They are getting a lot of satisfaction for their resentment, and the sub-personalities want to hold on to the condition because it provides a means of controlling others.

Case #10. With an MS client, we begin with looking at the childhood programs that are similar to those held by many rejected children. Feeling unacknowledged at school and not appreciated for his work, he became a super-student, trying to impress his parents that he had value. Although he graduated from college at the top of his class, it seemed that nobody would validate his accomplishments. After a few failures in business, he began to develop MS symptoms, and they progressed to the point where he became wheelchair-bound.

When I meet him, he is making a commitment to recover. A controlling sub-personality is running his life and forcing people to take care of him. In this way, his mind's interpretation is that he is finally getting acknowledged.

After many sessions, we get him back on his feet and functioning. His Middle Self and Ego are intent on getting this end result, and they don't care how they do it. When he reclaims his power and regains control over his life, he recovers completely.

Case #11. At one of my lectures, a very intelligent woman asks me about MS. Apparently, brain scans and MRI showed lesions on her brain that indicate MS. She is an instructor at a college, but has become so debilitated she lost her job, which caused a rapid downturn in her health. She can no longer drive a car and is considered legally blind. She is losing motor control of her legs and arms. She is also trying to escape an abusive husband who is not functioning rationally. She is finally able to break free when he ends up the hospital and almost dies. When we look at her situation, we also find a very abusive childhood. I work with her over a two-year period and we recover her eyesight so that she can drive a car and walk again. At this point, she is recovering slowly.

Case #12. Another MS client drives over five hours to see me. In two sessions, we clear the total disease syndrome and she returns to perfectly normal health. Her base causes were the same as all the others, but the difference is that she is willing to let the past go and release herself from blaming anyone. When she accepts that she created the MS to get a desired result, she is able to break the disease syndrome completely. (This is the hardest syndrome to break down and get a person to reclaim their personal power.)

Case #13. When a client was not validated for his ability, he became a bookworm to prove that he could be someone. He graduated from UC Berkeley, *magna cum laude*, but the only problem was that he had cut himself off from everybody and everything in his life to succeed.

He had joined a group led by a guru, who insisted that his followers had to do everything his way. This matched his program because he wanted someone to run his life for him. He had met his wife in this group, and she was very controlling. This also served his need to be validated. He had worked for a bank with good performance reviews, so he had been promoted, but this validation had come from the outside, and not from within, so it was worthless.

A week after he had started his new job, he'd had a *grand mal* seizure at work and been taken to the hospital. He had also had his driver's license revoked so his wife now had to drive him to work . . . and to my appointment.

He was able to recognize the program, release the pattern, and reclaim his personal power, but once he did, he started to have relationship problems. His wife objected to him taking back his power, because she had enjoyed their "mother/son" relationship as it was.

The more he tried to regain control of his life, the more angry she got, and eventually she divorced him. At this latest rejection, down he went and had to have friends drive him to the appointments. We finally got him back on his feet so he could function once more.

Case #14. A women comes to me because she has just lost her job for the sixteenth time and has been through a divorce from her fifth husband, all five of whom parallel her father's behavior. She is looking for a "father" who will love and validate her, and faces the timeworn challenge of standing up, taking her power back and validating herself.

Her problems had started when she was three days old, and lying in the hospital bed with her mother. Her father had walked in and begun to berate the mother for almost dying in childbirth, and for having a fourth child that they could not afford. He had been irate that she had had to stay in the hospital for another week under observation.

(I witness this dialogue coming directly from her Subconscious Mind, yet she has no knowledge of the incident at all. When she goes to her mother with this information, her mother denies it.)

When we get her strong enough to confront her parents, she tells them that what they want to believe does not make

242

any difference, that she has released their lies, and feels great. She tells them she has forgiven them, and that she loves them for who they are. They all break down and, in a "happily ever after" outcome, talk the situation out.

She soon finds a great relationship and new job that's better than the last one she lost. Six months later, she calls to tell me she is now married and life is beautiful. All this took only six sessions.

Case #15. In 1986, a female client has the most interesting disease I have ever seen: breast cancer for the third time. However, she'd had cancer twice and had both breasts removed at different times. This time, the tumor was attached to the ribcage. I ask her, "Are you sure you want to live?"

Although she says "Yes," I find that she is in denial. Even though we release her "I want to die" program, it's back the following week. In her Middle Self, we find a program about wanting to die because she cannot control her husband (of which she is in total denial). We make peace with her attitude about her husband, and the "I want to die" program is gone.

Next, I ask her to put her cancer in my hand. She refuses, saying she doesn't want me to get cancer. I assure her that getting her cancer is not in my karmic pattern. She lets go of the cancer, and the force of it knocks me to the floor. That is my first experience of the power of vector disease energy when it lets go. (Now, I sit down when doing that treatment.)

I have encountered at least ten clients with the desire to die rather than deal with a personal confrontation. In the following three cases, I was unable to redirect the "I want to die" program.

Case #16. My father had four life-threatening diseases, including pancreatic cancer. The doctor gave him three months to live. He tried chemotherapy, but found it too painful and upsetting, so he followed my suggestions and, with the help of a sympathetic doctor, it was gone in six months. (In this country, of course, cancer is big money, and so the medical profession, FDA, and the medical boards conspired to run that doctor out of California and then out of the U.S. He is still very successful at treating cancer with alternative methods, and the vested interests wanted him out of business.)

Four years later, my father was totally clear of cancer, but needs an operation for an obstructed intestine. When he died about a year and a half later, the hospital tries to list his death as cancer, so I forced them to perform an autopsy, where they found no cancer at all, and so listed his death as "lung congestion."

In truth, he left because he did not want to confront my mother anymore. She was a master controller and he had given his power away to her. He gave up rather than follow his own desire to move near us to be close to his grandson. (He died at 76 and mother lived to 94. When she decided to go, within 24 hours she was gone.)

Case #17. A client who has been doing very well goes into decline when her husband leaves her alone for two weeks. He has taken elk-hunting trips for many years without any ill effects; the difference now is that she wants to hire a person to clean the house once or twice a week. The husband objects and says that because he is now retired, he will help her.

However, he is unwilling to clean the way she wants, and this blows up into a major conflict in their relationship. When he leaves for his trip, she feels overwhelmed and stops coming to me. When he returns, he does not support her desire to resume treatments.

About six months later, he calls to tell me that his wife wants to see me, but can't leave the house. I make the house call and find her withered away and barely able to talk. I give her the last rites, help her forgive herself for allowing this to happen, and give her permission to leave. I tell the husband that she will be gone in less than 24 hours. He calls me the following morning to confirm that she died during the night.

Case #18. Recommended by a friend, a man with colon cancer comes to see me. He and his wife are very wealthy and own a multimillion-dollar business. The wife is a workaholic and wants her husband to be the same.

Colon cancer is invariably caused by repressed anger, so that's where we start. Over time, I think we've cleared it all but am unaware of active sub-personality problems. He starts taking time off in the morning to play handball, which infuriates his wife. He convinces her to see me, but all she does is complain about how lazy he is.

For some reason, that marks the beginning of the end. He just starts withering away, with no real definable illness. He has many sessions with me, for which they pay well, but I am unable to pull him out of his downward spiral. He hangs on for a long time even though I give him permission to leave. What he wants is the love and attention that he never received from his mother or his wife. When he finally dies, I tell his wife why, but she totally denies any part in his death and criticizes me for my opinion.

Case #19. Another colon cancer client with a controlling workaholic wife comes to me after surgery, in the hope that I can find the cause so it will not reoccur. We clear all the usual causes for the cancer, but he chooses another means of death in order to escape his wife's control. He is completely unable to stand up to her and take his power back, and I am unable to stop him from creating his own death. He is very wealthy and she is angry that he is not putting in the hours that she wants him to devote to the business. In fact, she gets mad at me for recommending that he take time for recreation and exercise. Unable to digest food, he starts to lose weight and falls back.

Since there seems nothing I can do, I suggest that they go to a clinic in Mexico. The doctors at the clinic say they cannot do anything either, because he no longer wants to live and is not making any progress. I spend many hours with him trying to turn him around, but his wife has such control over him that

I am unable to do so. He is suffering, so I suggest to his wife that she give him permission to die. She does, and he is gone the next morning. (Since I discovered how to defuse the "I want to die" program, I haven't lost another client.)

Case #20. At a conference, a man asks me if I've had much luck with diabetes, a condition from which he almost died a year earlier. His eyesight is deteriorating, and his body is covered with large red splotches and bruises. His blood-sugar level is 410 (normal is 150), and he has to take insulin twice a day. In about an hour, we have cleared all the causes. I meet him six weeks later, and he tells me that his doctor confirms that he no longer has diabetes. All the symptoms have cleared, including the bruises and red ulcerated spots on his legs. I compliment him on his commitment, and tell him that if a person is as committed as he is, it works every time. Miracles are in your control and you create them.

Case #21. Many clients suffer from sciatic nerve pain, and I have found that it is invariably connected with an "I'm not all right" program, one of the most prevalent I see. In my case, sciatic nerve pain crippled me, almost to the point that at times I couldn't walk. It is almost always rooted in pre-birth rejection that keeps on building from many other situations throughout life.

Almost every client has anywhere from ten to several hundred programs locked in many body locations besides the sciatic nerves in the legs. Many clients cannot sit for more than an hour or so without needing to walk around for a few minutes. In addition to the pain, this rules out lengthy auto trips.

In all cases, this program stems from feeling rejected and abandoned as a child, and is compounded by rejection before birth. The parents' actual treatment of the child is not always the problem, but the child's perception of how it is treated. They can give a child all the right material comforts and educational opportunities, yet a child may still feel unloved and rejected. It is the personal touch and sense of love and acceptance that is required. Another child can grow up in what would be considered a deprived family, and be showered with far more love, support and encouragement to succeed in life than the pampered child.

Case #22. A new client comes to me because he cannot hold his head up without a brace. Take the brace off and his head falls down and rests on his shoulder. He has no strength in his neck muscles at all and is unable to work. He is also controlling of his wife. Neck pain is caused by not wanting to take responsibility for one's life. When I tell him that if we clear up his dysfunction, he will have to go back to work and must work at not controlling his wife, he refuses to continue the session.

Case #23. A man comes to one of my lectures, on the recommendation of his friend. He knows nothing about alternative healing or personal transformation, but starts attending my weekly lectures, and even comes for a session before the lecture, during which we start breaking down problems from his childhood.

One day, he says, "I want to work on my eyesight. You say that if a person wants to see their life clearly, they can regenerate their eyes. I'm ready for that."

We begin working on the reason why his eyes have deteriorated, and soon his eyes begin to clear up. One day, he announces that he is able to read without his glasses. A year later, he tells me, "I can see so well now that I don't even carry my glasses around any more."

This has happened to many people. There is only one catch–seeing your life clearly takes great commitment, because this is where denials really come into play.

Case #24. A client has serious breathing problems, yet the doctors cannot discover why. As I probe the area where she says it hurts, I find a very interesting program: fear of vulnerability and conditional acceptance. The programs are along the edge of the last rib from the side all the way to the center. When we clear all the programs, she can breathe normally.

Case #25. A man comes to my lecture with the intent of having me clear a diarrhea problem. He has to take the pills every three to four hours to keep it in control. His doctor (authority figure) has warned him that diarrhea is one of the side effects of the heart medicine he is taking. He stops the heart medication and uses chelation therapy instead, but, the diarrhea continues.

We release the doctor's proclamation and instructions in twenty minutes; the diarrhea stops immediately. (If the program is a belief and not a reality, then it can be released with a simple affirmation.)

Case #26. A woman client has the same back pain problem that I did. About twice a year, she has to go to the hospital and get an injection of muscle relaxant.

Middle-back pain can cause major problems. Self-rejection will cause the muscles alongside the spine to contract. I got to the point where I could not lift more then ten pounds without throwing my back out. The muscles would go into spasm and I could not move. The doctors wanted me in the hospital for traction to stretch it out, but I refused their kind offer. Today, with the help of the people who learned N/CR, my back is normal. (We cleared this client's problem in about five sessions.)

Case #27. At one of my lectures, a concert cello player asks about scleraderma, but I have not heard of the condition. We set up a session so that we can explore the cause. Apparently, her mother had forced her, as a child, to play the violin for three to six hours a day to get ready for a recital. Having had enough abuse, she had quit playing after the recital. Eight years later, her high school orchestra h a d needed a cello player so she volunteered.

After high school, she had continued with the cello and joined the Palo Alto Symphony Orchestra, but her mother had refused to attend any of the concerts, triggering a sense of rejection. Many years later, her local Unity Church h a d asked her to give a solo performance, for which she had gotten a standing ovation. Her mother, however, had still refused to attend. Shortly after this, she contracted this case of scleraderma. There is no known cure, and it's just a matter of time until the body simply ceases to function. The cause was an inability to handle her audiences' unconditional acceptance. In three sessions, we cleared the causes and the disease disappeared.

Case #28. My son believes totally in the N/CR process, and anytime anything happens to him, he asks for a session with me. One time, he'd fallen off a earthmover and injured his leg and hip. When the doctor prescribed pain pills and set up a physical therapy program, he checked first with me. We found that he had been offered a promotion at work, and had hurt himself to avoid taking the position. At least, that was what his mind was projecting. Once we cleared the fear of taking more responsibility, the pain disappeared and his injuries quickly healed up.

Case #29. At a lecture, a man describes himself as successful at everything he does. He has the big home, several cars, a plane, a yacht . . . and all the right memberships, in all the socially and politically correct organizations. However, he has recently realized that all his success is in the material world, that he is a workaholic, and that all his success and validation have come from his ability to create wealth.

After attending my first lecture, he knows there is something missing in his life. When he discusses the direction of their marriage with his wife, she tells him that she is well satisfied with their lavish lifestyle and does not share his curiosity about the spiritual aspects of life.

In session, we discover that his motivation to acquire material things and give his family everything they want is about getting validation and self-worth. He realizes that his parents had never given him the unconditional love he craved. They'd given material things, calling that love, and he was now doing the same thing. We clear the program and reinstall the self-love and self-validation program.

However, when he tries to discuss his new focus with his wife, she wants nothing to do with his new direction, nor is she going to participate in it. As a result, they divorce. He decides to drop the superficial social life style and simply enjoy the money he has. He tells his wife he is dropping out, and if she wants to continue the old way, she can pay for it herself. He changes his life completely and finds genuine happiness.

Case #30. A women volunteers at one of my lectures. We go through the basics of clearing and find that she has a severe thyroid deficiency, about which she is concerned because she is pregnant. Six months earlier, her doctor had told her that her thyroid test showed very low, so he prescribed a thyroid supplement. However, she was under extreme stress at the time of the doctor visit, and that's why her thyroid function had been down. The doctor was an authority figure, so her mind accepted his diagnosis. We forgive the doctor for making the statement, and reprogram the mind's belief. After about fifteen minutes, her thyroid resumes normal operation and has continued to do so for many years since.

Case #31. Another major find is the discovery of the denial and denial-of-denial sub-personalities. In this case, I have been working with a client for a few sessions and he seems to accept and hold the love program, yet I notice in his relationship with his family that he doesn't seem to follow through in how he communicates with them. In the next session, I check for denial-of-denial in the love program.

It appears that he loves himself and will receive love from others, but when we check denial sub-personalities, they indicate he is in denial and does not love himself, nor will he accept love from others. When we release the denial sub-personalities and begin tracing back for the core issues, we find tremendous anger and suppressed resentment at his mother, which in turn has created a resentment toward all women. This, too, is in denial. As we process through this, it opens many other doors to other suppressed denial programs and sub-personalities.

Case #32. Love and validation are the most important issues in a child's life. In my case, it was the base cause of all my problems. My parents did not know how to express love or give validation so it was the core issue in most of my dysfunctional behavior.

With one client, we found that his parents had provided all the things that a child would want, private prep school education, and all the trappings to go with it. However, all they had provided was material objects; there was no love, validation or acceptance. Meanwhile, the child had tried to satisfy his parents for providing all the proper things in his life, but could never perform up to their standards. No matter how well he had done, they had always wanted more or better. Most of time, he had received invalidation rather than acceptance.

Being a survivor, he'd gone into business for himself and succeeded, but again had received no support for his success. Finally, he had even rejected his own self, and manifested a life-threatening disease to win his family's acceptance. He had been willing to destroy himself for acceptance.

This shows how far the mind will go to get love and acceptance. He was unaware that his disease had been caused by his mind setting him up. The doctors h a d given him a "no way out" diagnosis. He had turned to alternative processes and nutritional programs, but they had not worked, either.

Finally, he had been referred to me by a friend who'd had positive results from our work together. In four sessions, we created a miracle. We cleared the dysfunction with reprogramming and let go of his anger and resentment, s o h e could come to peace with his parents. Most of the programs were in denial so he was not even aware of them. Once we let go of all the denial, and he could love and forgive his parents, and the miracle of healing happened naturally.

Case #33. A couple is trying to sell their house but they are not sure where they want to move to, so they have not made any plans for the future. The house is not overpriced or in disrepair, but it just does not sell. The couple is really frustrated because they cannot move forward. They come to me, assuming that there must be a curse or hex on them or the house, but we find nothing that is stopping them.

However, we do find a tremendous fear of not having an anchor or security. The house is security that they cannot let go of. Although they have consciously decided to sell it, their fear of not having security is blocking the sale. It is hard for them to let go of this. For the next 30 days, they write out longhand, 21 times a day, "It is safe to sell the house. Security is an internal personal quality, not an outer physical situation." As children, neither had had a solid home, and now they both felt that if they let go of the house, they would be homeless. The mind is not rational, nor does it see how it acts out its fear. This is actually a double-bind. Consciously they wanted to sell the house, but they were subconsciously blocking the sale. This is one of the main reasons we have to locate and release all our childhood fears and emotional trauma. I had worked with them on other issues, yet this one had escaped our notice until the house was on the market. Denial is so insidious that it's almost impossible to see its covert operation.

Case #34. At a lecture, a woman asks me what causes hypoglycemia. I explain, "Almost all sugar-based problems are caused by lack of love, and sugar, especially chocolate, which responds in the body like feeling loved."

"I was helping a friend put out a newsletter," she says, "and we planned to stick the address labels and take the newsletters to the post office by three. I was supposed to be at my friend's house at noon but I didn't show up until two. My friend was angry at me for not showing up on time, and had almost finished the job on her own."

"What was your reaction to your friend's anger?"

"I felt unappreciated for the work I'd already done, and headed directly to the candy shop. I bought a pound of jelly beans and ate them all in less than an hour. As a result, my hypoglycemic condition kicked in and I had a low-blood-sugar blackout. At the hospital emergency room, they gave me an insulin shot."

I ask her, "So, what do you think the lesson was in that incident?"

Typical of a person in denial, she says, "It was my friend's fault. She made me go to the candy store."

"Okay, I suggest a session to clear the programs that are causing the situation."

During the session, she disagrees with me about the cause, and claims she has had perfect parents, so they are not the cause. I agree that they are not the cause, but that it is her reaction to how they've treated her that's causing the problem. She disagrees with my interpretation, and I do not see her again. (Unfortunately, this classic case of denial-of-denial occurred before I knew how to deal with it.)

Case #35. My client has a controlling mother-in-law who can't help taking over every dinner party, whether it's at her house or the homes of her adult children. We go over the issue and it find that it is non-acceptance coming directly from childhood. My client's mother has passed on but had the same controlling qualities. She could not keep her comments or her need to control to herself.

The client recognizes her mother's controlling patterns and lets them go. We release all the "I am not all right" programs, the rejection as a child and the feeling of inadequacy, along with adding loving and forgiving her mother and her mother-in-law.

We then work on reclaiming personal power and taking control of her life so she will not react to her mother-in-law. We release her fear of standing up for herself and speaking out about how she feels.

When she hosts the next Christmas dinner, she tells her mother-in-law, "I can handle the kitchen. Why don't you spend time with the family. Dinner will be ready in a couple hours."

The mother-in-law grumbles at first, but finally complies.

When my client asks for clarification, I explain, "The only reason your mother-in-law took control is that everyone let her. They were reacting from their own childhood programs. Now that you've taken your power back and no longer have any feelings of inadequacy around your mother-in-law, she can't grind with you. You are stronger than she is, so she backs down. Controllers are only as strong as other people will allow them to be. They'll always defer to a person who is in their own power. They can't intimidate those who are in control of their life."

Case #36. It seemed that everything this client did was intended to reject self, and that his parents had deliberately set out to destroy his self-worth as he was growing up, because nothing he did was right by them. They had found fault with everything he did, no matter how well he did it. He'd done well in school in the lower grades, but they had offered no support validation, so he'd just given up and barely graduated. As an adult, he had received validation for the work he did, which helped some. Even then, however, he would sabotage himself. I was surprised that he came to me for help, because the more ingrained the behavior, the longer it takes to clear it. It was hard for him to understand, however, that he had drawn people into his life who would validate his self-image.

Many clients come with some form of back pain along their spines. In his case, it was middle-back pain, just below the shoulder blades. (This almost always signals self- rejection, and usually it begins in utero.)

He had been going to a chiropractor twice a week but the adjustments would not hold. However, as we worked out the self-rejection, his back pain began to lessen and eventually disappeared. It took many sessions to finally clear all the childhood programs and resultant patterns as an adult. I was surprised at his commitment; he persisted until we had cleared them. Most people give up when the going gets rough.

Case #37. In 1998, we discovered how powerful the Conscious Rational Decision Making Mind is. I was shifting my focus from the Subconscious Mind and Ego being the control factor, yet I had not encountered the true power in the mind. When I ran headlong into autopilot, I knew I had hit the jackpot. I was working with an established client and we encountered some locked-in programs when I discovered autopilot in his Conscious Mind. It partitions off a segment of the Conscious Mind and sets up its own operating system with sub-personalities to drive it. After discovering this, I decide we must erase this system so we could take its power back from it. Little did I know how powerful it was. We were removing some of the sub-personalities when the client started browning out, so I decided to clear the whole thing at once with the help of my cadre of reprogrammers: Ego and Subconscious Mind, Holographic Mind, Higher Self, Holy Sprit and Presence of God.

We began with our affirmations to clear the programs and asked them to uninstall the operating systems of auto-pilot and then delete, erase and destroy all the operating programs, patterns and operating instructions in the autopilot. I reasoned that if we could get them all before she passed out, we would have it cleared. All I'd have to do then was get her back in her body and we'd be finished.

However, I didn't realize that we'd crashed her entire operating system. (She'd been on autopilot control for 85 percent of her life.) I now couldn't wake her, and it took two hours for her mind to reconfigure the operating system, plus another hour to get the programs functioning in the proper manner.

Now, before just destroying autopilot, I ask how much control clients have over their lives. I then chip away at autopilot until I can de-install the operating system with knocking the person out of the body. (In her case, the client was wondering why she had behavior patterns she didn't like yet they manifested anyway. She was running double-binds, fighting autopilot for control. Fighting sub-personalities was disconcerting and exhausting, but now she has her power back, she sleeps less and has more physical energy.)

Case #38. At a lecture, a woman asks, "Is it possible that I set up my husband to beat me up? He denies hitting me, but I have the bruises to prove it. Our relationship is good and this only happens once in while. There doesn't seem to be any reason for it as far as I can see."

When we begin testing for the indication, we run into major denial. The husband is not consciously aware that he is beating his wife, even though he can see the bruises. We establish that he blacks out during the episodes. I am actually seeing what has happened, but I have to get him to experience it himself to break out of the denial and illusion. So I ask him, "Who appears or what happens before you black out?" I cannot get any further. Conventional psychology would be stumped at this point because, due to denial-of- denial, he has no recall whatsoever. It simply does not exist in his reality.

We have to access the fear causing the denial, so using the acupuncture points with N/CR, we see that his mother abused him as a child, and that he would escape into his magical child to avoid the yelling and pain. He would actually escape this reality into another magical reality that he had created.

With this established in his mind, we can then recall the incident. When we go through the process of releasing his mother and forgiving her, we open the door to reconstructing the incident. I explain to him what has happened and what he did to escape.

He describes it thus: "When my wife starts ragging on me, I don't see her anymore. All I see is my mother's image overlaid over my wife's. I become a child and go into a place of seclusion to escape her. At that point, I don't remember anything until I come back. When I do come back, I'm disoriented and it takes a while to regain my balance."

We work on her need to attack him verbally, and get over her need to control and manipulate him, so the whole behavior pattern for both of them is cleared. A few months later, the wife tells me there have been no more incidents since.

With conventional psychology, this would probably have ended in divorce, which neither one wanted. How many of these types of cases have the same root cause, but end up in divorce court or jail time, when they can so easily be resolved?

Case #39. Many clients have said, "I knew getting married was a mistake, but I did it for my parents."

Many people get married for all the wrong reasons. Most of time, we marry the one of our parents with whom we have not completed our lessons. We then transfer our neediness from that parent to the other person, which creates a new mother/son or father/daughter relationship. This will work until one partner gets tired of being controlled or not being given the desired amount of attention. (In men, it will result in sexual maladjustment, because you cannot have sex with your mother. In women, this does not seem to cause any problem.)

Many people are caught in relationship addiction, so they will say they are addicted to the love they never get. Usually they do not have a functional love program in their mind's computer, so they keep chasing what they think is love, when it's usually sex, which they interpret as love. I find very few people who are actually happy in their marriages. Most of them coexist because it's "the right thing to do." Society and religion place so many rules and pressures on people that very few even really know what true happiness is.

If both people are willing to work on it together, a couple can sometimes resolve their differences and create a good relationship. When I have been able to work with both partners, we can release all the childhood programs with their parents and put the marriage back together. However, if one person changes and the other wants to continue on the same path, irreconcilable differences will probably lead to divorce.

In Studs Turkel's book *Working*, he interviewed 30,000 people and found that only five percent were actually happy to the point that they would not change anything in their lives. fifteen per cent were relatively happy and had a few things they would change. Another twenty per cent were trying to change their lives, but felt frustrated in their effort. But a whopping sixty per cent were not happy with their lives, and felt locked in with no way out. (*This is a pretty sad commentary on life.* And worse, this book was first written in the seventies; things have gotten much worse since then.)

Case #40. Many clients have faced a major battle due to their bodies being toxic and out of balance, both in electrolytes and homeostasis. Candida is primarily a breakdown in sugar metabolism, and is one of the most difficult dysfunctions to overcome because it also has an insidious emotional component.

Many of my clients with Candida have victim tendencies and a hard time disciplining themselves. in one case, the client had followed the candida diet rigorously, yet was making no headway. After about three years, she was so weak from the diet that she quit her job. Then her disability ran out. When we started working, her ability to withstand cold was gone to the point she kept her apartment at 80 degrees. She was so careful with her diet that it seemed almost obsessive.

After five sessions, she was again functional in her life. The base cause had been childhood rejection. She had been an only child and a "mistake," since her parents had not wanted any children. However, they had felt sorry for her and enabled her candida by giving her money when the disability ran out.

Her base feeling was that nobody liked her and they would dump her from a job at the first chance, which she had proven correct by setting herself up to get laid off. I was able to break through the denial that she did not want to work because she would get fired. We cleared the program and the sub-personality, and her candida began to clear up. Once she felt empowered to stand up for herself, she risked eating foods that in the past had caused flare-ups. She was surprised when this didn't happen.

She knew now we were making progress where no medical doctors had been able to find an answer, and after almost a year of weekly sessions, she started sponsoring me and setting up lectures. However, after she recovered, her empowerment went to the other extreme. Her anger at men came up, something that often happens when a female client reclaims her power. Resentment surfaces from having been held down in the past, and they become aggressive and arrogant. Fortunately, most clients recognize their misplaced anger and recover.

Case #41. I meet many people who run into major blocks while working out, almost all of them caused by emotional limitations. When we release the emotional causes from the body, miracles happen. A weightlifter is upset that he has paid his entry fee into a weightlifting contest but cannot lift more than 175 lbs, when the minimum to enter the preliminary level is 300. He is at a loss as to why he is suddenly so weak. By asking a few pointed questions, I see the base cause, so I offer him a free session. He has had a fight with his girlfriend and she's left him for another man. His interpretation is that the other man was more desirable and had a better-looking body. First, we release all the anger at his mother, and then at the girlfriend. We recover from his failed relationship, and from his not being acceptable because he does not physically match up to the other man. We recover his self-esteem and clear the need to have someone else validate him. Two days later, he lifts 325 lbs. He remarks that he has no idea what we did, but that it worked.

Case #42. At a lecture, a woman asks me, "Do you believe in hereditary diseases?" As I have noted earlier, I do not accept the concept of the hereditary passing on of disease. Both her husband and her son had died recently of a heart condition they believed was hereditary. When we check her with kinesiology, her Body/Mind confirms that they had both died from a belief. If they had not held that belief, they would be alive today. (I have proven over and over that beliefs can kill.)

Case #43. A client tells me she is affected by environmental illnesses. We trace her belief back to her arrival from Europe at Ellis Island. It was an old ship and the odors of bunker fuel permeated the decks of the ship. The day before the ship docked, she had lost contact with her mother and didn't find her until they disembarked. Her allergies and her sensitivity were directly connected to the fear of losing her mother. Once we released the fear, the sensitivity immediately disappeared.

Case #44. A client capitulates to anything her husband wants. She puts up with his verbal abuse, because that is the way she was treated as a child. One of the main blocks to awareness is giving power away to an authority figure, regardless of who it is. It could be a parent, a friend, an employer, or a marriage partner. Outside observers will puzzle over the person being treated badly or with no respect, but the codependent accepts the mistreatment because of the fear of being rejected.

This usually goes back to childhood where children felt they were not accepted. As a result, they rejected themselves as "not all right." To get the "alrightness" back and get validated, they look for a person who appears to need them. I always warn clients with this complaint that they should ask their partners to participate in the process, or they may have fireworks when they become aware, empowered and reclaim their personal power.

After five sessions, the client asks her husband for a divorce. In an attempt to save the relationship, he has a few sessions with me, but refuses to do any follow-up. They divorce soon after.

Case #45. The other side of the coin are the counter-dependents who are actually more fragile than the codependents. It's hard for them to see their need to be in control all the time. Most are so in denial of their behavior that they justify all their reactions to a given stimuli. When confronted with an issue, they will go into either flight or fight. To give in is to lose their power. Quite often they will resort to verbal abuse to maintain control.

It is hard to get a counter-dependent to recognize that civilized behavior does not mean losing your power. I strive to work with the client's partner in hopes that if the codependent reclaims his or her power, the partner will see the light, but this seldom happens. Although a few clients are able to change the course of their future to happiness, joy and unconditional love, most of these cases sadly end in divorce.

Case #46. Many people who maintain "I have been on the spiritual path for twenty years or more, and have my life together" will volunteer to work at N/CR lectures and workshops. However, I contend that spiritual work cannot begin until we have built the foundation. All but three people I have checked who claim to have been on the spiritual path for fifteen years or more have accomplished little if any real growth on their path. The cause is clear.

One such woman, a twenty-year veteran of spiritual work, volunteers to demonstrate with me at a lecture. As I go through my basic checks, we find that her polarity is switched and she's out of her body. She does not love herself, nor can she receive love from others.

I check for the cause, and find that she had a controlling mother who rejected her before she was born and didn't want any more children. All her life, she has felt rejected and abandoned by her mother. Her list of programs is endless, so I suggest that she see me for a session, where we could release all this and get her on the track to reclaiming her personal power and empowering herself.

The first treatment appears to work but blows her out from her reality even further because we destroyed her fragile operating system. In in a second session, we build a new operating system that allows her get on with building the foundation to launch into her spiritual work.

This has happened to more people than I can count. Instead of starting on the bottom step, they jump up to step twelve. With a crumbling foundation under them, they crash when we bring up the emotional dysfunction in their life that has been covered up in denial-of-denial sub-personalities. The illusion is that they were growing, but because it's not done thoroughly, the mind just runs with an illusion. They assume that they've done all the basic work, when in fact, none of the releasing has happened, other than cathartic release. This unfortunate experience often happens because of misdirected teachers and pseudo-shamans. Quite often people embark on a spiritual path and assume that they can acquire the tools without guidance. In my experience, true clearing requires an accomplished teacher who can direct one on the path. The "I can do it all myself" attitude simply does not work.

Case #47. A person at my health club had a tragic experience because of his daughter's relationship addiction. She had broken up with her boyfriend because he was verbally abusive. He would alternate between staying away from her and harassing her. The father had gotten a court restraining order to keep him away, and he had disappeared for about six months. She was living with her father for protection so he felt safe for her. The old boyfriend had called up and wanted to see her one last time before he moved out of state. She had agreed to meet him at a restaurant nearby to talk with him. Her father had wanted to go along for protection, but she had declined, saying that it was a large, busy restaurant. Apparently, their discussion became an argument, and the boyfriend had pulled a gun, killed her, and then himself. "Why?" asked the father. When one person gets paranoid over another, the latter becomes the medicine. If the aggressor cannot have his medicine, then no one else can. They see no reason to live, and feel they can take the person with them in death. Until we recently stopped looking at crimes of passion as criminal acts, they were inexplicable.

Case #48. With many clients, I find that the mind seems to be our enemy. As we saw before, the problem is not our Ego at all, but the Middle Self and its autopilot programs. Our mind decides it will protect us from the ultimate enemy: rejection, abandonment, invalidation and fear of failure. In an effort to protect us, it sets up sub-personalities to keep us from situations that might cause us to face what it feels will be failure. We can use willpower to force the issue and punch through it, but unfortunately that creates an inner conflict that wears us out. Clients often tell me that they know that what they are doing will work well, but for some reason, it's not successful. The base cause is always: "I'm not all right," and "I'm not acceptable." Self-rejection and invalidation are the core issues. When we clear these programs, things begin to work out. I have studied people who succeed in their life pursuits, and they always come from a functional family. You might ask, "Why not me? I've tried hard to be successful." It all comes back to karma and the lessons you have to clear up now. The sooner the better. Do it now!

Case #49. A psychotherapist who specializes in children's issues brings a young client whose parents are involved with a cult that practices Black Magic ritual abuse. The child has been subject to the cult's practices and has been the target of ritual abuse.

When the mother had divorced the father and broke away from the cult, she'd taken the child to a psychotherapist to deal with the fear laid in by the ritual abuse. After three fruitless sessions, the young boy would not talk at all. The therapist had told the mother she could do nothing and suggested a session with me.

In the session, I suggest going into the records to discover the source of the child's resistance to the therapist. We find that the child was reacting to the therapist's Meta-Communication, which was being influenced by a past life when the therapist had practiced ritual abuse. Amid much emotional release and tears, we cleared the past-life record and locked it in the archives, so there would be no Meta-Communication about this experience.

The next time the child saw the therapist, he opened up and would not stop talking. In two sessions, using some N/CR processing along with conventional therapy, he was cleared of all the ritual abuse. This case shows how Meta-Communication functions: neither person knew what they were reacting to, but it stopped the therapy cold. Resolution was a win-win for both therapist and client.

Case #50. The issue of attraction to the same sex is one of the most controversial issues I've had to deal with in my practice. Are gay people actually born with a homosexual pattern in their life? My answer is no, and I have documented proof. I have worked with many women and men on the issue, none of whom actually came to me to deal with that issue. Most of the time, they just have the same issues that everyone else has.

The client's mother had been a U.S. Army nurse who had married in the Philippines during WWII. The daughter was born in the Philippines, into a functional and financially stable family, from whom the child received much love and affection. After the war, the parents had returned to the U.S., where the mother's family had not accepted the Filipino father at all. In this family group, the mother and her family had rejected the child, and the father was the only person who had given the young girl any affection and love.

After about five years, the father had been unable to handle the abuse and rejection, and had returned to the Philippines. If she'd been older, the daughter might have gone with him, but she had grown up feeling rejected and abandoned by her father. The mother wouldn't let her visit her father, for fear she wouldn't come back. It was like ownership, but with no affection or love. Assuming that all men would reject her, my client had gravitated to same-sex relationships. I asked her, "Why did you come to see me, when you hate men so violently?"

"I feel that you're here to help me through the problems in my life. You never tell me how to run my life because you always give choices. I feel that you are a historian, giving me back my childhood and helping me release the hatred and misplaced anger I've held on to until now. I feel at peace in my life, now that I understand the causes for my behavior. This doesn't mean I'll be attracted to men, but now I know I have choice. Thank you for giving me back my life."

Case #51. At one of my lectures, a man asked, "Do you really believe that AIDS is not a disease?" I replied, "It's not AIDS that kills people, but the other viruses and bacteria that the immune system is unable to control because of the low T-cell and leukocyte blood count. In fact, the AIDS virus mutates so fast that it destroys the immune system, and there is no way to control it."

"Okay, are you willing to work with my friend?"

"Of course," I replied. "AIDS is not contagious."

For such an advanced case, the results were dramatic. After just a week, the client stopped needing blood transfusions and his T-cell count shot up at an unheard of rate. The couple went on a vacation they'd been planning for years, but had had to postpone indefinitely.

The client died within two weeks of their return. The official cause was listed as AIDS but, on further pathological studies, no cause of death could actually be pinpointed. The friend (who had attended my lecture) was HIV-positive and now wanted to ensure that it did not develop into AIDS. We cleared up the HIV status in two weeks, and he continued to have sessions with me for about a year. By the end of the year, he was even questioning his same-sex attraction, and is now in a heterosexual relationship.

Case #52. A psychologist friend referred a lesbian who was having relationship problems with her partner. After a basic session, she wants to know why she took on the lesbian lifestyle. We unwind the core issues and the original cause: intense anger at her father and all of the men in her life. During the sessions, she releases her anger, and decides to opt out of the lesbian lifestyle. Her partner is furious and comes to see me. The session with the partner is one of the most tumultuous ones I've experienced. She begins by screaming at me, "You destroyed my relationship. I feel like committing suicide. Carolyn left me for a man. She has penis envy, and I can't provide satisfying sex for her."

After she gets that off her chest, I ask, "Well, what do you want to do about it?" Apparently, she just wanted to unload on me. Soon after, she calls to apologize and book a session. In several sessions, we release the anger and many of the issues around the rejection, and she reclaims her personal power which opens her up for more effective relationships.

Case #53. I was invited to present a lecture by a woman who had attended my lecture with a friend from distant city. Unknown to me, of the 28 attendees, only three were heterosexual. In my ignorance, I answered questions without any withholds and the audience accepted my answers without much resistance. At the end of the lecture, a women asked me if I would stay after the lecture and work on her. She'd been afraid to volunteer during the lecture, because she could feel her anger rising. She warned me that she would probably begin screaming during the release. She was right; she did, and at the top of her voice.

Afterward, she told me she felt like a piece of spaghetti. In a further session, we cleared mountains of rejection and anger against her father and men in general, which gave her a new life. She had no intention of relinquishing her lesbian lifestyle, but the clearings had given her a whole new life. Her "male rejection" issues were the same as for many women, yet her interpretation had guided her into a lesbian lifestyle.

Case #54. Two of my clients are cross-dressers. One keeps trying to start relationships with women, even though he knows they will eventually reject him. He also reacts as a man or woman depending on the situation, although he seems happier in the female persona. Either way, his intended female partners reject him. His background was typical of transsexual men, as covered in Chapter 2, but he was terrified of the sex-change option. (Unfortunately, he stopped the sessions, so we didn't reach resolution.)

Case #55. The client's life-stress was simply breaking his body down, and his adrenal function was so low that he should have been totally shut down by clinical depression. Yet amazingly, due to the power of the mind, he was still somehow able to function, even though he was exhausted all the time. He was a survivor, and was using pure will power to drive his life. Once we released all the childhood trauma and he reclaimed his personal power, he began to recover and is now able to function normally.

Case #56. Occasionally a sick client is getting a payoff from his or her illness, often related to control of others. Asthma is commonly the illness of choice to manipulate other people who then give their power to the controller. I have explained to many controllers what they're doing to get the payoff, yet most deny it. In some cases, we may have cleared all the programs, beliefs and sub-personalities, from every level of the mind, yet if they retain the concept of payoff in the Conscious Rational Mind, it will rebuild the program, and the disease syndrome will return. I have cleared some clients of asthma for up to two weeks, yet it returns with more intensity than in the past.

Case #57. Fear of stepping forward or reaching out in life can result in pain or physical breakdown in our arms in legs. At an Expo, I met a women with a paralyzed arm who had no use of the fingers on her left hand. One morning, ten years ago, she woke up with her hand in this position. After much physical therapy, she could move her arm, but nothing seemed to help her hand.

In the first session, we traced the original cause to her childhood, when her parents had told her she would not succeed at anything. They had invalidated everything she did. Ten years ago, she had been about to start a new job, in which she would have to use her hands, and to make sure she couldn't fail, her programming had kicked in to prevent her from taking the job.

Once we released the parental programming and the fear of failure, she was able to reclaim her personal power. We also reprogrammed her love program so she could love herself and allow herself to receive love. We released the fear of reaching out to new situations and new realities. Her arm loosened up, and her hand uncurled, right in the session, to give her full use of her fingers for the first time in ten years.

Case #58. A client lived only a few blocks from my office, and was a virtual prisoner in his house. He was afraid to go out due to what he described as "environmental illness" in that he was allergic to everything. We began with his pre-birth rejection by his mother—she hadn't wanted any children. She had verbally and physically abused him, and worn strong perfume all the time, so he had connected rejection and abuse with strong perfume. With a shy victim-type personality, it was no surprise when he had married a strong, controlling woman who verbally abused him and controlled his life. He was seeking a mother-son relationship, so that he could continue to work out relationship lessons with his mother. (She also wore strong perfume, which was the core issue.)

The client had used to work at a scientific laboratory that used strong-smelling chemicals (the catalyst). He had developed reactions to those chemicals, and had finally retired on disability. His allergy syndrome had built on itself until, today, he was afraid to go anywhere. We cleared all the childhood programming with his mother. Then we tackled the beliefs and sub-personalities that were driving the concepts about environmental illness. Once clear, we took a field trip to a lecture to try out his new-found freedom.

As fate would have it, a women with strong perfume sat down right behind us, and he bolted for the door to get some fresh air. Outside, I managed to convince him that his environmental illness was a self-created illusion, and we went back in and enjoyed the rest of the lecture. Over the next few sessions, we cleared his remaining problems, finally releasing him to find happiness and joy for the first time in his life.

Case #59. A prospective client called from Florida, but since I live in California, meeting was a problem. As it happened, Ft. Lauderdale was hosting an upcoming Expo, so we arranged to meet there. He had been diagnosed as a classic case of learning-disabled, coupled with ADD. His family had sent him to many therapists but to no avail. At their suggestion, he had enrolled in a college that helped learning-disabled people, but after five years, he was still in his junior year. He was listless, and had difficulty getting out of bed each morning and just making it through the day.

As usual, his problems all stemmed from childhood during which he had collected the usual rejection programs in addition to his father continually putting him down. He had done poorly in school, and was unable to fit into the social scene. When his school had labeled him learning-disabled, he'd bought it hook, line and sinker.

In the first session, we cleared the ADD label and the learning-disabled belief, along with all the traditional programs. Immediately, he began to find school easy. He was amazed that we could release pain in his body and change his programming and belief by just holding acupuncture points on the body and saying an affirmation. Over two more sessions, he reclaimed his personal power and took back responsibility, and he perked up in every area of his life. He now jumped out of bed, eager to tackle each day, and wanting to be up and around. He told me, "I've never felt like this before. Now I have this drive to succeed and get going in my life."

Case #60. In the mid-80s, a woman came to my lecture dressed like a construction worker. She wore Levis, heavy work boots and a flannel shirt. She said, "I fit into one of the categories you talked about, and I want to find out why."

For the last 15 years, she'd installed new electric lines for the power company, and was the only woman she knew of in construction. She had been the youngest of three girls. Her parents had wanted a boy, but were unwilling to have a fourth child. She'd been a tomboy all her life, playing sports and generally spending most of her time with men, stopping at bars with her crew for an after-work drink. She had no boyfriends or intimate relationships, even though men would show interest in her.

She'd never had lesbian tendencies, nor did she want any part of that lifestyle. Interestingly, she didn't feel rejected by her parents, or that they'd treated her like a boy. She had just taken on that lifestyle herself, to prove to her father that she could meet his demands on her.

We released the programs about needing to please her parents, and she reclaimed her personal power so she could live her life for herself. She came to her second session wearing a dress, and I ask, "What happened?"

She replied, "The need for the challenge isn't there anymore. I don't feel I have to prove anything to my parents. I just want a lifestyle where I can live a normal life, so I applied for a transfer to the dispatch department with an inside/outside combination position."

This client was typical of people who just flow with the river, not really directing or controlling their lives, but who do not experience happiness and joy. Once she got in touch with, and understood her choices, she changed paths to one more in line with what she desired. Her new lifestyle brought her peace, harmony, happiness and joy. She began a good relationship with a new male friend, with whom she could work on the love aspect. She also began to make women friends.

Case #61. One of the questions that puzzles many people is, "I want to clear up patterns in my life, so why can't I accomplish what I set out to do?" One client had cleared all the blocks to accomplishing her goals, yet in the next session, she found that she was self-sabotaging. The culprit was a program buried in her Conscious Rational Mind, hidden in denial. Its thinking was that if she does not keep her commitments, nobody could hold her responsible, so she could never fail. She would get migraine headaches to stop her from achieving her goals, but then she'd feel guilty for not keeping to her commitment, and she'd berate herself for not following through. She justified the pattern by saying that she needed compassion, but that others were critical of her, and withheld it. Breaking this pattern took several sessions, because between sessions, she recreated the programs and beliefs for the mileage she derived from them. When she finally realized that her soap-opera drama was costing her jobs and friends, she decided to reclaim her personal power. Her life rapidly turned around.

Case #62. During childhood, this client had lost his father to serious illness, and his mother had seriously neglected him. He came to me claiming that outside forces were plaguing him. I had my doubts but went along with the possibility. We began on the premise that outside forces were affecting his health, and over a few sessions, we cleared all the outside effects being caused by other people. In his own mind, he had created blaming belief patterns that spawned many "denial-of-denial" blamer sub-personalities, connected with a number of denial and "refusal to take responsibility" sub-personalities.

All told, we cleared over 45 sub-personalities, but then his entire operating system crashed. He felt drugged, sick and congested, and unable to function. A later session uncovered a whole other set of the same programs and patterns. The problem was that with "denial-of-denial," a person cannot access the programs or patterns, so they seem real since, as far the client is concerned, the feelings are real. When we access the records, we find that some are old, but others are new, created to justify the aberrant behavior and feelings. So we keep chipping away at the programs, and at some point, we will clear them all. This process continues until the client either sees the truth or gets fed up with the way he feels.

Case #63. Similar cases arise when clients live in a dream world of fantasy. One client came to me quite disoriented, in a condition psychologists call 'bipolar' or manic depression. As usual, I looked for the original cause of his dysfunctional behavior, which was that when the client had been very young, his father had died. His mother had never remarried and retreated into a dysfunctional state so she didn't have to take responsibility. As a teenager, therefore, he had ended up taking care of her. An aunt had helped out, but he essentially had no adult model to follow and felt massive rejection. As a survival mechanism, his mind had suppressed the programs under layers of denial. (Of course, the rejection lesson would recur later in life.)

We found that the base cause was denial of reality. He didn't want to accept the lesson or what was happening to him. We found the core issue was not wanting to accept responsibility, plus denial-of-denial of responsibility sub-personalities, plus about thirty denial-of-denial blamer sub-personalities. He couldn't even recognize his trait of walking into situations and setting himself up, because in his mind, everybody else was causing his problems.

When we started to remove all the blocks and erase the denial sub-personalities, he almost passed out. At the end of the first session, he was exhausted. In future sessions, we kept finding the same programs, but when we found the catalyst, he made a major breakthrough and was finally able to get his life back on track.

Case #64. In my seminars, I always assert that any allergy is a belief that has no program driving it. Instead, it is driven by a sub-personality activated by the catalyst, something we can clear up in one session.

The client came to me after falling down in tall grass while running her dog, and within hours, suffering an allergic reaction. Her face swelled up and she got a red rash, with spots all over her body. However, her doctor couldn't find any actual allergy. In session, we found the original cause was, as a child, being frequently beaten up in the tall grass by her older brother. He had been angry that she'd been born and was "stealing" his parents' attention away from him. Beating her up was his means of expressing his anger.

The core issue was created many years later when she'd gotten into a knock-down fight with her now ex-husband, also in tall grass. Tall grass became the catalyst, so every time after, if she fell down in tall grass, her irrational belief said she was going to get beaten up. The allergy simply delivered the message that there was a lesson she had to deal with, but she wasn't able to hear it. When we cleared the belief, sub-personality, core issue and base cause, within fifteen minutes, the swelling and rash disappeared, right before our eyes. Since the catalyst was now permanently erased, there was nothing to activate the issue, so the grass allergy would not recur. All it took was an appropriately-worded affirmation.

Case #65. At one of my lectures, a woman asked, "Your theory sounds great and I'd like to believe it, but I had back surgery and four ruptured disks removed. I can't deal with the pain any longer. It's so bad that I'm contemplating suicide."

I told her, "Please don't put the responsibility for your life on me because I'm only a programmer, not a healer. I don't heal anyone, but I can show you how to heal yourself. *You* have to rewrite the scripts and install the programs I provide you with."

In her first session, I learned that her parents had been career Air Force officers and hadn't wanted any children, but if they did have one, they'd wanted a boy. She was an only child and had seen very little of them, so she had installed the self-rejection programming: "They don't want me; I'm not accepted."

Her back problems stemmed from her spine contracting from the trauma that was locked in by the programming. When the pressure of the muscle contraction had become too intense, the disks ha d ruptured. Doctors had tried to fuse them, but it hadn't worked, so two years later, they had surgically removed the disks and tied four of the vertebrae together with stainless steel wire. This hadn't worked either, so it was obvious to me that she was still not getting the message.

She decided to go for it, committed to healing herself, and the results were amazing. In the first session, we released the rejection, and the pain disappeared. In the second, we discovered and released some traumatic past lives with the same parents. But what we didn't know was that a miracle had already happened.

The client then set up an auto accident and had to have back X-rays. Her doctor in reading them assumed he'd mixed up two patient's X-rays, but when it was eventually proved that these *were* her X-rays, he was completely baffled: they showed that the stainless steel wire had disappeared, all four disks were now present again, and the vertebrae were in perfect condition! (*Let me repeat that: The four discs that had been removed surgically were back in their original locations, and perfectly healthy!*) Some follow-up work with her clears the balance of the trauma, and over the last ten years since, the client has had no back problems. Her body had been talking very loudly, screaming even, but she was just not getting the lesson. The fact that her health turned around in just a few days proves the power of the mind.

Case #66. One of the most phenomenal cases I have had involves a client I met at a lecture I did in Las Vegas. He is an extraordinary example of someone who succeeded against incredible odds. Born with cerebral palsy, he couldn't speak until he was six. He was confined to a wheelchair and unable to move himself until he was eight. He started school late due to his disabilities, yet he graduated from high school in the normal time. He had a college degree, a B.Sc. in mechanical engineering; he built race cars, and had won many races. He started his own business and was an inventor, patenting and building some of his own inventions. When we met, he still had some spastic body movements and slurred speech, one would assume from a stroke, say, but was able to live an almost normal life.

Very few people with cerebral palsy live beyond age thirty-five and they can seldom take care of themselves or perform in a job above minimal responsibility. At sixty-two, he has outlived anyone with cerebral palsy in past history. He had the usual quotient of human emotional programming, plus tremendous anger at people who treat him as a disabled person who cannot do anything for himself. In his business dealings, people had taken advantage of him because they felt he could not defend himself. But he had proved them wrong time and again, and succeeded beyond any expectations.

When I started working with him in 1996, he was beset by people trying to sabotage one of his inventions, so we changed the negative programming causing the problems. We are still a "work-in-progress" today, but I know nothing will stop him. His life path proves that nothing can stop you if you have the courage, commitment and the discipline to move through your limitations. He has never considered himself a victim. He sees life as a challenge that one can overcome with commitment and consistent work.

Cerebral palsy is a Karmic genetic situation filed in the pre-birth flight plan. The Soul knows it can take this lesson on and overcome the effects of the so-called birth "defect." Here is a man who on his own was able to work through the disabling effects of cerebral palsy, and succeed at making a life for himself, with very little help. He is an excellent example of a person whose mind tells him he can't do what he's attempting, yet he does it anyway. How many of us could even begin to overcome such a challenging genetic life controlling "defect"?

Case #67. We were participating in a health show in February of 2001, and hoped to see a friend who had helped me set up seminars and workshops for many years. When he came up to our booth, his condition appalled Susie and me. I had assumed he would be participating at the show himself, but he was in no condition to do so. He was a well-known healer and reflexologist whom I had known for over 15 years, but I had not seem him for over a year.

Therefore, I was shocked to see him so badly crippled that he had to use a walker. He could not talk clearly and was shaking with Parkinson's Disease.

"What happened to you?" I asked him.

"I don't know," he told me. "No one seems to be able to help me. I've been to many practitioners I know who tried to work with me, but to no avail."

"I suggest you make an appointment with me, so we can clear all of the dysfunctional programs and heal your afflictions," I advised.

He did so and, when I worked with him, tracking the programs and clearing the files was quick and easy, because we had done so much work together in the past. In one session, we healed the Parkinson's Disease and cleared his speech problem. He left the session without the walker and taking very clearly. Two days later, his lady friend called to say, "You have given Jim back to me. It's amazing what you have done with him."

Six months later, none of the afflictions had returned. All neuro-motor diseases are easy to clear once you find the base cause and clear the programming. The "Catch 22' is that the person has to let go of the need for the illness. He was not getting any mileage out of his affliction, so it was easy to reprogram and release.

Case #68. I work with many people who cannot seem to get their lives in gear, so they procrastinate all the time until a major crisis wakes them up. This happened to one client who was forced to take action in his life. When he was able to handle the situation, he found that it was so easy once he took responsibility, that he decided to go forward on all his unfinished languishing projects. I saw him less than a month later, and he had gained total control over his life; auto-pilot was gone and he had no more control sub-personalities.

I thought this was a miracle; the month before, he'd been loaded with sub-personalities that caused avoidance, disorientation and procrastination. And now they were all gone. Sowing the seeds over the past year had worked. Once he reclaimed his personal power, he was on track.

The last time I saw him, he commented, "When you are on the other side of the fence, you can see all the denial and illusion other people are in, but they will not listen to you when you observe it in them." I then asked him, "Does that phrase sound familiar from our sessions?"

He grinned and said, "Now I'm in your shoes, I can see why I did not want to admit where I was. It sure is a lot more comfortable to be where I am now."

Case #69. One of the more amazing experiences I have had came with a client who was slowly dying, and we could not seem to stop her life from simply slipping away. Eventually, we found that she had regressed into a past life where she'd had a condition similar to Alzheimer's. It was as if she was living in a parallel lifetime, even though she generally seemed to be cognizant of things around her, though at other times, she would slip away into this other lifetime.

The family had significant funds, so it was not a matter of money. Our work revealed that she felt that she no longer had any opportunities in life. We would heal one condition and she would pull up another affliction until she became unable to move on her own. Over a six-month period, she progressed from simple problems to life-threatening conditions, where she could not eat much at all. When I told her what she needed to do to halt the progression she was creating, I noticed myself getting to a point where I almost passed out. When I told the client's daughter what was happening, she astounded me by saying, "You actually did. You passed out for four minutes. It was like you just faded out and stopped talking for no reason."

Checking with Kinesiology, I discovered that her mind had knocked me right out of my body. It was intent on killing her and did not want me interfering. Nothing I could do could turn that intent around, even though the client was aware of what was happening. She finally died in her sleep about two weeks later. The power of the human mind sometimes amazes me. Not only did it destroy her, but it also stopped me from helping her.

Case #70. During 2001, I began to find that many clients who have had a life-threatening illness feel that the battle of life is futile. To a few of them, this is a startling and shocking

278

revelation, but most do not even recognize that it's happening to them.

This attitude is activating what I call the Instinctual Mind's files, and few people know about this mind or what it can do to them. When these files are opened, they begin to create "I want to die" and "fear of dying" programs. In extreme cases, clients can have as many as 150 files open. The root cause of Alzheimer's is the battle between the "I want to die" and "I'm afraid to die" programs. When the programs are active for a long time, they create an Alzheimer's program that will advance slowly until short-term memory starts to be affected. Clearing and erasing these programs clears suicidal feelings and restores short-term memory.

In one of the most advanced cases, the client had written two books, but could not seem to get them out to the market. We cleared her fear of failure around the books, and assumed that everything would fall into place. However, the following month, the Instinctual Mind's file was open again with more "I want to die" programs.

Then we found so many programs in denial-of-denial about her self-worth that had not been cleared that she was setting up a program to escape from life rather than confront potential failure. We finally broke through when we discovered a string of past lives paralleling her current challenge, where she had backed out rather than confront the fear of success or failure.

A lesson you avoid in past lives will be forwarded to the current life until you get the lesson. Each time, the lesson is more intense until you recognize it. Here, the client blamed her failure on people who would not accept her work and others who dropped the ball when she needed help. They were unknowingly just cooperating with her program, in order to force her to recognize the lesson. When she contacted these same people again, everything went according to clockwork and fell into place and on time. This is an example of something I tell many clients: this is an interactive universe and we all work in each other's lessons, whether we want to or not.

Case #71. Our fear seems to surface when we least expect it. With the downsizing of companies, many of my clients are in fear of being downsized out of a job. I had two recent cases involving downsizing, both very different.

One client knew that he was going to get fired, so he retrained in another sector of the same field and became a consultant, making more money than he had before.

Another very inventive client made herself indispensable. She performed all the backup work for her supervisor, who then had more free time to do the things she wanted to do, but which were not really part of her job. When downsizing cut the department from forty-five people down to five, my client had no problem, since she had been working with me to build her self-confidence and self-worth, and reclaim her personal power. She was able to weather the storm since she could handle the workload increase, but her supervisor could not because she hadn't been keeping current with the workload (since my client had taken so much of it on). Both of them had an increased workload, and now my client refused to carry her supervisor's extra load as she had in the past.

The supervisor is now trying to find a way to leave the company. Even though my client knew she might get laid off, she was able to handle the stress. (She did activate a few programs around it but we were able clear them easily.)

It is clear to me that the reason some people succeed is that they do not see themselves as losers, and then they evaluate what they can do to succeed. The most important qualities are self-esteem, self-worth and self-confidence, and that you know that you are entitled to abundance in your life. You can do anything you want to, if you believe that it is possible. Victims do not hold that belief.

Case # 72. I had been working with Sam three or four times a year for about four years, but we were unable to alleviate his elbow and knee pain until we could access the programs and sub-personalities that were causing it.

His programs were in denial-of-denial, so we had no access until we released the programs attached to issues above them. (Peeling off the programs and issues above seems to pull up the denial issues to replace the programs that we've just cleared, usually around the same or similar issue.) When we were able to deal with these new issues, the pain from both the knee and the elbow were released.

Sam had had the habit of starting a project but not finishing it. The sessions revealed his concern that if he finished anything, he would be judged on it. His interpretation was that he would be rejected for not doing it correctly, as had happened in his childhood. So, to avoid being judged and rejected, he never finished anything. Having released that, he can now finish everything he starts, without fear of rejection.

Case #73. In Jill's mind, she had been replaying past-life programs about how to get attention. During four sessions, we uncovered all the attachments and programs that had been transferred from those lifetimes to this one. But first, we had to release the standard "rejected before birth" program before we could access the major root causes that we found in the past lives.

Her main challenge was her feeling guilty about not having properly brought up her children. They were not meeting her expectations, and she blamed herself for this failure. As a child, she had not gotten enough attention and had been required to take of her younger brothers and sisters, so she had not had a happy childhood. As a mother of her own family, she had gone overboard to make sure that the same thing did not happen to her children. According to her, their failure to succeed was her fault.

To release the guilt, we had to release all her attachments and expectations. Then we found a headache syndrome, which was a means to get attention from her children, who otherwise did not pay much attention to her. However her self-persecution was not getting the desired result. We were finally

281

able to locate all the sub-personalities and programs to get Jill on an even path to transformation.

Case #74. Since I have had considerable experience with hearing loss, I have attracted many clients with that issue, although most of them did not have the same causes that I did. The majority were unsuccessful in trying to cut someone out of their life, and they shut down their hearing so they wouldn't have to hear them anymore. The mind is very literal in its attempts to meet our needs.

An interesting example of this syndrome is a man who was always jumped on by his wife about many of his habits and how he did the jobs around the house that she wanted done. His hearing ended up so poor that he needed hearing aids. In a few sessions, we cleared all the domestic difficulties, which brought his hearing back, so that he could dispense with the hearing aids.

When his hearing began to go downhill again, we found that he was still dealing with feeling unappreciated and unaccepted for the things he did for his wife. When we finally got him on even keel again, his wife began to get various aliments, including a bout with cancer. I was able to clear most of them for her, but she kept getting more, and continued to get progressively worse. She finally died after about nine months of illnesses.

The final prognosis was that she could no longer get her way because her husband had taken control of his life and would no longer let her discredit or control him, so she passed on. I would be interested in her perspective now.

After his wife's passing, his hearing came back perfectly and has never been compromised since.

Case #75. The more we are confronted by change, the more we back out of life. I have seen many more people simply backing out and going on autopilot in the last year than ever before. Some are backing out of life and dying because they cannot have life the way they want it to be. Taking responsibility and recognizing that we cause all of our issues is not a reality for many people.

Nowadays, in my sessions, we are moving through them much faster; we can accomplish as much in one session as we did in three ten years ago. Recovery of our separated selves can be an ordeal if we are not in control. It's not that people do not want control consciously, but more the fact that they've never had control, so they don't know what it is.

I am amazed at the frequency of this. In this case, whether I was going to be able to get the client back in control of her life was questionable. When I tested her for control on a scale of 1-100, she scored zero. Her life had been like a log in a flooding river, crashing into every obstacle in the way. When we tried to clear a few issues, she just left her body, and would not get back in no matter what we did.

I spent twenty minutes trying to convince her Conscious Mind that she was in no jeopardy or vulnerability to misdirection from me. For a long time, her mind would react to the reprogramming and cancel it, so new programs couldn't be installed.

After numerous attempts, I told her, "If you will come back for a second session, we should be able to break through the barriers that your mind is putting up. Meanwhile, if you follow the homework and read the affirmations every day you will be able to take control of your life."

She agreed, and we did finally break through the barriers and empower her to take control. I gave her the affirmation program homework (21 times a day for 21 days) and got her to keep a personal journal to track her progress.

Case #76. I have seen this woman four times in the last ten years. I lost contact with her a few years ago when she moved. When we cleared the rotator cuff in her shoulder, I knew that at some time in the future the other shoulder would go out, since she had not cleared and completed the clearing about being able to stand up and say what she wanted to say. She had just gone through a divorce, and it had activated her shoulder problem. She remembered my website and called me to make an appointment. She said I was the best alternative to surgery, so she was willing to drive six hours to her sister's home then over two hours more.

We cleared the pain in a two-hour session. Now she has full use of her arm again.

Case #77. A woman came to my lecture with a question that was interesting. "I would like to believe what you are talking about," she said. "I don't think you could help me with my problem. My parents and I have spent over $40,000 in the last thirty years trying to activate the muscles in my legs so I can walk normally. As you can see I have to shuffle along which is exasperating.

"I had polio at fourteen. I was in an iron lung for a year and then in a wheelchair for five years. I would like to try your work, but I cannot see paying for something that might not succeed. I've done too much of that over the years, and it was very disappointing to work with people who failed to deliver and still charged me. What can you offer me?" I told her I would offer a double-or-nothing deal.

"If I can not do anything for you, you do not owe a penny. But if I do you will pay double. We will sign a contract, so you know I will do what I say." She decided to take me up on the deal, and made an appointment.

What we found out was her brother had been born when she was five. She had ended up out in left field, as he received all the attention. He became the Little League baseball star, then a soccer star who got straight A's in school. She had ended up sick all the time to get attention. This got old with her parents by the time she was fourteen, so even that attention stopped. The next step was Polio, which worked. The only problem was, she'd now been locked into her disability for the past thirty years.

We went through the forgiveness process, with her parents and her brother. we released all the resentment anger locked into her cellular memory, plus the self-rejection and the "I don't fit in." She walked out of my office moving normally. She paid me double, and said if she had $1000, she would have paid me more.

"You just released me from the prison of my mind," she told me. "I did not know I was holding myself prisoner. My next stop is a bicycle shop. I have not ridden a bicycle for over 30 years."

Case #78. I had a woman call me who had MS. "The doctor told me it was incurable," she said, "and that I would eventually die from it. A friend sent me one of your articles. You say you can clear MS. I just read your book so I am ready. When can I see you?" We got together the following week. All MS stems from the same issue of wanting to be taken care of, but they do not know it. She was the oldest of seven children, and had not had a childhood. Her mother had basically set her up as a servant by the time she was six years old. She took care of the other children and helped her mother clean house and wash clothes. She said she had not been allowed to play with other children. So what does she do? To get out of the house, she gets married at eighteen, to a man just like her mother. She has four children even though she did not want any. When her children reach junior high school, she contracts MS. She can no longer do all the housework, so her husband hires a maid three days a week. What she really wants is attention from him. He avoids it by hiring the maid.

It is the same programming all the other symptoms have. So we clear all the childhood programming and the anger and resentment at her husband (which was just continuation of the childhood programs). A month later, she calls me to tell me she needs to clear more of the husband stuff because it has created fireworks. She also wants to make sure all the MS is gone, so she can confront her doctor with "I don't need you anymore."

She does that the following week, and he does not believe the MS is gone, so he challenges her to have another MRI. He says he'll even pay for it if it comes out negative. It does and he has to pay. He won't even discuss with her what she has done. Needless to say, now she is empowered and will not take any more garbage from her husband. Now that she has a different outlook on life she says they may get a divorce.

Case #79. One of the major conflicts I run into is getting people to stay with doing their homework and reading the affirmations. When I found the Inner Conscious Mind was a saboteur, it really shocked me. I had thought for over twenty years it was supposed to support us and help us when we ran into binds. But what I found was that the longer it was in our minds, running programs from the back room, the stronger it would become. I tried to remove and delete it, and began to fight. I was reading the affirmation three times a day, yet that did not seem to work as it would weasel its way in and re- install itself. After one major battle I had with it, it shut down my intestines so I could not have a bowel movement. It was successful in doing this for almost five days.

The pain was getting almost unbearable. I finally had a colonic. It would not open up until we had put water in three times. The colon therapist was afraid we might blow a hole in my intestine. But it finally worked and broke the blockage it had created. What I finally did was read the affirmation for four hours straight. I have had others do the same.

The signal that says it is trying to get in again is feeling faint, sneezing, coughing, losing your place while reading, feeling like you are blacking out . . . anything that causes you to lose focus. Start over again at the point where it says repeated readings.

Case #80. This could have been in Placebo effect since I was working at a long distance. This man was 1500 miles from me. He had crushed his ankle when a 400-pound piece of iron fell on his foot. When he called me, he said, "They want to amputate my foot."

At this point, we are now ready to ask questions with Kinesiology, or go directly into program releases. We can go directly to the root causes and the core issues stored in the Subconscious Mind's files. This will reveal the programs that have become habit patterns that are causing dysfunctional behavior, illness, diseases or pain in any form. We can quickly release and heal any dysfunctional program using N/CR. *(See steps in a session in chapter 15 for the protocol for the process.)*

I recommend taping all sessions for the protection of both therapist and client. Also, the session can be reviewed and transcribed. There will be many parts of the session the client will not be able to recall because the mind may block it out.

Many people have found that repeating the affirmations will lock in the new programming.

Q. Why is this particular process so effective?
A. Unlike other therapy processes, the client is required to participate in the session. The client is not worked on. In most treatments, such as Rolfing, Trager, massage, acupuncture, and other body-related processes, you do not participate. In psychology, you will be asked what your problem is, but few clients know what the base cause is, so how can we work with a belief, concept, or a program when we are not sure of the cause? The body will always reveal the base causes and the core issues if we listen to it.

We must get Middle Self to cooperate with us, as it is one of the main players in the game. The Middle Self knows exactly what is happening in our lives, so we need its support. All levels are brought in to play, physical, emotional, mental, spiritual and etheric, all at the same time. The body being a hologram, we access all levels of the mind and body with Kineseology and with clairvoyance to access the records that we need in releasing the programs. We go one further by accessing the ability of the Higher Self to go to the akashic records for past life information. Any malfunction in a person's life at any level can be cleared up. There are no limitations.

Q. What should you expect during a treatment?
A. To understand what a treatment is like, you must first understand what it is not like. No special preparations or clothing are required. You will not experience any deep tissue work that is painful, nor will you be required to accept altered states of consciousness. We do not use hypnosis or guided imagery. You will not be expected to dredge up painful, emotional experiences from the past or "lead the discussion" as in analytical psychology. In fact, you do not need to tell us anything. Your body will reveal all we need to know, although we may ask some questions to establish some basic criteria. It's easier to access programs if you make up a list of the basic issues you would like to cover. This way, we can focus on the issues you want work with.

Emotions may come up and you may experience flashbacks during the process but they are all momentary and release quickly.

We use affirmations as the means to reprogram and rewrite scripts in the mind. The therapist creates the affirmation, then the client repeats the affirmation. The affirmations are software for the mind. The only person that can reprogram your mind is you; there is no such person as a healer of others. You can only heal yourself. As such, we are only facilitators to direct the process.

Q. What goes on during a treatment?
A. When we began this work in the 1980s, we jumped in and started releasing programs from the body. As we progressed through the years, we found we had to take control of our mind so we developed affirmations we now describe as "dialogues with the mind." These can take up to an hour to complete.

When we locate the cause or core issue with kineseology, we must determine if it is a belief or reality. If it's only a belief, it may be controlled by a sub-personality. In either case, we can release it with an affirmation that will reprogram the software. If it is body-based, then we have to locate the acupuncture point that holds the incident we are releasing; a momentary pain will occur at that point. As we bring up details of the incident and forgive the cause, it will disappear immediately.

We do not experience the mind's action during the process; it instantly communicates to the body through neurosynapses and signals the muscles to let go of the tension. At the same time, it is rewriting the programs in the computer.

Through affirmations, we communicate what we want to happen. It is important to understand that you are giving permission and removing the programs yourself. As the therapist leads you through the affirmation, you are healing your own body. The therapist is actually just a facilitator who has agreed to let you release the negative energy through him/her, providing an opportunity to experience love and forgiveness to release the incident.

Q. How long does this take and how much?
A. The number of treatments depends on your willingness to let go. Taking responsibility to see life differently without judgment, justification, rejection or fear/anger helps. A typical average is three to ten sessions. Some clients have had over 50 sessions, while others have cleared most of their issues in four to ten. There have been miracles in one session, but they are rare. The cost of a session is
$250 and typically lasts about 2 hours.

Q. How do I make an appointment?
Call 916 663-9178 office or cell phone (916) 710 6413 for an appointment. Check our website at:
www.transformyourmind.com.

If you want to sponsor a lecture or seminar we offer free sessions for helping us promoting the word about this work. If you are interested in spreading the word of this work please call us. We would be happy to work with you. We are setting up a network of practitioners that will be listed on our website.

Q. How can I become a sponsor?

A. If you would like to help us present lectures or introductory workshops, please call the number above. We provide a free session if you set up a lecture for us (a minimum of ten people). If you are interested in setting up appointments for me at a designated location I will provide you with a free session for each day I work at your location (there is a minimum number of sessions each day to qualify). We teach the Energy Psychology Neuro/Cellular Repatterning process in a five-workshop series. If you would like to sponsor a workshop we allow you to attend free.

C: The StressBlocker™

Disclaimer:

The following is a description is of an experimental device intended for research in electronic medical experiments. We report on the results of our research and from our customers Report to us. We do not make any claims for what it will do for you,

Due to FDA regulations, we make no claims as to what the Stress Blocker will accomplish. We can only report what users have relayed to us. We check out the testimonials to find if we have multiple responses that verify the experiences people are having. Many claims have been made by users of the Stress Blocker, but we can not recommend it for anything as it has not been approved by the FDA. We are not Psychiatrists or doctors. We are not allowed by law to diagnose or prescribe. We have come to a conclusion over the past 15 years that based on the testimonials listed here these are accurate depiction's of their experiences.

What is the StressBlocker

StressBlocker is based on the research and theory by Nicola Tesla on Coils and Scalar fields. Tesla was the Einstein of the electrical field. He invented the AC motor that we use in all most of the appliances today. The StressBlocker is small pocket sized unit about the size of Garage door opener. It has a radiated field 15 feet in diameter described as Scaler Field. These are based on quantum physics formulas developed by Nikola Tesla a contemporary of Thomas Edison. Tesla's field was electrical research. He developed many theories on the use of coils and antennas.

The StressBlocker Concept

This unit acts as both an ELF generator that radiates the Schulman earth resonance signal and a high frequency field which is the ideal frequency for functioning of the body. The body/mind will intrain itself with the frequency that has the strongest effect on it. The Stress Buster creates a fifteen foot wide circle of energy around the body which causes the body to identify with this frequency level and block out other frequencies that are stressful to the body. All of the brain chemicals such as Interlukens, Serratonin, Interferon and L dopa etc. all function best when our body is at about 25 to 50 Hertz. The immune system and the endocrine system work more effectively when there is no load on the adrenal glands. The stressBlocker will activate and cause the endocrine and immune system to regenerate itself and become stronger and more effective to protect us from stress. It take about three weeks to recover from Adrenal Gland burnout.

What are the physical effects one can expect?

Most people are operating at 9500 Hz which overloads our Adrenals trying to keep us functioning in this stressful society we live in. With the StressBlocker the body can recover bringing the frequency down allowing the body to operate at 35 Hertz. The Adrenals can heal and resume their normal operating level within three to five weeks.

These testimonials are from only a few of the reported users. We have delivered over 2500 units. The most often reported effect is clearing stress, depression, lack of energy, sleeping better and being able to slow down. Many people have reported it causes an accelerated healing of cuts and wounds on the skin. It apparently is activating some cellular response as skin cuts and abrasions seem to heal 10 times faster than normal. Skin scars begin disappearing. The unit is activating and supporting the immune and endocrine system. It seems to build up a persons immunity to illness. The only one negative aspect that we have found is sometimes it pushes up Emotional programs that have repressed in the past

We hesitate to list many results people have received due to the fact that people tend to expect certain results from the Stress Blocker as such many results might be placebo effect. It is an adjunct that responds to your body like a bridge to better health. It can be a catalyst for miracles, It is an adjunct for healing. . You have do your part in releasing your emotional trauma that is causing the results that you experience. You have to work with it. You can expect it to do things for you but, please do not put unrealistic expectations on the StressBlocker. It can have a placebo effect if you believe it works om some issue have you want healed, it works on almost anything. We can give others experiences such as many people have said that it pulled them out of depression in five days to five weeks without any drugs. Many have stopped using mind altering psychoactive drugs in two to five weeks. Two Psychiatrists worked with some their patients which did validate this information from their experience with patients, but would not write testimonials due to their reputations being challenged.

It causes accelerated healing by activating the cellular restructuring in the body to cause cellular regeneraon at about ten times faster than the time it normally takes to heal. In my case I took a chunk out of my foot with a chain saw which was not healing very well. As soon as I received the new redesigned STRESS BLOCKER V my foot began to heal at level I had not seen before. The only way I can describe what I saw was like freeze frame photography or watching it heal in slow motion daily. You could actually see the hole heal from one day to the next. The hole closed up and healed over in less than two weeks. The keloid scar caused by the gash is gone, all one can see is a red spot in the location of the wound for about two years Now we can't see any mark at all. Generally in my experience I have found that deep cuts like this one took many months to heal and they leave keloid scars that very seldom ever disappear. The DPDT immunizations we received as children leave a big scar. It has disappearedon most people. I had two large keloid scars on my body that have disappeared or smoothed over. A birthmark which was on my arm for 65 years is gone. I have keloid scars from the operations I had when I was child which never changed for 65 years. They are half the size and the keloid is smoothing out. Many people have reported the same effects.

StressBlocker effect on the body/mind

Negative sensory input or negative thoughts and emotions cause the neuropeptides to break down the bodies cellular structure. The same effect happens to the immune and endocrine system which causes them to lower their ability to protect us against stress and illness. The electrical field around the body must be strong to ward of disease factors. As the body frequency rises the electrical and auric field weakens. This electrical field is described as Chi, Ki or Prana. It gives a person more overall strength, vitality and protection

The following is a greatly simplified explanation of the theory behind the Stress Blocker. The information which causes the various parts of the body to operate is carried by the body's neurological network system. The brain serves as a "switching network center" that directs the information across the network to the appropriate parts of the body with electrical impulses through the meridian system and with chemicals known as neuropeptides and cytikinins. These are all connected through a computer network from three levels of the mind. Each computer system networks with a mainframe computer known as the Inner Conscious Mind and the Subconscious Mind. The Subconscious mind acts as the data base storage memory or hard disc for all programs and habit patterns. All three systems must work together or we will encounter malfunctions in the software that we describe as anger, fear, I am not all right, rejection, abandonment, resentment, need for control, manipulation and relationship conflicts. This causes breakdowns in the hardware which we describe as disease and illness or mental depression etc. Each cell is mini network computer that receives its orders from the minds operating system through the neurological system meridain transmitters . Electrolytes, neuropeptides, and cytokinins in the body are carriers. When operating properly they maintain a delicate balance of chemicals, like the storage battery in your car.

When they go out of balance or get run down and the electromagnetic fields breakdown. The result is your batteries are run down. The body loses its ability to protect itself properly. The ability for the brain/mind to communicate with the cellular computers breaks down and the body becomes subject to attack by diseases, illness and outside forces. When the physical body is in harmony, it functions at 25-35 Hertz. However, stress and emotional conflict cause the internal frequency to rise to 9500 Hertz. When this happens, it becomes more difficult for electrical, neuropeptides, electrolytes, and the neurological system to transmit electrical impulses through the body/mind network. The rise in frequency causes all body tissues from the skin to the organs and endocrine system to be subject to stress, breakdown causing *accelerated aging.* This is the most damaging effect of increased stress and high frequency. The result is illness, disease, depression, chronic fatigue, emotional instability and life threatening disease. Metabolism is affected due to breakdown of the function of the endocrine glands as a result, nutrition supplied to the body slows down and is not assimilated properly. Feeling tired and depleted causes chronic fatigue and depression is the result. As the internal frequency rises past 150 Hertz the good happy brain chemicals begin to shut down and the adrenals kick in larger doses of adrenaline to keep you functioning. The end result of this is adrenal insufficiency as the adrenals are overworked. They begin to produce less and less adrenaline. when production drops to 20% or less chronic fatigue begins set in as Cortosols are now replacing adrenaline. It is similar to low blood sugar caused by hypoglycemia which leads to diabetes but, high frequency causes breakdown in all systems of the body. The end result is Chronic Fatigue, Epstein Bar or other forms of distress which leads to clinical depression. many people run to the doctor and begin taking Prozac, Zantac, Zolov, Valeium, Paxel or other mind altering drugs. These are described as anti depressant drugs. You can get addicted to these feeling good drugs because they suppress the symptom and cause the brain switching network to believe the symptom of total body malfunction is a false message. The major dysfunction most people suffer from is adrenal exhaustion. When

Adrenal function drops below 20% you go into adrenal exhaustion which is clinical depression in medical terms. Cortosols are toxic to the body but are a last ditch efforts to keep the body functioning. **If this keeps up day after day it begins to break down the body.**

Are there any negative side effects   Q and A

We have been building and selling the StressBlocker under the Names StressBuster, Harmonizer and Body/Mind Harmonizer for the last 15 years. As you can see from the testimonials following everybody has had positive results. We have found that the power of the mind can stop any positive effect if the person does not want to believe in the product or the process. It does not make any difference what it is or what can do for other people. What we have discovered was at some level in their mind they did not want it to work

In a sense we can state that beliefs, attitudes, perceptions and interpreations control everything so all results can be placebo effect since the mind controls the outcome of any, drug, supplement, product or therapy process. If we let it work it will, but if we override the effect with our mind it will not work. We make the choice. Nobody is conrtolling our decisions. We are the conttroller of our life. What we perceive is our reality. Right or wrong it is our perception.

find out what they are and release them if possible. Multiple Personalities and sub personalities can cause uneasiness if they feel that they are losing control over you. Our intent is to get control over our mind so it will work for us not against us. Be aware that Stress Blocker can and will activate programs or activities in your body.

It is best to keep the StressBlocker within 5 feet of your body at all times 24/7 as it works as a bridge to balance your body. If you leave it somewhere, check yourself out to see it you have attached beings on you as they see you as a target when you are using the StressBlocker. Generally after the first week everything calms down and you will experience a sense of well being when your body slows down operating at 25 to 35 Hertz

Are you ready to get up each day to peace, happiness, harmony and joy fully rested sleeping less hours from a perfect nights sleep with limitless energy. Stress will not have any effect on you any longer. Depression and feeling burned out will fade into the past. Being dragged out with lack of energy from long flights across multiple time zones from jet lag will be a eliminated. Arrive at your destination ready to go to work. No down time or need to sleep to off the jwer lag to readjust and regain your stability. See enclosed sleeping affirmation which work with the unit. **Our mind is so powerful you can defeat the StressBlockers positive affect on you. We have witnessed people who claim it does not work. That is there conflict not the StressBlocker. We have checked many people finding their resistance was a belief or an attached entity,** People have returned units claiming it was making them sick. The few comments from people who have returned has been "it did not work for me." **now it works.**

Operation of the Stress Blocker ---- Electronic Medical Research

Every living being in the universe has a particular frequency that it resonates at when it is in perfect health. Each component of our body also resonates at a particular frequency. If the stress places conflict and disrupts this frequency the particular cellular structure the organ or gland is weakened and will be subject to breakdown, disease or illness   The Stress Blocker balances all the electrical, metabolic and electromagnetic systems that are dysfunctional shutting out the disharmonious stress that causes the body to elevate its frequency. It is operating at fifth dimensional energy so third dimrnsional endergy has no effect on it.. It strengthens all the systems of the body by bringing down the frequency to the optimum level for perfect health which 25-35 Hz. To be in balance, most devices, plants and animals have positive and negative energies that rotate clockwise and counterclockwise. This creates a balance in the electrical system. A few plants such as Garlic, Onion, and some herbs radiate a double positive field, hence their antibiotic, healing qualities. The StressBlocker also radiates a double positive field which explains the response it creates.

For more than 200 years of recorded history the earth frequency or Schuman Resonance was 7.83 Hz or cycles per second. Recent research has shown that it has risen to between 13 and 14 Hz. Our original Harmonizers were built at 7.83 Hz. We had been increasing the frequency along with Schuman resonance.

The body will identify with this frequency and resonate with this frequency blocking out other interference. When it is subjected to contact with the StressBlocker for a period of time the body will duplicate the StressBlocker frequency. It may be up to three days to a week depending on the level at which your frequency has risen. When you are inside the 15 foot diameter bubble of the electromagnetic field you will notice your body begin to slowdown and relax. When your body/mind resonates at this optimum level for a period of time the body begins to heal. You may notice that the Stress Blocker needs to be recharged more often than every four to six days in the beginning. If your body energy is low and you have been under considerable stress this will draw the battery down faster as the unit interfaces and responds to your body energy level. We have had reports that people have had to charge the battery as often as every day in the beginning.

Tesla Theory and Technology

We were asked by some electronic wizards, radio frequency engineers and some physicists why we were getting a clear AC sine wave coupled with a scalar wave without the circuitry to produce it. All they could say was that we are in hyper dimensional physics and it over their head. They could not explain it. One comment was you are into Tesla and Einstein's realm we do not understand what you are doing. We are apparently producing an output that no one understands nor has any history of this effect been recorded as far as we can see from our research. Many people claim their product produces a Scalar field, yet they do not under what a Scalar field is nor what it appears like on electrical laboratory instruments.

The StressBlocker generates a bio-electrical magnetic field using electromagnetic Scaler field technology developed by Nikola Tesla in the early 1900's. The coil-antennae produces a *Scalar Wave Field* described as a longitudinal wave field that functions outside of third dimensional space/time. Since it operates outside of space time in our third dimensional world based on hyper dimensional physics it is unencumbered by the limitations of conventional physics rules. Scalar waves operate within the etheric field which surrounds the body.

When we shifted to the new unit we were working with three new research consultants and a builder that was a project engineer we now have on our team a Radio Frequency engineer and Physicist. They seem to understand what we are working on and have offered suggestions on how to improve the StressBlocker.. They have said, " It appears as far as we can understand, that we are in at the threshold of a new discovery that has not been experienced in quantum physics at this time." They had not been able to measure the Scalar fields output as it functions outside of conventional physical principles. We now have been able to measure the radio frequency which indicates that it is the carrier wave field. We will have picture on our website.

Testimonials:

1. It seems to bring programs to the surface which I did not have awareness of in the past. It is the best therapeutic tool I have come in contact with. – B.E., California

2. I strapped the Stress Buster over a broken leg on the cast where the break was and the break healed four times faster. The doctor was amazed that we could take the cast off in less than four weeks. – J.S., California

3. Chronic Fatigue that has been existing for years with no way out as it seems from past experience. It disappeared in less than a week. – J.C. Arizona

4. I am feeling better as general well being and ability to handle stress more effectively. Not getting angry as easy as in the past. I left the Stress Blocker home and I noticed my stress level began to rise at work. My co-workers noticed the result. – C.D., California

5. It has been reported to us by Psychiatrists that have purchased the Stress Buster that it indeed does work with depression very well since it reactivates the brain chemicals and supports the rebuilding of normal production of all the essential brain chemicals allowing the adrenals to slow down and heal. As a result people seem to pull out of depression. – R.N., Virginia

6. I put it on a plant that was seemingly dying. It revived in one day when the StressBlocker is placed next to them for 24 hours. – T.K., California

7. A burn totally disappeared in three days. This was apparently caused by the activation of the cellular restructuring. – J.T., California

8. It apparently has caused my immune system to recover because I am recovering from a long term illness that has hung on from a long time. It is feels great to get my stamina back. – W.B., New Mexico

9. It activates programs in the mind that have been c for years. Apparently denial programs are forced to the surface. – H.M., California

10. I am finding I have more energy and I sleep less now that the stress is relieved. – G.B., Colorado

11. I have been taking drugs for depression and low thyroid and adrenal function. I continued to take the drugs until they ran out. I noticed that I was getting the same effect from the Stress Blocker so I did not renew my prescriptions. That was three years ago and I have not had any depression since. The new one is even better. Thank you so much. – AP, California

12. The new model is so much better. I have more energy and can do things I had given up in the past – G.V., Florida

13. I had been to the doctor for my high blood pressure and he suggested that I should be taking medicine to control my blood pressure because it was 190 over 120. I decided that I would come back next month to check it again. It was still the same. I bought the Stress Blocker started carrying it with me all the time. I went to see the doctor again and my blood pressure was down to 120 over 80 in less than a month. The doctor felt the nurse had made a mistake, so he checked it himself with the same result. He could not understand how my blood pressure would come down to normal. His statement was "that just does not happen to someone your age." I cannot attribute it to anything other than the StressBlocker^{TM}. – CS, Arizona

14. It is amazing. I felt burned out and the doctor said my adrenals were very low and wanted me to take drugs to build them back up. I told him I did not take drugs of any kind. I would find a way to help me out. This is it. My adrenals recovered in 10 days. I do not feel as stressed out anymore. This is truly electronic medicine. – K.S., Oregon

15. As a doctor working in an Operating room almost everyday it can become very stressful. My stress level has been reduced to almost zero. I also notice the people who work with me are operating under less stress. Everything goes like clockwork with no conflicts. – R.O., New Jersey

16. My husband ended up with the cold/flu twice this winter and I usually get it from him and end up down for a week. This time no flu or anything. I can only assume the StressBlocker protected me and keep my immune system up to par so I was not affected. – C.H., California

17. For me it is a miracle because I seem to go out of my body quite often. It is very dangerous for me to drive when this happens. Since I have using Dr. Art's polarity exercise and I have been using the StressBlocker^{TM} I have been solidly in my body all the time. – J.S., California

18. I have had serious Immune system problems for years. It seems that everything that comes along catches me. The Stress Blocker has upgraded my Immune system to the point that I am very seldom sick now. – C.K., California

19. When I called to find out about the unit I was willing to try anything as my blood pressure was 210 over 120 and I had lung congestion. My legs hurt so much I could not walk around the grocery store. In five weeks my blood pressure went down to 130 over 90 and it continuing to go down. I have no lung congestion and I can drive trucks again. I have gone back to work full time. – H.N., Colorado

20. I would not be without my boogie buster because it protects me so well. I touch many clients in my work. In the past I was picking up their energy attaching to me from my clients. – J.N., California

21. I have had low adrenal function almost all my life. Stress really takes me down the point I can't work. My downtime has been increasing too. With the Stress Blocker I have recovered totally. I have not experienced any depression or lack of energy sine I have been using it. – C.K., Colorado

22. Accelerated healing of burns has been amazing. I spilled boiling water on my face when I dropped a teakettle. The burn marks began clearing up in two weeks. In a month they were almost gone except for redness on the skin. There is no scaring as the red burn marks are gone now. – MK., Arizona

23. One of the most amazing sights that I have seen is old burn scars and keloid scars are disappearing. Most of these

have been on my body for twenty to forty years. It is truly amazing. – H.M., California

24. I finished a motorcycle race and took my protective leather cloths off and stepped into an exhaust pipe from a racing motorcycle. It must have been 1300 degrees when I brushed it with my leg it caused a serious third degree burn. The burn healed in less than one month. In six weeks it just a was just a dark spot on my leg. In the past it has taken six months for burns like this to heal and the skin is scared. The burn marks are gone with no scaring. – KG., California

25. I have had panic attacks for fifteen years and can not drive in traffic. I am able to drive anytime now without taking medicine.
– K.W.H., Pennsylvania

26. I have been running at high speed all my life. The doctor told me to slow down. Being a workaholic it was more stressful to push myself into slowing down which caused more problems. The StressBlocker^{TM} did it I am back to normal. – J.C., Washington

27. I have been using psycho active drugs for over 15 years or I go upside down emotionally. After using the StressBlocker^{TM} for four weeks I cut back on my drugs for two weeks until my prescription ran out. I have not taken drugs for two years now I feel great with more energy and happiness in my life. – Ivar. Ikstrums, Washington

28. Most people say I am hyperactive. I tend to tap my feet and have uncontrollable arm and leg movements all the time. I didn't even notice this. With the StressBlocker^{TM} this has all stopped. – C.F., Florida

New Products and upgrades

1. The price of the Portable 800 millivolt Body/Mind Stress Buster is $297.00
Price outside the US varies based on exchange rate which fluctuates. Plus USA $10.00 shipping. Canada Approx. $15.00 to $30.00 USD; outside of North America varies

Older-model StressBlocker™ can be exchanged for an updated StressBlocker™ for $100 to $200, depending what age they are. Plus shipping $10 US; $20 to $30 Canada and other countries varies.

2. A new Stationary StressBuster unit operates on 120 volts for clearing offices and homes and creating a overall balancing/clearing effect in offices, houses, seminar and workshop facilities. We have been able to shield it so it will not effect TV and Short Wave Radios. The challenge is to build a stronger unit that will not interfere with short wave or TV reception. What we have is a signal generator that would be classified as a portable radio station if we get to strong. We would run into trouble with the FCC. **Price: $297.00**. Plus $10 shipping In the US $20 to Canada

Operating Instructions:
Please read carefully before using the StressBlocker™

TAKE NOTE: **If you Choose to return for a refund we charge a $50.00 Inspection charge to make sure we can resell the unit as a used product.** *We have a very strict return policy. You must use the unit for at least six months. We will not accept returns until after six months from purchase date. (This eliminates the tire-kickers who order and return the next week.)*

If you are unsure or do not understand these instructions please contact the person who sold you the unit. Please do not order just to look.

Stress blockers are shipped fully charged.
If your unit arrives and is not charged follow the instructions below:
To charge: plug the charging unit into a 120 outlet (the black unit with the plug) plug the charging cable into the USB port on the charger. Plug the mini USB charging plug into the front panel on the StressBlocker (similar to a cell phone plug) into

the charging socket above the blinking light next to the switch. The blinking green light indicates the units operating properly and is charged. When the green light goes out charge immediately. Red light is on during charging.

Use only the charger supplied with the StressBlocker. The StressBlocker has a charge limiter so it can not be overcharged. **When you are charging, the red light will go on.** When it is fully charged the light will turn off and the green light comes on. If you are unsure if it needs a charge, plug in the charger. If the red light goes on continue to charge. **It does not make any difference how often you charge it.**

If you purchased the Stationary StressBlocker^{TM}, you just plug it into a 120 volt AC outlet in your house or office. Try to center it in the building so it has maximum effect throughout the building. The StressBlocker^{TM} has a lifetime warrantee. Return it to us and we will repair it. We will repair any malfunction in the units at no charge if it is a breakdown in the unit. We charge for repairs for mishandling or damage caused by the user. We provide a one-year guaranty. We will refund your money anytime for one year if the unit is returned in good condition. Subject to any damage or repairs that may be needed to repair the unit.

To Order the StressBlockerTM call or write:

Energy Medicine Institute
9936 Inwood Rd, Folsom, CA 95630
Voice: 916-663-9178

Do not send checks to Energy Medicine Institute, make them out to Art Martin (we do not have a bank account in the name of Energy Medicine Institute)

E-mail: Mailforart@gmail.com
Web Site: http://www.stressblocker.net
We take PayPal on website and Phone orders

D: CDs, DVDs & Books

The first two books are available in most bookstores in the U.S., and in some countries around the world The other five are available in spiral bound pre-publication format from the publisher, Personal Transformation Press.

2011: The New Millennium Begins
$13.95, ISBN 1-891962-02-7

What can we expect the future to bring? How do we handle the coming changes and what do we look for? Prophesy for future earth changes and new planet Earth as it makes the quantum jump from the third to the fifth dimension.

Becoming a Spiritual Being in a Physical Body
$14.95, ISBN 1-891962-03-5

The "operations manual" for your life. Recreating your life for peace, happiness, harmony, and joy. Changing from being a physical being having transitory spiritual experiences to becoming a spiritual being in a physical body. Letting go of the duality of life.

Journey Into The Light
$15.95, ISBN 1-891962-05-01

The process of ascension and the steps that govern the journey to a light being. Looking for the missing link in evolution. Stepping out of the cycle of reincarnation.

Opening Communication with GOD Source
$14.95, ISBN 1-891962-04-1

The author's search for God uncovers the shocking truth that it's actually a group of wise and ancient beings who have been involved with Earth since the beginning. Packed full of usable and powerful techniques, this book takes you beyond the blocks that most of us have and puts you on the spiritual path.

Recovering Your Lost Self
$14.95, ISBN 1-891962-08-6

The author's journey from victim to cause in his life. How you can find your true self and have abundance in your life. Accepting unconditional love in your life through forgiveness and acceptance. Coming to the point where peace, happiness, harmony and joy are reality, not an illusion.

Behavioral Mind Body Medicine: Exploring The New Frontier of Psychoneuroimmunology, Energy Medicine and Energy Psychology
ISBN 1-891962-07-8

What is psychoneuroimmunolgy and the mind/body medicine connection? An overview of the modalities and processes. Integrating the concepts. Research on the modalities. The mind as network computer. Affirmations, software for the mind. Neuro-Kinesiology. Using muscle testing for clearing beliefs and concepts, programs, patterns and records that are causing allergies, emotional behavior patterns, disease, illness and physical breakdown in the body. Neuro/Cellular Repatterning, a method to access the mind's programs, beliefs and interpretations and release them to heal any disease, illness or dysfunction in the mind/body. Miracle healings on demand with love and forgiveness. Supporting the body with nutritional and herbal products.

CDs and DVDs

Tapes are available on the guided imagery to train yourself to access the records and on the process for contacting your teacher and accessing the Hall of Records.

1. The Seven Chakra Guided Imagery:
   Train yourself to step out of the body to enter the Temple and the Hall of Records.

2. Accessing your Akashic Records:
   On the process and the various forms and methods of finding the answers to all your questions.

3. Psycho/Physical Self Regulation:
   Originally a tape for runner and walkers to regulate, flush the body of toxins and burn fat for energy. Can be used to train yourself to eat properly and reduce weight.

4. DVD Your Body is Talking Psychoneuroimmunology
   Dr. Art Martin is interviewed by Dr. Patricia Hill

Epilogue

This volume of *Your Body Is Talking; Are You Listening?* subtitled *How the Mind Works: The Mind/Body Medicine Connection,* has examined the body/mind as a vehicle for spiritual transformation. We have looked at the origins of illness, disease and behavioral dysfunction, in terms of how body cells communicate and how beliefs serve as agents of cause and effect. We have examined how the mind functions, and the origin and effects of sub-personalities. And finally, we have looked at meta-communication and how we project our deepest self-image to anyone sensitive enough to pick it up.

Volume Two, subtitled *N/CR in Practice,* begins with how my personal journey into healing led to a deeper understanding of the human condition. Volume Two then looks at the history of Energy Psychology and Energy Medicine, and how I coupled these fields with the new therapeutic process of Psychological Acupuncture, to develop the unique practice of Neuro/Cellular Repatterning. Over the years with N/CR, I have witnessed countless remarkable—some claim miraculous—recoveries, many of which are documented in the chapter titled *Case Histories.*

This two-volume set includes so much new material that a single-volume book would have become unwieldy; in fact, many readers were already complaining of the size of the single volume. Our aim is to bring you as much information as possible about the rapidly growing field of Energy Medicine so we decided to opt for two volumes to make the information manageable. I urge you to now read Volume Two as the natural sequel to the book you have just finished.

I have tried to present a balanced view of Energy Medicine, Energy Psychology and Neuro/Cellular Reprogramming. I always feel one should should present both side of the practice.

The best way to lose people's confidence and respect is to present a one-sided view only listing the success stories.

We have had thousands of them and we have had few that were failures. So we balanced the presentation with a few failures, so we can be real. . . . Many practitioners only want to show you their success stories. I would assume that they have had more failures than success stories, but they do not want them out.

About The Author

In today's world, the issue of credibility often comes up. *How many degrees do you have? What colleges did you attend? Who did you study with? Who were your teachers? How do you know this works?*

When I needed outside validation and acceptance, those were valid questions. Now I do not consider them valid, nor do I care if others reject me because I don't have the credibility they seek. What I learned in college has no relevance to what I do now in my practice. What I know is far more important than my background. Therefore, I am not interested in listing all my credentials.

Neuro/Cellular Repatterning is a process that was developed by myself and three people who worked with me during the research period: Dr. James Dorabiala, Mike Hammer and Bernard Eckes. And new information still pours in even today. This is basically a self-taught process, and everyone who has worked with us over the last 20 years have been our students and our teachers.

What *is* relevant is that we be open to new ideas. I will attend others' workshops and experience their treatments. Healing is an open-ended and ongoing process in which we need to be open to new ideas. The "sacred cow" syndrome is outdated and does not work for me.

Someone once attacked me with, "You think you have the whole pie, don't you? You believe that nobody can match up to you." My response was, "I don't think I have the whole pie, but based on the success of the last 20 years, maybe I have a few more pieces than some other practitioners."

Art Martin was born into a family where his father wanted a child and his mother did not. As an only child, he did not have any sibling interaction, so his only contacts were at school. His dysfunctional family laid down many problems, which he has come a long way in clearing, thanks to discovery of the process he developed—Neuro/Cellular Repatterning—and the people who worked with him over the years.

In 1963, he quit college after receiving a degree in Advertising and Journalism. After five years feeling frustrated with the educational system, he worked for a newspaper for a year. He then became a Real Estate salesman, but found that it was not his calling, and went back to a newspaper.

In 1965, he married Susie, his partner ever since. Their sons, Ross and Ryan, were born in 1971 and 1976. Very few people in the field of therapy work seem to be able to stay in relationships, due to the fact they do not want to deal with their own issues. Art was committed to finding himself and went on a path to do so. He stabilized his own relationship by working out his issues.

In 1968, he and Susie moved to St. Helena, CA, rebuilding an abandoned winery. To clear the land to plant grapes, Art became a logger. To support his family while the winery was being rehabilitated, he purchased a D8 Caterpillar tractor for land-clearing and vineyard preparation. Many people said, "how are you going to learn how to operate that huge tractor"? He hired a man to work with him and learned how to operate it.

After getting the winery set up, he discovered the big-money interests were pushing grape prices above what was economically viable for a small winery to stay in business, so he sold it.

His next venture was a restaurant which he built himself, but he found the restaurant field one of the most demanding there are. Working twelve to eighteen hours day was not what he wanted to do as a career.

However, Art met his first teacher at the restaurant, someone who planted a seed of doubt about his life path. After closing time, while cleaning up the restaurant, they would spend many hours talking about their paths. He decided to sell the restaurant and retire, since Susie wanted to go back to work. Art became a house-husband, taking care of the children and the house for the next four years.

In 1980, the buyers of the restaurant went bankrupt, so their payments stopped. Art had to return to work and his quest was disrupted. Fortunately, Susie was working full- time, but in 1980, she was laid off, so Art, who had a green thumb, worked as a gardener at a senior citizens' complex.

Having closely studied the Findhorn community, he took the opportunity to apply what he had learned about the earth spirits. He found, from the plants themselves, that the landscape architect had put many of them in the wrong places. Over the next year, he transformed the grounds into a magnificent flower gardens, and even built a passive solar greenhouse to grow flowers year-round.

By 1982, he had begun to establish his healing practice, so he quit the gardener job and concentrated on researching healing practices.

Art soon found that Santa Rosa, CA, did not support the type of work he was doing, and when Joshua Stone invited him to go to Los Angeles to give readings to clients, he jumped at the opportunity. He and Joshua found they worked well together as a team, and Art was able to provide a unique and valuable service to many therapists. However, the traveling almost broke up his family, so they moved to Sacramento, CA, and opened a bookstore and metaphysical center.

While Art received considerable support for this venture, he didn't anticipate how few people had the money to support it financially. Having invested all the family's savings, and refinanced their house, he managed fairly well for almost three years until he took on partners in order to expand. However, his partners did not understand the law of cause and effect, and when they embezzled an undermined amount of money, the business went under. They had invested over $300,000 in the Wellness Institute, with their life savings from twenty years in business. They lost it all, and had to start over again.

Knowing that "What goes around comes around," Art managed to accept what had happened, forgive them and get on with his life. However, trying to understand the lesson in this was hard to accomplish. Angry at losing his life savings and 20 years of hard work, the clarity and acceptance that he had set it all up came slowly. Even though he knew this at one level, it was a hard lesson to learn. The lesson was that while he had received much verbal validation from those who supported the center, he had been paying over half its operational costs.

The failure was a mixed blessing. It put him on a new path, one in which he traveled and spread the word of his work, and really had to get down to business. He did finally recover, even though they lost their house and one of their cars. Looking back, Art recognizes the many great strides forward that he has made. Today, he travels extensively, giving lectures, seminars and workshops on a variety of subjects. He also has a circuit of cities he visits regularly for individual sessions.

He has set up a publishing company to promote his books (see the list in the front of this book), and these are available through the Wellness Institute. Many of them are in bookstores now and also available through the following website:

http:// www.transformyourmind.com

He may also be reached at:
(916) 663-9178
or by email:
mailforart@gmail.com

PAGE 143
Hunting Touch

CPSIA information can be obtained at www.ICGtesting.com
Printed in the USA
LVOW10s1651270315

432319LV00002B/437/P